The Royal Gwent & St. Woolos Hospitals

A Century of Service in Newport

Compiled and Edited
by
Professor Brian Peeling CBE

Contributors
Cliff Knight
and Members and Friends
of the hospitals

Editorial Group
Joanna Dundon
Gwilym Griffith OBE
Rosz Howell JP
Julian Hayman
Andrew Ponsford

Forewords by
The Rt. Hon. Paul Murphy MP
and
Denis Jessopp OBE

OLD BAKEHOUSE PUBLICATIONS

ISBN 1 874538 08 5

Published in the U.K. by
Old Bakehouse Publications
Church Street,
Abertillery, Gwent NP13 1EA
Telephone: 01495 212600 Fax: 01495 216222
e-mail: oldbakehouseprint@btopenworld.com

Made and printed in the UK
by J.R. Davies (Printers) Ltd.

British Library Cataloguing in Publication Data: a catalogue
record for this book is available from the British Library.

Index of Contents

Her Majesty Queen Elizabeth, The Queen Mother
Patron of The Royal Gwent Hospital 1948 to 2002.

(reproduced by kind permission of Her Majesty The Queen)

Foreword

The Rt. Hon. Paul Murphy, MP

House of Commons
London
SWIA 0AA

I have great personal delight in writing this foreword to Brian Peeling's history of hospital care in South Gwent. As a former lecturer, I congratulate one of our most distinguished urologists on compiling and editing a finely written book, which will be the standard work on healthcare in Gwent.

The story started in 1839 - not long after my mother's own ancestors arrived in Newport and at the time of the Chartist riots. We are told of the progress made in healthcare and hospitals in South Gwent during the 19th and 20th centuries, and of course, of the impact of the creation of our own N.H.S., created as it was, by the Monmouthshire M.P., Aneurin Bevan. It is a tale of dedication and commitment, of charity and of local national government, against an enormously changing background of a rising population and of huge industrialisation accompanied often by widespread poverty and disease.

It is also a story of hope and of huge progress in medicine and science, with chapters on medical and surgical developments over the years. The book covers a wide spectrum and the reader will be rewarded with a knowledge of our county's medical history unrivalled by any earlier studies.

My own family over the last 160 years has been served by the specialists, nurses and doctors who feature in this book, and I am especially pleased that Brian Peeling and his team have devoted so much energy and skill in telling us such a fascinating story.

The Right Honourable Paul Murphy M.P.

Foreword

When we were planning the celebrations for the centenary of the Royal Gwent Hospital it became clear that there was no comprehensive record of the hospital for the whole of that century. Moreover, we felt that there was a real danger that essential and valuable history could be lost completely, given the speed of change in the National Health Service.

Brian Peeling, to our great relief, agreed to tackle the job of producing such a history and this volume is the result. He, and his willing collaborators, have compiled a history that goes well beyond the story of the Royal Gwent; it traces the complete development of institutional health services in the Newport area right back to the original Dispensary in 1839. It also serves as a tribute to so many people who have striven to improve the health of the community for nearly two centuries.

It really is a momentous story and shows just how close has been the relationship between the hospital services and the community, how great have been the problems and how often they have been overcome by collaboration between hospitals and public. It is not difficult to understand why the people of Newport and beyond hold the hospitals in such regard.

Our profound thanks go to Brian and all his contributors especially Cliff Knight. The research and compilation have been a huge task but they have produced a live and fascinating record of the past that should be an inspiration for the future. We have a lot to live up to.

Denis Jessopp OBE
Chairman (1996-2003)
Glan Hafren/Gwent Healthcare N.H.S. Trust

Preface

In the Foreword to the book *'The History of the Royal Gwent Hospital'* published in 1948 (compiled by T. Baker Jones and W.J.T. Collins), a plea was made for the history of the hospital to be updated when the first century of The Royal Gwent's existence had been reached.

This book fulfils that wish. It comes from the suggestion by local historian, Mr. Cliff Knight, that part of the celebrations planned for the Centenary Year of The Royal Gwent Hospital, should be a record of the hospital to the year 2001, the Centenary Year. This idea was accepted by a Centenary Group set up by the Chairman of the Gwent Healthcare N.H.S. Trust, Mr. Denis Jessopp OBE, and an Editorial Group was invited to take the matter further on behalf of the Trust. This book is the outcome.

However, purists could argue that 1939 should have been the Centenary Year, not 2001, because the first glimmers of a hospital service in Newport date from 1839 when the extremely modest but far-sighted creation of a 'Dispensary' in Llanarth Street occurred to start the process that led to the large hospital of today. Therefore, this book starts with events of 1839 but the record has been stretched beyond the Centenary Year to the year 2004 as it has taken three years to compile. The sequence of events between those dates forms a logical progression of the development of hospital services in Newport with The Royal Gwent and its predecessors as the focus of attention. However, after absorption into The National Health Service in 1948, its work became more closely linked with other hospitals in the area, especially St. Woolos Hospital which had developed from the Newport Poor House or Workhouse that had started its existence in 1838. Therefore, the book has inevitably become an account of the history of Hospital Care in Newport and the South of the County, based upon The Royal Gwent and St. Woolos Hospitals.

Much of the historical research and fact-finding about the hospitals up to 1948 has been made by Cliff Knight who is a main contributor to the historical parts of the narrative. However, accounts of more recent developments and professional changes since then have come from the experience of past and present people who have worked in or have been associated with the hospitals. We are most grateful for their contributions, cooperation and especially their patience while the book has been put together.

Radical changes of structure, administration and professional aspects of hospital practice have occurred since The National Health Service took over hospital services in 1948 so that an account of these aspects of health care provides reference points for the past as well as a general picture of the hospital service in Newport as it is today. Members of the public have entered into the spirit of the project by supplying information and several hundred photographs about the hospital often following published requests for assistance made by *'The South Wales Argus'*. However, in a publication of this size, only a limited number of these illustrations can be used. Every effort has been made to present accurate information and involve as many people as possible but we trust that any errors and omissions of fact or omissions of individuals will be forgiven. We also have endeavoured to provide interest to the readers, although it has been inevitable that some sections will acquire a more specialised flavour to give a reasonable record of the work of a hospital and the growth of the Newport hospitals in recent years. Some repetition of detail appears in the text but this could not be avoided when topics overlapped between different chapters.

The book is dedicated to all who have served the hospital over a very long time for it has been their efforts, skills and determination that have built up and established the role of the Newport Hospitals as principal sources of excellence in Health Care entering into the 21st Century. Whether The Royal Gwent and St. Woolos Hospital will still exist in fifty years for a follow-up to this book, only time will tell especially as recent press reports have indicated that the Royal Gwent may be replaced in 10 years time by a major hospital development on the other side of Cardiff Road on the Corus Steel site. If that happens, then this book could take on the role of a definitive history of the hospital.

It is intended that any proceeds from the sale of this publication will be directed towards amenities for patients because the hospitals exist for their benefit.

(Editorial Group - 2004)

Footnote: it is a great sadness to us that our colleague and friend, Mr. Gwilym Griffith OBE FRCS, died in January 2004 after a long illness and so was unable to see the final publication of this book. We have been most fortunate to have had the benefit of his advice, interest and support during its preparation for which we remain most grateful.

Gwilym Griffith (1933-2004) after receiving the OBE from The Queen at Buckingham Palace in 2001.
(photograph courtesy of Mrs. Elan Griffith)

Chapter 1: Early Years of Hospital Care in Newport (1839 to 1901)

Cliff Knight

The Royal Gwent Hospital owes its origin to a modest establishment which opened in Llanarth Street in the centre of the town on the 3rd April 1839 known as *'The Dispensary'*.

To understand why this happened one needs to take a glimpse into the conditions prevailing in the town at that time, and why those administering it felt that it was necessary for something to be done to help those who were without medical care. Previously the only help given to the underprivileged and especially the sick had come from monks. Monasteries had an *infirmitorium* which was a place in which sick monks were taken for treatment but in addition to caring for their own, monasteries opened their doors to pilgrims and other travellers. However, their services had ended with the dissolution of monasteries in the 16th Century. After that time, organised and institutional medical care was sporadic and virtually non-existent, certainly outside the great cities.

During the first part of the 19th Century Newport was described as a filthy, unsanitary town. Some properties had no sewage connection but merely drained their effluent into low ground to form a permanent, foul smelling mire. Irish immigrants who had come to the town following the potato famine wandered the streets without shoes and stockings, finding shelter in overcrowded lodging houses with men, women and children huddled together on their beds of straw and shavings, the sick lying next to the healthy, the young to the old, and the smell was intolerable. Soup kitchens were set up to alleviate hunger and misery and affluent members of society gave bread and potatoes to the poor and starving.

Under these conditions cholera, malaria, typhus and tuberculosis reached almost epidemic proportions and to try to alleviate the suffering, residents were ordered to ventilate and clean bedrooms, to clean yards using plenty of lime, to remove all heaps of foul matter and to clean out cesspools. In an attempt to control an outbreak of cholera the local press suggested that suspected cases take two tablespoons of the following mixture: six drachms of prepared chalk, two drachms of white sugar, two drachms of gum Arabic, thirty drops of tincture of opium, thirty drops of essence of ginger, half an ounce of cayenne and seven ounces of water.

The mortality rate was alarmingly high particularly among children and with the lack of burial grounds and no money to pay for burials, deceased children would be buried in shallow graves in ships' ballast which was being spread over the Pillgwenlly area to raise the level of the land to make it habitable and partially protected from high tides of the Severn Estuary.

The Newport Dispensary (1839)

Such were the horrifying conditions that prompted the Town fathers and the medical men of the town to take some action. In those days, there was no Town Hall so a meeting was called for 27th December 1838 in The National Schoolroom in Commercial Street at which Sir Charles Morgan of Tredegar House presided. The meeting was attended by local Members of Parliament, 'gentlemen of the town', the Mayor, clergy and medical men of Newport *'to establish a general dispensary'*. A resolution from the meeting reads: *'That it appears to this Meeting, from the great and increasing population of the Town and Neighbourhood of Newport, that the establishment of a General Dispensary is desirable as an object of great importance and of much public utility'*. A working committee was appointed consisting of the

Mayor and fourteen others to move the resolution forward. On 9th January 1839 the committee's report was presented and was recommended by a meeting of subscribers who had chosen, with some modifications, to establish an institution based on the lines of the general Dispensary of St. Mary-le-Bone in London. The committee *'found it desirable to encourage in the poor, a reliance on themselves, and to stimulate them to secure as a right, by small contributions, whilst in health, that assistance which, when disease overtakes them, they may be unable to obtain except by the charity of others'*. In other words, it was an invitation to poor people to join a local health insurance scheme!

at Llanarth Street

On 30th March 1839, the Monmouthshire Merlin announced that the Newport Dispensary would be ready to receive patients on Wednesday 3rd April and so the first voluntary movement in Newport was started in Llanarth Street to create a Dispensary for the treatment of those who were too poor to pay and were not eligible for poor relief. (Map 1 - Site 1) The announcement stated that *'Mr. J. Jones and Mr. Jehoida Brewer will attend on Mondays, Wednesdays and Fridays at ten o'clock: Mr. H. Parry and Mr. James Hawkins on the alternate days'*. Patients were requested to *'bring their own bottles'*. The Dispensary was to be staffed by local doctors on a voluntary (honorary) basis and Mr. R.F. Woollett was appointed in 1840 as the first Secretary of The Dispensary as well as Resident Surgeon. Over the years to come, he became a champion for the care of poor people in Newport. Although the 'ordinary citizen' was encouraged to subscribe to the

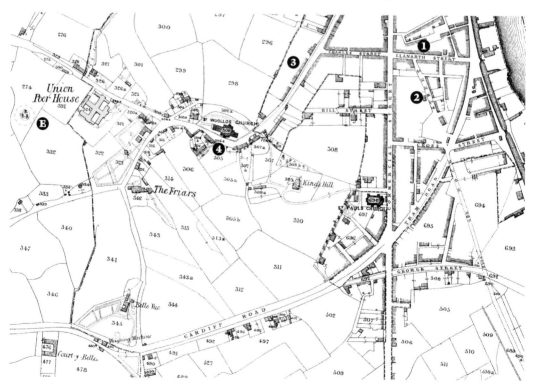

Map 1. *Tithe Map (undated ?1841) of St. Woolos Parish, Newport (Gwent Record Office reference D917.11) shows estimated sites of Newport Dispensary at Llanarth Street (1), at Dock Street (2), and known site on Stow Hill (3). Note location of Tithe Barn opposite St. Woolos Church (4) and the presence of the Union Poor House (ref. p.44) off the Turnpike Road to Bassaleg and ultimately to Penylan and Cardiff. Note earthwork (E) in section 274.*
(For higher resolution see Pull-out Map 1).

(photographic copy Andrew Ponsford)
(reproduced by kind permission of the Very Reverend Dr. Richard Fenwick, Dean of Monmouth)

Dispensary while in good health, most of its upkeep seems to have come from the better-off residents of the town who, having paid a more generous subscription, were given access to care which presumably was passed on to selected patients who would either attend the Dispensary or be visited in their homes. A further means of income came from local churches whose ministers were encouraged to preach 'charity sermons' periodically, with donation of collections made to the Dispensary.

On the 25th April 1840 a record of the patients admitted during a week to the Dispensary was published as follows:

Patients admitted	27
Cured	14
Discharged	2
Dead	1
Total number of patients under medical care	73

No patients were lodged in the Dispensary which might be compared functionally with a present-day Out-Patients Clinic.

In the meantime, the Board of Directors was obliged to inform the public that monthly meetings, presumably of subscribers, would not be held until further notice. This was apparently due to the trial at Monmouth Assizes of John Frost and others following the Chartist Riots in Newport and it is likely that some of the Directors would have been among jurors, magistrates and witnesses concerned with the trial.

About this time the Dispensary experienced some difficulty due to serious friction between several honorary medical staff some of whom resigned. This was followed by a special meeting of subscribers called under the chairmanship of a local Member of Parliament, Mr. Reginald Blewitt of Llantarnam Abbey. A committee was formed with the power to fill vacancies of consulting and visiting surgeons. Dr. W.W. Morgan of Corn Street, Newport was appointed.

However, having solved the problem of medical staff cover, debts began to mount and there were fears of closure. A report in August 1841 showed that the supply of medicines was almost exhausted largely due to unpaid bills despite vigorous efforts to increase the list of subscribers as well as fundraising activities such as a bazaar organised by the ladies of Newport and an increase of charity sermons from the town's pulpits. At the same time, the governors resolved that Mr. Woollett should continue at the Dispensary for one year at a salary of £100 provided that he, or his assistant, should be in attendance every day except Sunday between 9am and 1pm and between 4pm and 5pm. He relinquished his role as Honorary Secretary and handed over to Mr. Henry Williams from November 1842 who also assumed the duties of Treasurer. Mr. Williams eventually became highly regarded as an outstanding and much respected official - his portrait used to hang in The Board Room of the Royal Gwent Hospital.

The weekly reports of the Dispensary had not been published in the Monmouthshire Merlin for some time but they reappeared in June 1843 with the news that, because of an upsurge in subscriptions, the institution's debt had reduced from £237 to £53. The Annual Report also revealed that 860 patients had received attention that year and that almost 3,000 had been seen since the establishment of the Dispensary in 1839.

at Dock Street

The finances were, therefore, considered to have been sufficiently healthy for a move to larger and improved premises to have been considered. This took place in 1843 to 17 Dock Street. (ref. Map 1 - Site 2).

Nevertheless, Newport continued to be an unhealthy place. Mr. Woollett reported to the subscribers in 1843 that *'there are accumulations of filth in the heart of the town, amidst a population huddled in ill-ventilated apartments, and more liable to be affected by the malaria, from their frequent want of the necessities of life'*. Apparently, at least 149 cases of fever had been attended at that time. Again in 1846, Mr. Woollett drew attention to Newport's streets *'disgraced and rendered noxious by open drains and collections of filth'*. There had been 163 cases of fever out of 1294 patients seen in the Dispensary in that year as well as 248 cases reported at the Fever Hospital established in the old Tithe Barn above St. Woolos Vicarage and opposite St. Woolos Church (ref. Map 1 Site 4 area 306a). *(There is still a building on this site and part of its wall consists of stonework that could be from the original building. It is now a business concern - Editor)*

In 1849, cholera hit Newport, and in September of that year 272 people received treatment but with 28 deaths in one week.

There were no Medical Officers of Health in those days but the remarkable Mr. Woollett's persistence about the evils of poor drainage bore fruit in 1858 when a proper drainage system for Newport was introduced.

Meanwhile, medical science, such as it was in those days, had improved nationwide and must have spread to Newport as is evident from the following notice that appeared in The Monmouthshire Merlin in March 1847: *'William Wilson of Pillgwenlly has finger removed by operation using* 'ethereal vapour producing insensibility'. *First time used in Newport. Patient said that he had no sense of pain during operation and expressed great surprise, on arousing from his happy slumber at seeing his finger on the floor'.* (*This apparently innocuous event is really very remarkable because it had been only one year previously that the great Scottish surgeon Robert Liston (1794-1847) had for the first time in Britain used ether as a general anaesthetic in a public operation. That had occurred at University College Hospital, London, on 21st December 1846. For 'ethereal vapour' to be used as an anaesthetic in Newport only four months after its first public demonstration in Britain meant either that a local surgeon was well ahead of his time or was chancing his arm (and the patient) with a new-fangled idea. There is no record of the surgeon's name but the operation was clearly very successful! - Editor*)

By 1850 the finances of the Dispensary had improved and a reserve fund of 500 guineas was formed which was increased after one year to 850 guineas. These were deposited in The Monmouth and Glamorgan Bank in Newport. Unfortunately, the bank got into financial difficulties and the Trustees had to accept 15 shillings in the pound on the deposited amount.

Nevertheless, by 1856 the idea of an Infirmary was discussed. The Dispensary had remained at Llanarth Street from 1839 and in 1843 it had moved to Dock Street until 1857 when it moved for a short while to 'The Mount', 11 Park Square.

In December 1857 a deputation had called upon Sir Charles Morgan, Bt. to request that he might provide a suitable site on which to build a new Dispensary, and vacant land at Park Square was suggested (ref. Map 2 - Site 4). However, Sir Charles would not entertain the suggestion as he intended using the site as an ornamental park. This land still remains as an open space and contained a statue of Sir Charles until it was removed to Bridge Street in the centre of the town in 1992 where it remains today. Instead of this site, Sir Charles offered the Directors of the Dispensary a site on Stow Hill nearly opposite Charles Street, known as 34 Stow Hill. (ref. Map 1 - Site 3) This was readily accepted.

Building work commenced in 1858, the estimated cost being £8,000. It was estimated that £572 per annum would be needed for maintenance of the institution made up as follows:- Surgeon £100, Dispenser £50, coal and gas £30, rates and water £12, Matron £20, drugs etc £120 and six beds £240.

In March 1860, Mr. George Mayou of Monmouth was appointed as the first House Surgeon to the Dispensary on 34 Stow Hill which opened on the 14th May. There were six honorary surgeons, Dr. Christie, Dr. Davies, Mr. W. James, Mr. O.H. Jennings, Mr. L.W. Yorath and Mr. W.H. Brewer.

In the Medical Report of The Dispensary for 1861, 1909 patients had been admitted that year and 168 were under care at 31st December 1860. The Report stated that 1428 patients had been cured and 473 had been 'relieved'. It is interesting that only 32 had been admitted with fever but not surprising that 315 had been diagnosed with respiratory diseases of whom 20 had died. However, the infant mortality rate was horrific for, of fifty-eight recorded deaths, the Report stated that thirty-five had been children under five years of age. In modern terms, it is astonishing that the budget for the year, according to an audited balance sheet, had been for costs (including salaries) of £279.5s.6d against receipts of £297.5s.6d and outstanding bills of £93.6s.4d.

Therefore, by 1862 the Dispensary was about £200 in debt which seems to have caused some dissension amongst the medical staff for Mr. Mayou (who signed these Reports) resigned. Subsequently, the post of House Surgeon was advertised but it was indicated that applicants should possess qualifications of MRCS and Licentiate of the London Society of Apothecaries. A salary of £160 per annum was offered together with furnished accommodation to establish the first established post of *resident* medical officer in Newport.

Although in 1864 a Dispenser was appointed, the institution was beginning to perform as an Infirmary rather than a Dispensary although no In-Patients were cared for. Despite the fact that the finances at the time were reasonably satisfactory, the Directors felt that a house-to-house canvas might boost the coffers of the Dispensary. As it turned out there was an increase in donations but not annual subscriptions and local ministers were asked to continue the practice of 'Hospital Sundays' and 'Charity Sermons'.

The Newport Infirmary & Dispensary, 34 Stow Hill (1867)

By 1867, the first In-Patients were accommodated at Stow Hill and a Matron appointed. The Dispensary was now ready to call itself an Infirmary so that its title changed. At this time it was announced that donations of fifty guineas would entitle the donors to become Vice Presidents and Governors for life and the donation would also entitle them to nominate one patient and twenty-four dispensary patients per annum. For smaller donations lesser 'privileges' were granted.

The Newport Directory of 1878 contained the following notice: *'The Infirmary and Dispensary at No. 34 Stow Hill was opened as a Dispensary in 1839 and as an Infirmary in 1867, and contained eighteen beds. Consulting Surgeon - R.F. Woollett (who had been Resident Surgeon at The Dispensary in 1840); Medical Officers - Drs. B. Davies and James Cheese; Resident Medical Officer - O.E.B. Marsh; Visiting Surgeon to South District - Robert Cooke; Matron - Miss Lewis; Treasurer - Thomas Gratrex; Secretary - L. Mullock. Hours of attendance - Outpatients half past nine till eleven.'* (The Matron the previous year had been a Miss Irwin).

It was about this time that the Inspector of the Board of Guardians issued a critical report on 'The Old Barn', a large wooden building in Pillgwenlly between Lewis Street and Williams Street which had been converted into an Isolation Hospital. The Inspector reported that the building was so overcrowded that the beds, occupied by males and females, were so close together that they were touching one another and the stench from the building was overpowering. He suggested that the patients be transferred to other buildings including the possibility of the Infirmary, and the building be closed.

In 1881 additional property on Stow Hill adjoining the Infirmary had been purchased and construction of new wards to accommodate twenty additional patients had commenced. These were opened on the 7th November 1882 and at the same time some improvements were made to the old wards. The provision of Isolation Wards was also considered.

Further income was provided for the Infirmary in 1885 by a private home nursing scheme for paying patients and by 1889 the income from this venture had risen to £403 for the year.

At about this time, interest began in Newport about the care of children. In the early 1800s there had been no such thing as family planning or birth control. Unwanted children were often born to parents in dire poverty and were simply a burden and nuisance to them. Some found shelter in filthy overcrowded lodging houses whilst others turned to the Newport Union Workhouse on Stow Hill to join the vagrants, tramps and homeless. This building had opened in 1838 and was called the Newport Union Poor House. (ref. Map 1 and see Chapter 4).

Accommodation at the Workhouse provided an adequate existence for most families for some years but in the 1850s the building became so overcrowded that it was decided that all children over two years of age would have to be separated from their parents and housed elsewhere. A building in Caerleon known as 'The Skinyard' was chosen for this purpose and converted into an 'Industrial school' where the children could learn to work and become useful to society.

In 1887, Queen Victoria's Jubilee Year was celebrated and in Newport it was commemorated by creation of a Children's Ward containing fourteen beds. The money for this ward was raised by the Mayor, Thomas Pugsley, who had the pleasure of opening it in 1888.

The Newport & County Infirmary (1888)

By now the Infirmary was beginning to be on a firm footing on Stow Hill and in January 1888 the name of the Institution was changed from 'The Newport Infirmary and Dispensary' to 'The Newport and County Infirmary' providing accommodation for fifty patients.

In 1887 Mr. R.F. Woollett died. He had been the first Secretary, Dispenser and Resident Surgeon at The Dispensary in 1840 and had been Consulting Surgeon since 1860. He was undoubtedly an exceptional person.

In 1890 a Dental Department was set up at the same time as another new Department which was financed by the Samaritan Fund for the provision of necessary nourishment and care, clothing, artificial limbs and appliances for those on discharge.

The Newport & Monmouthshire Infirmary (1892)

In 1892, the name of the Institution was again changed to 'The Newport and Monmouthshire Infirmary.'

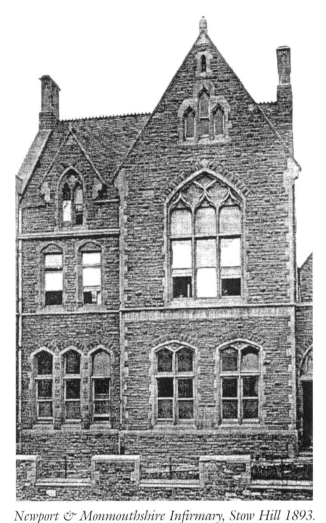

Newport & Monmouthshire Infirmary, Stow Hill 1893.
(photograph courtesy of Haydn Davies, Author 'The History of the Borough of Newport'; Pennyfarthing Press 1998)

By 1892 valuable financial help was beginning to come from bodies of workmen and as a reward for this, it was agreed that any body of workmen making donations should be entitled to 'Recommendation Notes' and might nominate one person to vote at Subscribers' Meetings. In addition a Workmen's Fund was formed, whose first subscription was £159. In recognition of the financial assistance that this fund had given, it was allowed one seat on the Board of Directors for every £250 subscribed and one Voting Representative at Subscribers' Meetings for every £100 subscribed. So began the active involvement of the working classes in the hospital until it was 'nationalised' in 1948. (see Chapter 5).

In 1895 an Eye Department was established and thoughts about building a larger Infirmary were born. To this end Dr. Garrod Thomas, who had done so much for the hospital in the past, offered £5,000 from his wife and himself provided that a further sum of £15,000 was forthcoming from other sources. Dr. Thomas' donation was a huge sum of money at that time. Encouraged by this offer Lord Tredegar offered a site on which to build a new hospital consisting of four acres of land at Cardiff Road. The Northern Boundary of this plot was marked by the houses of Clytha Square and a private dwelling called Richmond House and the eastern limit was the Cardiff Road which had the tracks of the G.W.R. Monmouthshire Railway running alongside.

The other boundaries of the plot were limited by the Estate of Friars House, which also belonged to the Tredegar House Estate and Lord Tredegar. (ref. Map 2).

The prospect of a new Hospital in the town kindled much enthusiasm and many functions were held to raise the necessary money. By 1900 £16,457 had been raised and the Directors felt that they were able to proceed with the venture. Conveyancing to The Trustees of the hospital of the site given by Lord Tredegar was completed on 22nd September 1900 with the proviso that the land was not to be used for any purpose other than that of a hospital 'without the previous consent in writing of the Vendor'.

From 1896, documents relating to this project are referred to by the name of the new hospital as 'The Newport and Monmouthshire Hospital' but in the meantime, until its opening in 1901, patients continued to be cared for at the 'Infirmary' on Stow Hill.

Hospital care in Newport had, since 1839, passed through its infancy as a Dispensary until 1867, continued through a period of adolescence as an Infirmary from 1867 until 1901 and was to emerge into an adult state in 1901 as a General Hospital, the new 'Newport & Monmouthshire Hospital.' The Infirmary building on Stow Hill was demolished in 1901 and replaced in 1904 by St. Woolos Infants and Junior School which opened in 1904 and remains to this day hoping to celebrate its centenary in 2004. A concrete gate post from the original structure still exists at that site as a reminder of the old Infirmary which in its last year in 1900, had treated 540 In-Patients, 2320 patients who had visited The Dispensary and 1268 patients visited in their own homes.

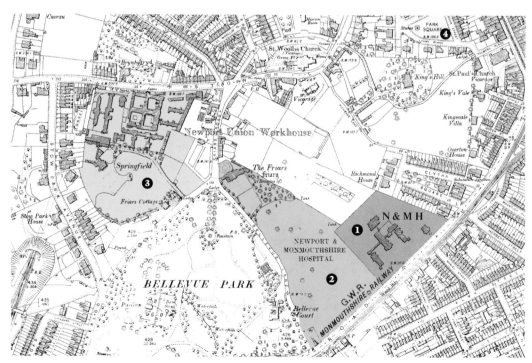

Map 2. Detail of Ordnance Survey Map, Monmouthshire Sheet XXXIII.4, 2nd Edition, 1902. Scale 25 inches to a mile. Showing central area of Newport with land donated by Lord Tredegar for the new Newport & Monmouthshire Hospital (1). Note its relation to Cardiff Road alongside The G.W.R. Monmouthshire Railway, to Clytha Square, and to the Friar's Estate owned by Lord Tredegar (2). Also the proximity of the Newport Union Workhouse/Springfield site on Stow Hill (3) and the location of Park Square (4) which was requested in 1857 as a new site for the Newport Dispensary (ref. p.4). (For higher resolution see Pull-out Map 2).

(photographic copy Andrew Ponsford)

Chapter 2: The Newport & Monmouthshire Hospital at Cardiff Road (1901 to 1913)

a) Design & Building
Terry Gale JP

Documents concerning design, contracts, drawings and planning of the new hospital have been generously made available by Mr. Terry Gale, Estate Officer of the Works & Estates of the Royal Gwent Hospital. He had acquired them by chance some years previously in Newport Market. These documents date from 1896 to completion of the hospital in 1901 and are the original papers used by the Committee, the architects and the contractors for construction of the new hospital. Therefore, they are the source of reference to the following narrative *(Editor's Acknowledgement)*.

A competition was set up for the design of the new building and submissions had to be sent to The Chairman of the Newport and Monmouthshire Hospital on or before 1st December 1896.

Instructions to Architects

Instructions to Architects for the 'Proposed New Hospital for Newport and Monmouthshire' stipulated among other conditions:
- that it was *'desirable that the competing Architects should make a personal inspection of the Site and its surroundings before sending in their design'*
- that *'a zone of 40 feet from the back garden wall of the houses in Clytha Square, forming the Northern Boundary of the Hospital Site must be left open and unbuilt upon'*
- that *'the Drainage to be connected to the existing sewer in the Cardiff Road. The approximate depth of this sewer is about 5 feet*
    Gas Mains are laid in Cardiff Road
    Water Mains (150lbs. pressure) in Cardiff Road
    Electricity Mains (alternating current) in Cardiff Road'
- that *'the present scheme is to afford accommodation for 84 patients, but the complete Hospital for 112 patients must be arranged for and the future extensions shown clearly on the drawings'*

The total Ward accommodation required was:

1 Medical ward	(12 Females)
1 Medical Ward	(12 Males)
2 Surgical Wards (12 each)	(24 Females)
2 Surgical Wards (12 each)	(24 Males)
1 Children's Ward	(12 beds)
	----------------
	84 beds
Isolation Wards (2 beds each) with each large Ward	12 beds

Total	96 beds

There was to be One Operating Room *'with all requisite fittings'*, an Anaesthetic Room and a Recovery Room.

A Casualty Room with Bathroom and Lavatory attached and an adjoining Padded Room.

A Mortuary and Post-Mortem Room (with fittings).

Patients' Lifts

An Out-Patients Department: Waiting Hall (say for 80 patients)
    Consulting Rooms with dressing rooms
    Lavatory & WC for Honorary Staff
    Lavatory & WC for Males and Females
    Casualty Room for Out-Patients (with Bathroom/WC)
    Dispensary communicating with hospital
    Drug Store
    Coal Store

It was specified that the Out-Patients should be in a separate Block and that the Waiting Room should be the equivalent of one storey in height.

It was also suggested that *it is desirable to adopt a fire-proof construction to all portions of the building used for the accommodation of patients*.

Accommodation for Administration was specified for:

Committee Room for 25 members
Secretary's Office
Waiting Rooms for Visitors and Patients
Library/Medical Staff Room
House Surgeons' Work Room
Separate Sitting Rooms for House Surgeons and Matron
Dining Room for House Surgeons and Matron together
Matron's Office
1 Bedroom for Matron
1 Bedroom for House Surgeon
1 Bedroom for Assistant House Surgeon
Day Room for Nurses
Dining Room for 26 Nurses
18 single bedded rooms for Nurses
7 double bedded rooms for Nurses
Cook's bedroom
2 double bedded rooms for Ward Maids
4 double bedded rooms for House Maids
Engineer's bedroom
Double bedded room for porters
Sitting Room for Engineers and Porters
and service facilities for kitchen, scullery, laundry
boiler room, disinfector, workshop.

(This inventory surely provides an insight into hospital staffing of those days as well as the culture that the hospital was the focus of the lives of these people. A residential commitment together with provision of day-to-day facilities was presumably normal for a hospital community at that time and this tradition lived on with some modification into the 1950s and 1960s - Editor's comment).

Finally, the bottom-line of the Instructions to Architects was that *'The total cost of the Hospital embraced in the present scheme is not to exceed £16,000'*. One can only speculate that this figure was chosen because a target of £15,000 had been the stipulation by Dr. Thomas in 1895 for his financial support and the Directors would have been satisfied that the sum received had been £16,457 (see p.8).

The first prize of the competition for design of the new hospital was £100 and went to Richard Lovell of London: the second prize of £50 was awarded to Mr. J.T. Harnet of Liverpool.

The plan for the ground floor of the hospital is shown below. The ward layout mirrors the accommodation of the wards of the second and third floors of the building.

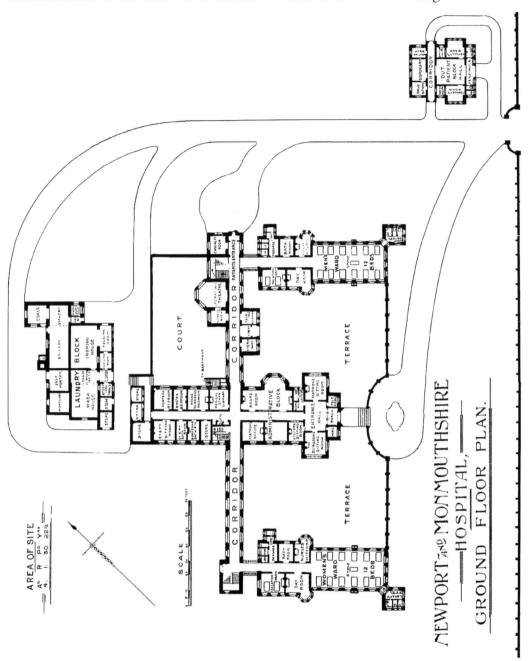

Original Contractor's drawing of the Newport & Monmouthshire Hospital. Note the position of the Out-Patient Department next to the main gate and the location of a Laundry Block behind the main hospital. Also area of site expressed in 'acres, rods, poles and yards'.

(*photographic copy Andrew Ponsford*)

Tenders and Construction

Thirteen tenders were received to build the hospital. Eight of these came from contractors in Newport and the remainder were from contractors as far afield as Barrow-

To
The Chairman
Newport & Monmouthshire Hospital,
Stow Hill, Newport.

Sir,

We the undersigned are willing to undertake the Erection of the Proposed New Hospital at Newport according to the Drawings prepared by Mr. Richard J Lovell of 46, Queen Victoria Street London, E.C. Architect and subject to all the clauses restrictions and provisions contained in the Architects Specification accompanying the Drawings for the sum of Twenty nine thousand nine hundred and fifty pounds.

£   s   d
29950 . 0 . 0.

We remain, Sir,
Yours obediently,
Name   A S Morgan & Co
Address 1 Godfrey Road, Newport.
Date 6th July, 1897.
Amount of General Estimate £29950 : 0 : 0

Extra Cost of White Glazed Brick Dado in Operating Theatre, Waiting Halls and Lobby and Hall in Out Patients Block } £70 : 7 : 8

Extra Cost of White Glazed Brick Dado in Anaesthetic Room and Corridors & Wards on Ground and First Floors and for lining the Walls of Operating Theatre with buff glazed bricks } £1364 : 19 : 0

31385 . 6 . 8

Contractors' Contract 1897.

(photographic copy Andrew Ponsford)

in-Furness, Banbury, Wolverhampton and Hereford. These varied up to £34,250 but the successful bidder was A.S. Morgan of Godfrey Road, Newport whose basic tender was the lowest, £29,950. Extras amounted to £70.7s.8d for white glazed brick dado in the Operating Theatre, Waiting Halls and Lobby and Hall in the Out-Patient Block and £1,364.19s.0d for white glazed brick dado in the Anaesthetic Room, the walls of the Operating Room and elsewhere in the hospital! The Grand Total of this tender was £31,385.6s.8d.

The contract for this work was signed on 6th July 1897 between The Chairman of Directors and A.S. Morgan.

The original designs specified installation of gas lighting throughout the hospital but this was changed to 'Electric Light, Telephone and Fire Alarm installations' at a cost

Original drawing showing design of stoves for ward heating. This is a lateral section of a stove showing a hinge to an upper grille that presumably swivelled to allow coal to be fed to the hearth below. Also, an in-flow air-duct is shown below the floor leading to a compartment for circulation of hot air. An exhaust vent via a 'smoke flue' exits below the floor to an external common chimney stack on the outside of the ward block.

(*photographic copy Andrew Ponsford*)

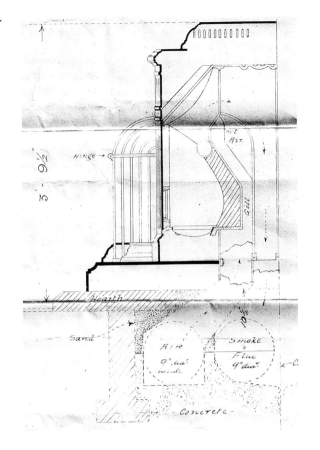

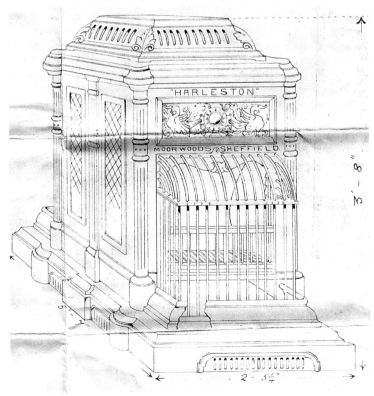

Original drawing showing external appearance of a ward stove. There was a hearth at each end and heating appeared to be a combination of radiation from the fire and convection from circulation of hot air from the grilles at the top of the stove.

(*photographic copy Andrew Ponsford*)

of £1,399.5s.0d to be completed within four calendar months of commencement of work. The contract for this work by Messrs. A. Alger of Dock Street was signed on 21st May 1899. The decision to change from gas to electrical power throughout the new hospital was undoubtedly a courageous one at the turn of the 19th to the 20th century bearing in mind the prevalence at that time of gas as a source of lighting and heating.

Another unusual feature of the hospital was the use of coal-fired stoves set in the middle of the wards to provide heating: these can be seen in the ground floor plan shown on p.11. Their design is unusual in that air inflow and exhaust outflow ducts passed to the stoves under the floorboard joists (see p.13).

The cost of Steam Laundry Machinery and fittings by Moorwood, Sons & Co. of London was quoted at £1147 and the Laundry had its own Boiler House. There was no general Boiler House.

A Tender for Fire Protection Appliances was received from Messrs. A.G. Arnold & Co., Electricians and Engineers, of 19 High Street, Newport for the sum of £450. This firm is still in business as Electricians working from 13 Skinner Street, Newport which at the time of the Tender for the new hospital was their subsidiary place of work *(information from present proprietor)*.

b) Laying of the Foundation Stone (1897)
Cliff Knight

Plate to commemorate the laying of The Foundation Stone (1897).

(photograph courtesy of Mr. Rex Moreton, Newport)

14

The Foundation Stone was laid on 2nd August 1897 by The President of the Hospital, Lord Tredegar, with a silver trowel that can be seen today in the town's Museum in John Frost Square. The Foundation Stone Plaque was salvaged when the old hospital was demolished in 1991 and was re-located in the year 2001 outside the modern Royal Gwent Hospital as a reminder of days gone by (see p.236). The captions indicate that the new hospital was built to commemorate the Diamond Jubilee of Queen Victoria.

The Foundation Stone ceremony was accompanied by a great Trade Union demonstration and a procession of some thousands of people marched, drove and rode through the town to the site of the new hospital. This large gathering of people at the opening was made even larger by a great influx of visitors to the town who had come to attend the Welsh National Eisteddfod which was being held during the same week at the nearby cattle market in Tredegar Street off Commercial Road in Pillgwenlly.

This was, of course, the time of the Boer War in South Africa, and despite an urgent need for funds to build the new hospital, the medical profession at the hospital dispensed, free of charge, prescriptions to the wives and families of soldiers engaged in the war.

c) The Grand Opening (1901)
Cliff Knight

The new Newport & Monmouthshire Hospital was completed four years after the Foundation Stone ceremony and it was built, as planned, alongside Cardiff Road (Map 2). The hospital was opened by Lord Tredegar on the 5th August 1901 accompanied by the Mayor and Corporation, and a great number of local people. It must have been a great occasion.

Opening of the Newport & Monmouthshire Hospital on its new site in 1901.

15

The Commemoration Plate for the Opening was also salvaged in 1991 and cites the names of the architects and also the Newport company, Messrs. A.S. Morgan, who were the contractors.

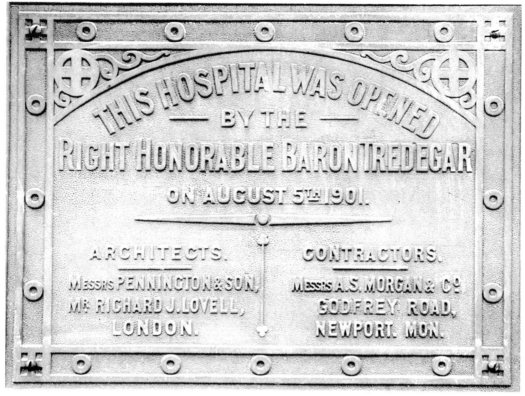

The Plate commemorating the opening of the new hospital in 1901.
(photograph courtesy of Mr. Rex Moreton, Newport)

In a leaflet advertising the event, the general public was encouraged to make Donations and take up Annual Subscriptions to defray anticipated annual maintenance costs of £5,000. It was stressed that the future was *'dependent entirely on voluntary contributions'* which proved to be a most prophetic statement. Building the new hospital had increased In-Patient accommodation to 100 patients over 45 provided in the old building on Stow Hill.

Principal Features of the New Hospital *(Terry Gale JP)*

The Contractor's drawing of the Site Plan (p.11) coincides precisely in overall design and detail with the photograph of the hospital taken in 1901 (p.17).

The hospital was built on a three-floor plan and the building was entered through a front hall in a centrally placed Administrative Block. On the ground floor alongside the entrance were a small Porter's room and a single room for a telephone. Also, there were sitting rooms for surgeons (no physicians mentioned!), the Matron and a room for visitors. Further in was bedroom accommodation for house surgeons, engineers and porters as well as a Library for Medical Staff. Ward blocks were sited on three levels as wings at each end of the building, each with 12 beds and a single Operating Theatre was situated off the main corridor at ground level. However, other drawings suggest that it is likely that an earlier and more ambitious plan had been put forward and turned

Photograph of the new Newport & Monmouthshire Hospital at the time of its opening. Note the chimney stacks arising form the ward blocks venting the ward stoves. Also, the towers at the end of each ward block; these housed toilet facilities for the patients and were in use until In-Patient accommodation moved to new buildings in the 1980s.

down. This had included a wing at the east end of the building for a dispensary and possibly an Out-Patient Hall or Casualty. It is of interest that the next phase of the hospital's development included an extension in 1916 for these same services at that end of the building. One can only speculate that, in 1901, the Directors postponed this expansion for financial reasons.

In the Entrance Hall of the hospital, the title of the institution was portrayed by floor mosaics and stone inscriptions that read 'N&MH'. There are still many medical and other staff who remember this unique feature for it was a striking introduction on entering the hospital by the front door (which for many years could only be used by consultants). The mosaic had to be removed at the time of demolition of the old hospital in 1992 but it has been preserved and is in safe storage at St. Woolos Hospital at the present time *(information from Mr. Noel Bellamy)*. There was also a Committee Room which was in continuous use as a Board Room until 1974 and was used as a Meeting Room for many years after that.

A Casualty department was built at the east end of the building and there was a small dispensary on the ground floor opposite the Operating Theatre; presumably this was for In-Patients' medications. An Out-Patient Department was a stand-alone building at the entrance gate off Cardiff Road with its own dispensary.

A Laundry and a Mortuary were built behind the main hospital. However, there was no general Boiler House for the hospital as heating for the wards came from coal-fired stoves already mentioned and which are indicated in the hospital plan (p.11). Presumably elsewhere heating would have come from open coal fires in rooms and offices. The Laundry had its own Boiler Room.

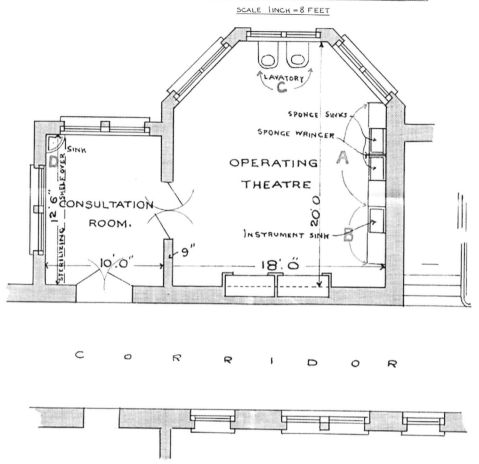

(photographic copy Andrew Ponsford)

The single Operating Theatre opened off the main corridor of the Ground Floor through a Consultation Room.

The layout of the Operating Theatre shows two sinks and draining boards designated for cleaning 'sponges' (used in those days instead of linen swabs) with a 'sponge wringer' between each sink. Over the 'sponge' sinks were overhead reservoirs for distilled water and solutions presumably used to clean sponges re-circulated for further use.

There was also a separate sink for 'instruments' and two fittings labelled 'lavatory' which, after reference to the manufacturer's design specifications, were hand-wash basins.

In the Consultation Room, there was a 'sterilizing shelf over' but there was no indication of autoclaves. One wonders whether the Consultation Room doubled up as the anaesthetic room and recovery room specified in the original Instructions for Architects.

The wards and many details of the original hospital will be very familiar to older and retired members of staff as well as older patients and visitors as these were still in use into the 1970s and 1980s. It is worth commenting that the design and layout of the 1901 hospital was far-sighted and ambitious and it served the community well for many years as it was destined to remain largely unchanged for many years to come.

Operating Theatre - Sponge Sink with solutions overhead.
<small>(photographic copy Andrew Ponsford)</small>

Operating Theatre - Lavatories. Note a foot operated tap for the left-hand basin.
<small>(photographic copy Andrew Ponsford)</small>

d) Developments from 1901 to 1913

New Facilities between 1901 and 1913 (*Cliff Knight*)

The layout of the original site of the Newport & Monmouthshire Hospital is shown by Map 2 together with the area of the property in relation to the neighbouring Friars Estate. This was the basic unit from which future developments grew during the following century, commencing within a few years of the hospital's opening.

In 1901, male patients were to be accommodated in the three wards of the east wing and the three wards of the west wing were for female patients.

Four wards of the new hospital were occupied at once and the first birth (a boy) was registered at the end of the month of opening. Home visiting by surgeons, which had been started in the Dispensary days, was discontinued. In March 1902 a fifth ward was opened but one ward remained closed because of lack of money needed for its maintenance. It was eventually opened in 1903, so that the hospital then became fully occupied. The number of In-Patients for the year was 898. In the meantime Miss Ainsworth, who had been the first Matron, resigned for reasons that were not recorded.

In 1905, the Directors equipped one room at the hospital for X-Ray purposes. (*This decision must have been a most inspirational piece of planning for it occurred only ten years after the first X-Ray had been carried out in 1895 when the German, Willhelm von Roentgen, had X-Rayed his wife's hand and laid the foundation for a revolutionary new form of medical investigation for which he received a Nobel Prize in 1901. It would be interesting to speculate on the number of other hospitals similar to the hospital in Newport that had invested in an X-Ray set so soon after Roentgen's work - Editor*)

Two years later, in 1907, the first of a number of endowed beds was established through the will of Mr. C.H. Bailey who had died that year of pneumonia.

Also in 1907, the hospital was in debt to a sum of £1,248, the first of a recurring and eventually familiar state of affairs. Local fundraising donated sums of £80 and £12 respectively in 1906 and 1907 as part of the proceeds of Fêtes held in Belle Vue Park and in 1908 £200 was received from a Carnival and Fête organised by the Workmen's Hospital Fund Committee. It was recorded at this time that four per cent of the total income of the hospital was supplied by the local churches.

It was in 1912 that Mrs. C.H. Bailey, the widow of the rich Newport ship repairer who lived in Stelvio House, Stow Hill and one of the town's most generous beneficiaries, gave to the hospital the Mortuary Chapel with its beautiful stained glass window in memory of her late husband.

Prior to 1904, the only training for midwives had been provided at the Maternity Nurses Home at the junction of Cardiff Road and Herbert Street (opposite the Royal Gwent Hospital) financed and run by Mrs. C.H. Bailey. In 1904, the Directors of the hospital set up a course to train midwives to nurse pregnant women in their own homes which was subject to regulations of the Central Midwives Board appointed by the Midwives Act in 1902. This development ended the unsatisfactory practice of untrained 'street midwives' which had grown up in the 19th century when no proper facilities had been available.

It is not widely known that, in 1905, the house at 13 Cardiff Road situated immediately opposite the present main entrance to the hospital was purchased as a temporary Home for nurses. This building now houses the offices of The Gwent Hospitals Contributory Fund.

Donation of The Friars in 1913 *(Cliff Knight & Brian Peeling)*

In 1913, the Right Honourable Courtney Charles Evan, Lord Tredegar, made it known that he intended to give the fine mansion house known as 'The Friars' to the hospital in memory of his uncle the Right Honourable Godfrey Charles, Viscount Tredegar, who had died after being President of the hospital for 37 years.

The Friars. Front aspect 2004.

On 1st August 1913, a letter to Sir Garrod Thomas from the legal advisors of the Trustees of The Tredegar Estate stated that *'it has been arranged that the Tredegar Estate Trustees shall convey the Friars house and the 5 acres of land adjoining which is the largest extent that under the Family settlements they are empowered to do, and that Lord Tredegar shall pay to his Trustees the value of the remaining 8 acres or thereabouts, so that the whole property can be conveyed as a gift'*. It is also of interest that later in this letter the following point to be settled was *'whether, should the Hospital... be taken over by the State or any Local body the land should revert to the Tredegar Estate'*. In later correspondence (19th and 22nd September 1913), the concept of *'nationalisation or municipalisation of Hospitals'* was again mentioned in relation to a reverter clause in the final Deed of Gift. With regard to the Conveyance, a small strip of land at the corner of Belle Vue Lane and Cardiff Road should receive separate attention presumably to protect tenants of a small cottage located there (seen on Map 2).

The final Conveyance of the Friars House and 13 acres that went with it was completed on 3rd November 1917 and the Conveyance of the small strip of land including the cottage was completed on 15th December 1920.

The Friars has, with time, become an integral part of the hospital scene in Newport but how and when it came into being is not clear. According to Haydn Davies (p.62 in 'The History of the Borough of Newport', Pennyfarthing Press, Newport, 1998) one authority (Archbishop Coxe) maintained that it had been a monastery for the White Friars of the Carmelite Order whereas another authority (Wakeman) considered that it had housed the Dominican Order of Black Friars. More recent research stated that there was no record of a Dominican Priory ever in Newport (*South Wales Argus* 12th January 1932).

Whatever the real background might have been, and whether it ever had connections with St. Woolos Church, it eventually became occupied as a manor house. In 1543, the property came into the hands of Sir Edward Carne but soon afterwards was bought by

Giles Morgan of Pencoed Castle who in 1547 became the first Member of Parliament for the Monmouth Boroughs. In 1730, it became the home of wealthy Newport lawyer, Thomas Clifford and in 1780 was occupied by Dr. Anthony Hawkins. Later, it was the home of Newport's rich, powerful, influential and infamous Town Clerk, Thomas Protheroe who later built and lived in Malpas Court now the site of Rougemont School. The next owner was Mr. Octavius Morgan, brother of Lord Tredegar, who lived there from 1841 to 1888. According to the well-known Gwent historian, Fred J. Hando, Octavius Morgan completely rebuilt the house into its present Gothic style. The Friars must have been a substantial home for its gardens appear to have been extensive and elaborately laid out (Map 2). The house remained in the Morgan family until it was given to the hospital in 1913.

There are several imposing features in the house especially in the entrance hall where there is a magnificent carved fireplace and screen. There is also much fine woodwork, said to be the work of William Mayo, in particular an imposing staircase with a small octagonal platform at the top overlooking the well of the stairs. From here, it is said, that Octavius Morgan led his assembled staff in prayer each morning, the housekeeper, the farm bailiff down to servants and boot boys.

Octavius Morgan died at The Friars on 5th August 1888 at the age of 84. There is an impressive brass memorial plate to him in St. Woolos Cathedral which tells us that he was educated at Westminster School and Christ Church, Oxford where he obtained MA in 1826. Later, he was made a Fellow of The Royal Society and of the Society of Antiquarians, was Member of Parliament from 1841 to 1874, and locally was J.P. and Deputy Lieutenant.

Fireplace in the Friars.
(photograph Nigel Pearce, Medical Illustration R.G.H.)

After his death, the house passed to Sir George Elliot MP until 1894 and then until 1913 was occupied by Mrs. E.H. Watts.

The house is reputed to be haunted by a ghost but it is not known whether it is an apparition of an earlier religious being or of an occupant from more recent times! However, Fred Hando recalls meeting a workman at The Friars during a visit in the late 1960s arranged for him by Miss Mary Coker, Chief Nursing Officer at The Royal Gwent.

The workman had discovered a secret passage leading from the Orangery of The Friars towards 'The Six Bells' public house (marked PH on Map No.2) which had been the ancient vicarage of St. Woolos Church. His progress along the passage had been stopped by 'a well of clear water' presumably a spring. However, this reminded Fred Hando of an account given to him by an 'ancient' organist of the church of a passage leading from beneath the organ when it had stood at the West end of the church. *'When the sermon began the ancient organist made his way down cellar steps under Stow Hill to the tavern for refreshment'*. The public house is still in active business but the cathedral organ has been re-sited to the chancel - near The Dean's Stall! Perhaps there had really been a connection between the church and The Friars in its early days of the Black Friars. However, there is no longer a connection between the modern organ loft and the 'Six Bells'.

The Friars is situated near the main entrance to Belle Vue Park on Friars Road and with it went 14 acres of land extending downhill from the building to the main hospital off Cardiff Road. This land was originally called 'Molly Rosser's Farm' and during the middle of the 19th Century was used for the renowned Stow Fairs when trades people from the surrounding areas would gather to do business and end the gathering with much merrymaking.

This donation from Lord Tredegar, therefore, increased the overall acreage of the land associated with The Royal Gwent Hospital to 18 acres.

After the Armistice in 1918, the Directors of the hospital decided to use the land for fundraising Fêtes each August Bank Holiday. (see Chapter 5)

Since that date the building has been used for many other purposes. In 1926, it was used as a convalescent home and in 1935 a fundraising Rose Show was held there. Later the Nurses' Preliminary Training School operated from The Friars and today it is used as a Postgraduate and Administrative Centre. (see Chapter 10)

In the 1960s, much of the land of Friars' Field has been used to build residential buildings to accommodate nurses and medical personnel working at the hospital at the time of expansion recorded in Chapter 6. It is interesting that many of the trees that had to be preserved for conservation reasons during building work on Friars Field in the 1960s and later, are original specimens from the late 19th century *(information from Mr. Terry Gale)*.

Chapter 3: The Royal Gwent Hospital
(1913 to 1948)

a) Principal Events to 1948

1913: The Royal Charter

In July 1913 the hospital was re-named by Royal Charter of King George V to be called 'The Royal Gwent Hospital'. This was a most prestigious honour to the Town which followed the investiture of Knighthood in June of the previous year upon the Chairman of Directors, Dr. Garrod Thomas, whose distinguished service to Newport and in particular to the hospital was, thus, recognised [1].

> [1] *There is difference of opinion regarding the correct spelling of Dr. Thomas' first name. In all references in the Royal Gwent and in the 'History of the Royal Gwent' published in 1948, his first name is 'Garrod'. In the Newport Encyclopaedia Coronation Year and Royal Visit Souvenir 1937, his first name is spelled 'Garod' presumably due to his Welsh origin and background (Editor).*

1914 to 1918: Care of Wartime Casualties

(Editor - information concerning wounded servicemen is based on 'History of the Red Cross in Monmouthshire 1910-1918' by Robin Jones RGN: Raven Press, Ltd., Pontypool 1988. Robin Jones was Charge Nurse to the Urology Unit at St. Woolos Hospital until his premature death from prostate cancer in 1997 at the early age of 59).

Soon after the outbreak of the Great War in 1914, beds for wounded soldiers and sailors at the hospital were offered by The Royal Gwent Hospital to The War Office. However, the hospital had necessarily to continue its work for the local population as well and at that time, the waiting list for the Royal Gwent was about five hundred patients. At first, fifty beds were allocated for service casualties but to support these an appeal had to be made to the public for beds and bedsteads. As usual with appeals from the hospital in Newport, these were provided. A further twenty-seven beds were added in 1916 when the new wing opened (ref. p.27).

The first casualties admitted at the beginning of October 1914 were Belgians. As the number of casualties increased, they were admitted to other hospitals in the County, such as the voluntary hospital at Pontypool and the Workhouse Infirmary Hospital at Griffithstown. Casualties usually arrived by Red Cross Train at Newport Station and after treatment in the hospital were discharged back to their units or transferred to an Auxiliary Red Cross Hospital for rehabilitation and convalescence. To illustrate the activity of the Royal Gwent during the war years, in one week in April 1915 there were eighteen sick servicemen in the hospital, and in the wards there were 112 patients, 24 further patients at The Friars and 395 who had attended the Out-Patients department. By November 1916, the number of wounded men in hospital beds had increased to 80. There were 40 beds in The Friars which were occupied by servicemen during their convalescence.

Wounded soldiers, while at the hospital, wore a distinctive blue uniform that earned them the name 'Blue Boys'. Many local people visited them while they were in hospital and sometimes took them out to parties, teas, concerts and bus rides which the men appreciated considerably.

The Newport Workhouse on Stow Hill also contributed to the care of wounded soldiers and sailors. In March 1915, the Newport Board of Guardians, which was responsible for its administration as both a Workhouse and an Infirmary, considered conversion of the institution to become a Military Hospital for wounded servicemen and later it became the Newport Section of The 3rd Western General Military Hospital whose headquarters was in Cardiff. It was therefore, under the control of the Western Command of the Military. In March 1916, 178 wounded and sick servicemen arrived at Newport Station from a variety of operational zones - the Dardenelles, Egypt, Serbia, Greece and Malta. They brought with them a host of medical problems ranging from typhoid and paratyphoid, malaria, septicaemia, various wounds and amputations, jaundice, ulcers, frostbite and other problems including some with heart disease. Then, again, in July 1916 the hospital had to accept at short notice 243 casualties, including 100 men on stretchers. In March 1917, 158 wounded men arrived, 123 on stretchers. These were followed by 137 men in April 1917.

Men admitted to the hospital were subject to military discipline because of its military status and there were proper rules that had to be observed. For example, smoking was not allowed on the wards so that smokers were forced to smoke outside the building (as they do in the Newport hospitals in the year 2004!). As a guideline, alcohol consumption was limited to two pints of beer per day per soldier to be taken at the end of the day and not on an empty stomach. However, strict discipline was applied to bad behaviour and drunkenness. Also, wounded or sick soldiers were punished if caught drinking outside the hospital and legal proceedings could be taken against members of the public providing alcoholic drink for these men.

As it was a Military Hospital, the hospital was staffed by Royal Army Medical Corps personnel from Medical Officers, orderlies, drivers, administrators, clerks and the nurses came from the Queen Alexandra's Imperial Nursing Service.

1914 to 1931: Further Facilities and Hardships (Cliff Knight)

Despite the hardships during the Great War and the next two decades, several important developments occurred at The Royal Gwent Hospital to give the local population ever improving clinical services. It is evident that the Directors of the hospital were people with foresight and vision who got things done. The basic layout of the hospital site of 1914 was unchanged from the building constructed in 1901.

The sequence of the developments that occurred during the next thirty years is illustrated chronologically by the site plan shown over the page. This can be followed during the account of developments at the hospital in the years up to 1948.

By 1915, all six wards were in action, all designed with the legendary Nightingale layout in which beds were placed in rows along the walls of the room and a central area was used as a rest and feeding area for mobile patients.

In February 1914, after internal alterations to the newly acquired Friars House, the overall accommodation of the hospital increased when sixteen patients were admitted there.

By that time the Directors had decided that it was necessary to build a new wing to the hospital, with a greatly improved Casualty Department, an additional male ward, two operating theatres and an Ear, Nose and Throat Department on the main site. Despite the increased burden of caring for soldiers and sailors, this extension opened in 1916 and was

ROYAL GWENT HOSPITAL
SITE DEVELOPMENT 1913-1948

1   FRIARS HOUSE 1913-1917
2   NEW WING 1916
3   RICHMOND HOUSE 1920
4a NEW X-RAY/PATHOLOGY 1921
4b NEW LAUNDRY 1924
4c BOILER HOUSE 1924
4d NEW KITCHEN 1924
5   OUT-PATIENTS/NURSES HOSTEL 1924
6   NEW NURSES HOME 1933
7   FRACTURE/ORTHOPAEDIC UNIT 1943
8   OLD OUT-PATIENTS UNTIL 1924 LATER WAS V.D. DEPARTMENT
9   64 CARDIFF ROAD FROM 1925

ROYAL GWENT HOSPITAL
SITE DEVELOPMENT 1948-1968

A NEW CASUALTY UNIT 1962
B SHORT STAY UNIT 1974
C POSTGRADUATE LECTURE
    HALL 1968

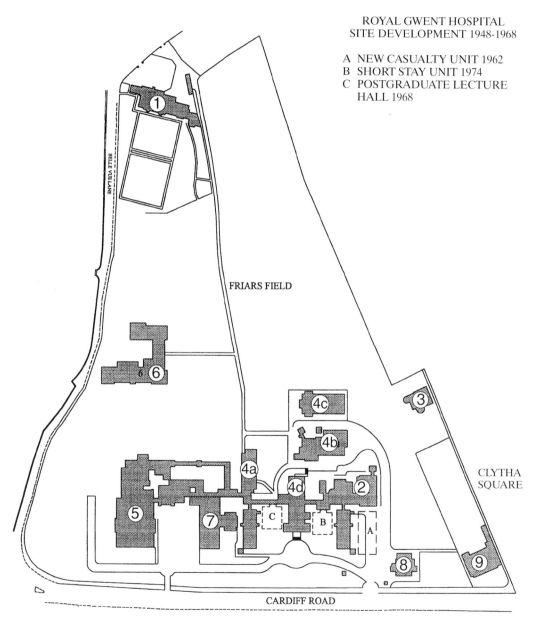

Women and Children's Ward, Christmas 1915.
Note the rows of beds peripherally. Also the nurses' uniforms and the polished floors.

remarkably similar in design to the wing at the eastern end of the hospital that is thought to have been rejected from the final design for 1901 (ref p.26/2 and p.28).

The Casualty unit was situated on the ground floor. The new ward situated on the first floor was intended for male patients. It was known as Grice Ward and later as Ward 7. Two Operating Theatres were located on the top floor of this wing and included Rest Rooms for medical staff and for nursing staff. This suite continued in use by all surgical specialties until 1943, when orthopaedic surgery transferred to its new home in the Orthopaedic and Fracture Unit. For a further twenty-five years, all general surgery was carried out in these theatres until 1968, and all E.N.T. surgery until 1977 when, finally, the suite was used as a medical endoscopy unit until 1990. This made a total active life for this suite of eighty-four years.

Almost immediately after the Armistice that ended The Great War, a most prestigious event occurred for the Royal Gwent Hospital when The College of Arms granted the hospital in 1919 a Coat of Arms on which were the Welsh words *'Goreu Olud Iechyd'* (*'The Best Wealth is Health'*).

During the Wartime years, the hospital had been continuously in debt and in October 1915 house-to-house collections had been organised. Eventually the debt was cleared largely due to a windfall of £10,000 received from the Central Demobilisation Board in 1920 together with £47,000 raised by contributions. These were, indeed, enormous sums in those days.

Heraldic Warrant 1919. Coat of Arms of Royal Gwent Hospital.

The first Extension of the new hospital 1916.
Ground Floor: Casualty. Middle Floor: Grice Ward (for men). Top Floor: Operating Theatres.

This encouraged the Directors to press ahead with plans for further expansion of the hospital.

Firstly, in 1920, they decided to purchase a house adjacent to the hospital site, Richmond House, to accommodate nurses (p.26/3). This building must have been a private house of some social standing with its own garden. Conveyancing documents and other records in the possession of the Gwent Healthcare N.H.S. Trust show that in 1862, Richmond House was leased from William Jones of Clytha Park to Peter Williams of Newport, a Master Mariner. His daughter, Mrs. Lydia Beynon and the wife of Thomas Beynon assigned in 1880 the residue of the Lease to Theophilus John Beynon a Shipowner, who, acquired the property fully in 1886. The house and its land was sold in 1897 to Mary Orders, wife of William James Orders of Newport, another Shipowner. In 1901, it was sold again to George Rudd Thompson, an Analytical and Consulting Chemist and again in 1914 to a Newport Merchant, Richard Williams. Finally, following Richard Williams' death, Richmond House was conveyed to The Trustees of The Royal Gwent Hospital on 16th October 1920. It is interesting that the house was associated with some well-known local names especially with Lydia Beynon Beynon whose son, Sir John Beynon donated 'The Coldra' to the Monmouthshire County Council in 1924 to be a Maternity Hospital in memory of his mother. This became known as 'The Lydia Beynon Maternity Hospital' which, in 1948, came under the control of the Newport & East Monmouthshire H.M.C. (ref. pp.72, 198) *(information from Mrs. Gill Winstanley, Facilities Department, Gwent Healthcare N.H.S. Trust)*.

Also, plans were made at that time for extensions including new X-Ray and Pathology Departments, a new laundry with a separate boiler house built behind the laundry block, a new kitchen, and a new Out-Patients Department with a Nurses' Hostel in its upper floor, and an Isolation Block (ref. p.26/4a, 4b, 4c, 4d, 5).

Richmond House as it is today. Its location at the northern corner of the original site of The Royal Gwent Hospital is seen clearly on Map 2.

In 1921, the new X-Ray Department and Pathological Department were equipped and a Skin Department was established with the appointment of Honorary Heads of all these Departments. That was also the year of the visit of the Prince of Wales to the hospital.

The new kitchen, laundry and boiler house were completed by 1924 and, presumably, some form of central heating was installed instead of the stoves in the wards that had been in operation since 1901.

Even allowing for the windfall from the Government received in 1920, fundraising always occupied much of the time of the hospital authorities. In May 1920 Newport R.F.C. played Pill Harriers in a charity match which raised a considerable sum and in the summer of that year £2,000 was raised at the Hospital Fête. Despite this, nurses continued to dress up in their uniforms to attend some of the local churches to take up collections on 'Hospital Sundays' as a further means of income.

All kinds of means were used to raise money for the upkeep of the hospital but in April 1923 John Cashmore Ltd., whose main job was dismantling ships which had finished their useful life, charged people to view H.M.S. Collingwood before it was broken up. This raised £816.

In 1924, the new Out-Patients Department planned by the Directors was opened by Lord Tredegar (ref. p.26/5 and p.30). This was built at the West end of the hospital and is still in use today (after several re-furbishings). The original Out-Patients Department built near the main entrance to the hospital in 1901 was later used for treatment of Venereal Diseases (ref. pp.26/9 and p.122).

The hours of attendance for Out-Patients in the 1920s were :
Eye Department - Tuesdays and Fridays 1.30-2.30pm
Ear Nose and Throat Department - Wednesdays 1-2pm
Dental Department - 9-9.30am
Medical and Surgical Departments - Mondays, Wednesdays, Thursdays and
Saturdays 10-11am

The new building opened in 1924 for an Out-Patients Department on the ground floor and accommodation as a Nurses' Hostel in the top floor. It is likely that this photograph was taken about 1935 in view of the sign appealing for £100,000 (ref. p.33).

No visiting was allowed to the Children's Ward, and no children under 14 years of age were allowed to visit patients in adult wards. The Adult Wards could be visited on Sundays, Wednesdays and Saturdays between 3 and 4pm and admission was only by ticket which had to be obtained at the hospital porter's lodge. The same regulations applied to 'The Friars'. There are still many citizens of Newport who recall these arrangements with some amusement. It seems that patients on admission to the hospital were allocated two tickets for their visitors and these became items of considerable value as others waiting at the gates of the hospital could only get in if the tickets were handed over by those leaving the hospital after visiting-time. The porter at the gate was, therefore, a person of great power for he controlled the flow of visitors. In fact, this system operated into the 1950s when the gate was controlled by a Mr. Wilson. He also meticulously opened and closed the main gates for each vehicle entering or leaving the hospital and is depicted at the gate on the watercolour of the hospital in 1950 shown on the front cover of this book *(information and painting by Mr. Stan Jordan, lately Superintendent Radiographer at the Royal Gwent).*

However, conditions in the hospital must have been hard for some people. In 1926 the Matron, Miss Foster Feather, publicly thanked the *South Wales Argus* for all the help that the newspaper had given to patients, including radio which had been installed throughout the hospital and toys to the Children's Ward. For some time prior to 1926 it had been felt that a great many of the In-Patients were in such poor circumstances that, although entitled to hospital treatment, they could not provide for their own non-medical needs while in hospital. A scheme was started to rectify this.

Also, the hospital became a complete Training School for Nurses.

In 1926, the Newport Directory recorded that 2,173 patients had been treated in the main hospital in 1925, 212 had been admitted to The Friars and 12,519 people had attended the Out-Patients department. The average daily cost for In-Patient care had been just over nine shillings (45p) per patient. The Directory continued with the names of all the medical staff and other senior staff members including the Matron, Miss Margaret Husband. Up to that time, the workload of the hospital since 1903 had shown a steady increase and The Quinquennial Statement of 1927 showed that since 1903 the number of Out-Patients and casualties seen and In-Patients treated had trebled leading to inevitable overall increase of costs but fortunately there had been parallel increased income especially from local working sources and especially from The Workmen's Fund. Otherwise, the hospital would surely have been in danger of foundering.

QUINQUENNIAL STATEMENT OF PATIENTS TREATED AND OF THE INCOME OF THE INSTITUTION. (1927)

Years.	Out-Patients and Casualties.	In-patients.	Shipping Contributions.	Contributions from Places of Worship.	Workmen's Contributions.	Workmen's Fund.	Hospital Balls.	Hospital Fetes and Carnivals.	Total Ordinary Income.
			£	£	£	£	£	£	£
1839—42	2133	—	—	—	—	—	—	—	—
1843	860	—	—	—	—	—	—	—	285
1848	1375	—	—	—	—	—	—	—	234
1853	1503	—	—	—	—	—	—	—	301
1858	2387	—	—	—	—	—	—	—	301
1863	2123	—	—	—	—	—	—	—	777
1868	2651	41	—	—	—	—	—	—	716
1873	3609	108	183	89	—	—	—	—	1696
1878	2750	154	297	96	50	—	—	—	1176
1883	2862	223	521	198	110	—	—	—	1606
1888	4837	360	586	162	225	—	—	—	2218
1893	4153	338	384	168	Not shown	159	—	—	2375
1898	4322	529	363	161	,,	1000	70	—	3162
1903	4497	883	488	260	,,	1450	—	—	4794
1908	7053	1173	551	387	778	2000	—	—	6528
1913	9009	1213	595	420	770	2600	301	479	9043
1918	8252	1777	347	824	1085	5400	—	—	13392
1923	10642	2009	755	937	976	9000	624	4616	24379
1927	14325	2290	613	792	1949	12000	524	6025	29766

1931: Sir Garrod Thomas (1853 to 1931)
(Editor - information about Sir Garrod Thomas from Miss Beryl Griffiths)

In February 1931 the death occurred of Sir Garrod Thomas, described as Newport's best beloved citizen. He had given 50 years of unselfish devotion to the town and especially to the Royal Gwent Hospital for without his drive and vision, The Royal Gwent Hospital might never have come into existence.

He had been born on 5th October 1853 at Panteryrod, a farm near Aberaeron in Cardiganshire and was the youngest of five sons of Lewis Thomas. His upbringing was frugal and Puritan and in his youth he attended school in Milford Haven where he became 'apprenticed' to a doctor. At the age of 18, in 1871, he studied medicine at Edinburgh University including instruction under the great surgeon, Joseph Lister. He had a distinguished career for he won a first prize and obtained the degree of MD in 1876. After studying at St. Bartholemew's Hospital in London, he became a Member of the Royal College of Surgeons and also proceeded to Master of Surgery, Doctor of Literature and Justice of the Peace.

Dr. Thomas settled in Newport in 1877 and in 1879 married Eleanor, the only surviving daughter of R.H. Richards. They had three children. Dr. Thomas set up as a General Practitioner with Honorary duties at the Newport Infirmary on Stow Hill. It was at that time that he had visions of a new, larger and better hospital for Newport for he was very concerned about the appalling conditions in the Infirmary and as has been noted earlier, donated a huge sum of £5,000 towards a new and better hospital. By his leadership and example the local community raised sufficient funds to build the new Newport & Monmouthshire Hospital, open it in 1901 and so on to The Royal Gwent Hospital in 1913.

Sir Garrod Thomas (1853-1931).

Dr. Thomas was a courteous man who was loved for himself as well for his medical service. He played an active part in church life (at Victoria Road Congregational Church as well as Mount Zion Welsh Church in Hill Street). He was a member of the Town Council from 1881 to 1897, was appointed High Sheriff of Cardiganshire in 1901, was a Director of the *South Wales Argus* and was one of the founder members in 1905 of the Newport Welsh Society of which he became President the following year. His knighthood in 1912 was the first to a person from Newport to receive that honour for seventy years and was a just recognition of his work.

He died in 1931 and requested that, after death, his heart be removed and buried with his ashes next to his wife who had died in 1926. That was done.

Following his death, a bronze bust of 'The Beloved Physician', as he came to be known, was sculpted by L.S. Merriefield. This stood in the entrance hall of the old Royal Gwent until 1991 when the old building was demolished. It now stands on a plinth made by the Works Department in the entrance lobby of The Post Graduate Medical Centre at 'The Friars'.

Sir Garrod Thomas and his wife lived at 'Bron-y-Gaer', 4 Stow Park Circle. This now houses The Mayor and Lady Mayoress of Newport during their year of office.

1931 to 1946: The Years to Completion of the Hospital *(Cliff Knight)*

Despite the great success of the annual Carnivals and Fêtes, in April 1931 the hospital still reported a deficit of £2,000. In December 1932, the *South Wales Argus* came to the rescue again and launched an appeal to renew the worn-out radio installation which they had provided eight years previously.

Nevertheless, in 1933 the Directors built a Nurses' Hostel on ground alongside Belle Vue Lane (ref. p.26/6)

New Nurses' Home 1933.

By the beginning of 1935, after years of trade depression and unemployment, the financial position of the hospital had been so desperate that it could only be cured by a superhuman effort. The bank overdraft was £65,000, developments and extensions were overdue so, to try to reduce this debt, 'pay-beds' were suggested!!

In October, in an attempt to clear some of the debt, John Cashmore Ltd. put on view the famous Cunard White Star Liner 'Doric' which they had bought for breaking up and promised all viewing entrance fees to the hospital. But this and other efforts only scratched the surface of the problem so that the Directors made the bold decision to launch an appeal to raise £100,000 The emphasis was not so much on the debt to be paid, but on new works to be done and further new services to be introduced such as a Fracture and Orthopaedic Unit which was urgently required. After two years from the start of the launch, £50,000 had been received as promised. The remaining £50,000 needed to achieve the target was more difficult to raise and an appeal was made to the Workmen's Fund. There was an immediate response as its members increased their individual subscriptions from threepence to fourpence per week. This was a great sacrifice especially in those days of hardship. However, these additional pennies brought in £30,000 and in recognition of this a ward in the hospital was named 'The Whitehead Ward' after the nearby Whitehead's Works whose workmen had shown unselfish generosity in their response to the appeal. Another welcome contribution came from the Miners Welfare Fund who contributed £4,000.

In March 1939, the hospital had planned to celebrate the centenary of the foundation of the Newport Dispensary for it would have been 100 years since it had been set up in Llanarth Street. The celebrations were put off presumably due to the imminence of war with Germany.

Then in September 1939 came the outbreak of the Second World War. Should the planned developments go on, especially a unit for Fractures and Orthopaedics? Should they be delayed until peace had been declared? The Directors were adamant that they must proceed and to demonstrate their intentions, a foundation stone for the Fracture and Orthopaedic Unit was laid in August 1940 even though that month was one of the darkest in the history of our country.

An incident involving the Royal Gwent at that time took place on the 13th September 1940 during the German bombing of the town. A German plane collided with a barrage balloon, crashed onto 31 Stow Park Avenue, which was a stone's throw from the back of Woolaston House Hospital. The son and daughter of the occupants of the house, Mr. and Mrs. Phillips, perished in the fire that followed. The pilot of the aircraft, Harry Wappler, landed by parachute in Queen Street, was captured by P.C. Cox and a Home Guard soldier and taken to the Royal Gwent Hospital with a fractured arm. He had arrived too early to visit the proposed Fracture Unit. However, some days after the event Mrs. Phillips very graciously went to The Royal Gwent to comfort the pilot. It is said that a cat had been aboard the plane and was found wandering in the streets of Newport after the crash but it is not known how it was identified although, presumably, it spoke German!

It was not generally known until recently that in 1940, Stanley Lewis, now still alive and aged 97, embarked on painting a large canvas measuring eight feet by seven feet with its main theme to commemorate Newport's civilian and rescue workers at the crash of the German aircraft on the town. At the time, Mr. Lewis was a lecturer at the Newport School of Art and the work remained incomplete because he was drafted into the Army. The painting would have remained unknown had it not been for the Keeper of Newport's Museum and Art Gallery, Mr. Roger Cucksey, who found it in the archives and arranged for it to be restored with aid from a grant made by the Council of the Museums in Wales. The restored painting has been on display since November 2002 in the Newport Art Gallery and Museum as well as a range of preparatory sketches made by the artist *(information from Mike Buckingham, South Wales Argus, January 24, 2003).*

Sketch by Stanley Lewis.
(reproduced by courtesy of Mr. Roger Cucksey)

34

Painting by Stanley Lewis.

(reproduced by courtesy of Mr. Roger Cucksey)

Recently, an elderly lady requested to meet Roger Cucksey at the Newport Museum and stated categorically to him that the nurses' uniforms in Stanley Lewis' painting were not correct. It appeared that as she had been a nurse at The Royal Gwent at the time of the crash she was a reliable authority. She had also witnessed the collision of the aircraft with the cable of a barrage balloon and its fall to the ground. Furthermore, she had nursed the pilot in the hospital and commented that 'he was nice young man - not like those awful Nazis'. However, he was not immediately told that his crew had perished in the crash but when he knew about this was inconsolable *(information from Roger Cucksey included with his permission - Editor)*.

During the earlier years of the war, Air Raid Wardens patrolled the hospital mostly on the lookout for incendiary bombs that might fall on the roof; presumably because of its close location to the hospital, Richmond House was made into an Emergency Centre for the Wardens.

Throughout the War, the hospital was still scraping for money. Churches still held 'Hospital Sundays' and at the Mayor-Making Ceremony a collection was made which raised only £10. In January 1942 the poverty of the hospital was reflected when an appeal was made for old slippers, old toilet bags, vegetables, old linen, hymn books and old jugs and basins. Although the nursing staff must have found the work hard during those difficult years, their morale was apparently high and in January 1943 demonstrated this by giving a variety concert for the patients.

In June 1943 the Annual Report indicated that 300 Out-Patients had been treated daily with ten operations performed each day and a special mention was made of the voluntary stretcher bearers. In 1944, at the time of the invasion of France, the hospital prepared itself to receive casualties of both sides from the Normandy Beaches. An entry in a book describing those times read: *June 1944 - British and German soldiers wounded in the invasion of the Normandy Beaches arrive at The Royal Gwent Hospital. Some German soldiers said to be arrogant and as young as 15.'*

Despite the War, the Orthopaedic and Fracture Unit was built and opened in February 1943. At the end of the war in 1945, it was found that the sum needed to complete this development had increased from £100,000 to £150,000. Undaunted, the Appeals Committee continued their efforts and were able to report that the Orthopaedic and Fractures Unit had been built and equipped at a cost of £151,000 (ref. p.26/7).

Fracture & Orthopaedic Department 1943.

The hospital's kitchen had also been enlarged, reconstructed and equipped at a cost of £4,700, and £50,000 had been paid to reduce the bank overdraft! Also, Richmond House had been refurbished and redecorated to house additional staff.

In December 1945 a Nurses Preliminary Training School at the hospital was proposed with the unusual suggestion that men as well as women should be attracted into the profession.

In 1945, as the War ended, the growth of Royal Gwent Hospital from its birth in 1901 had reached its final stage of structural development prior to handover to State control three years later.

To summarise the major events of the development and growth of The Royal Gwent Hospital since 1901, the following sequence had occurred:

1901:	Grand Opening of the new hospital
1905:	first X-Ray Room
1913:	donation of 'The Friars'
1916:	new wing for Operating Theatres (2), 'Grice' Ward (1) and Casualty; new E.N.T. Department
1920:	purchase of Richmond House
1921:	new Pathology and Skin Departments, new X-Ray Department
1924:	completion of new Laundry, Kitchen and the first Boiler House
1924:	opening of new Out-Patient Department, Nurses' Hostel, Isolation Block,
1933:	new Nurses' Hostel (adjacent to Belle Vue Lane)
1940:	F.O.U. Department Foundation Stone
1943	opening of dedicated Fracture and Orthopaedic building with Ward, Theatre (1), and Clinics

1946 to 1948: Transition to State Ownership (Cliff Knight)

In 1947 the hospital began to prepare for the time when it would change from a voluntary organisation to one funded by the Government. Lord Tredegar, who had supported the voluntary system, felt that there should be no change. However, change to Government control was inevitable as the National Health Service Act approved in 1946 was due to come into force in 1948, bringing all privately run hospitals such as The Royal Gwent under Government control. This was the final step of an evolutionary social process that had increased in momentum over many years beginning in the 19th century. The fundamental principle underlying such a radical change of Health Care was the undertaking by Central Government to fund services needed to provide free Healthcare to the nation. No longer would the community in Newport and its environs be asked to find monies to support The Royal Gwent and other Hospitals in Monmouthshire.

Therefore, the arrival of the National Health Service into the life of the nation created a formidable challenge to all concerned with health care, but was an exciting concept that intended to provide universal access to medical care especially for the poorer members of society. It was the brainchild of Aneurin Bevan who rose from representative of the people of Ebbw Vale as their Member of Parliament to the Cabinet as Minister of Health.

The giant leap forward when the National Health Service Act of 1946 came into force in 1948, was to be provision of a comprehensive health service for England and Wales linking the three major aspects of health care which were:

1. Hospital and Specialist Services
2. Family Practitioner Services
3. Local Health Authority Services supplementary to the Hospital and Practitioner Services

Prior to empowerment of the Act, and to lay the foundation required for the hospitals in Wales to fulfill their commitment to the first of these criteria, the infrastructure of the National Health Service as it would affect hospitals in Wales had to be created. The

Welsh Board of Health would take over financial responsibilities and from 31st October 1947 the Directors of The Royal Gwent Hospital were relieved of all financial matters including an overdraft of £91,000. However, day to day running of the hospital remained in the hands of the Directors until 5th July 1948, when The National Health Service came into existence.

From that day, consultants and doctors would no longer give their services on a voluntary basis to the hospital but would receive an appropriate remuneration from the Government on the basis of a Contract to provide services.

Henceforth, it was envisaged that the hospital should not need to rely on money donated from carnivals, fêtes, churches, voluntary donations and other sources of money because central funding from Government would take over responsibility for financial stability.

On the 15th June 1948 the hospital came to the end of its time as a Voluntary institution when the full Board of Directors met in the Board Room for the last time to pass over their power of authority.

Thanks were expressed to all those, both paid and unpaid, who over the years had played a part in the great enterprise of the new Newport hospital started in 1901. Those who spoke included the Chairman of the Board Mr. G.E. Dibdin JP, the Chairman of the Workingmen's Fund Mr. J. Bellew, Mr. W.S.J. Williams DL the Honorary Treasurer, Miss E. Frances Greene, the Matron, Mr. Trevor Jones, Secretary/Superintendent and Mr. P. Spencer.

The principal officials and officers serving at the time of transfer to The National Health Service were:

Patron:	H.M. Queen Elizabeth
President:	The Rt. Hon. Viscount Tredegar DL, FRSA
Hon Vice-President:	Mr. H.S. Lyne MBE
Trustees:	The Rt. Hon. Viscount Tredegar
	Mr. Noel Garrod Thomas CBE
	Mr. C.O. Lloyd
	Mrs. M.E. Coulman
Chairman of Directors:	Mr. G.E. Dibdin JP
Deputy Chairmen:	Mr. P. Fligelstone
	Mrs. M.E. Coulman
Hon Treasurer:	Mr. W.S.J. Williams DL
Secretary:	Mr. Trevor A. Jones

H.M. Queen Elizabeth remained as Patron of the Royal Gwent Hospital until her death as Queen Mother at the age of 101 years in 2002.

1948: The Newport & East Monmouthshire Hospital Management Committee
(*Editorial Review*)

When the National Health Service was introduced in 1948, the Minister of Health became responsible to Parliament for the efficient administration of the Service. For hospital and specialist services, Regional Hospital Boards were created to plan and administer hospital services in their areas and were responsible to the Minister. On a local basis, smaller Hospital Management Committees responsible to Regional Boards were set up to control local hospital services such as use of hospital beds in each area, and use of resources to avoid wastage by competition between hospitals. However, they only had limited authority over capital projects.

In Wales, the Regional Authority was The Welsh Hospital Board, and The Royal Gwent Hospital and other hospitals in the south of the county came under the control of The Newport & East Monmouthshire Hospital Management Committee (H.M.C.).

The H.M.C. was responsible for the following institutions:
In Newport:
    The Royal Gwent Hospital (259 beds*)
    St. Woolos Hospital (402 beds*)
    Allt-yr-yn Hospital (pre-convalescent and infections 57 beds)
    Lydia Beynon Hospital (General Practitioner obstetrics 24 beds)
    St. Cadoc's Hospital (psychiatric 380 beds)

In the Pontypool area:
    Pontypool & District Hospital (115 beds*)
    Monmouthshire County Hospital in Griffithstown, (206 beds*)
    Snatchwood Hospital, Abersychan (40 long stay beds)
    Sunnybank Hospital (children and women)

In the Chepstow area:
    St. Lawrence Hospital (150 beds*)
    Mount Pleasant Hospital (TB Annexe 150 beds)
    Chepstow & District Hospital (Gen. Practitioner beds - 20 beds)

Elsewhere in Gwent:
    Llanfrechfa Grange Hospital
    Cefn Mably Hospital (158 beds for tuberculosis).
    Cefn Ila (18 beds for maternity)

Bed complements taken from Second Annual Report of Newport & E. Mon. H.M.C. 1949/1950)

The Administrative Centre of the Hospital Group was located at 64 Cardiff Road in the grounds of the Royal Gwent Hospital at the junction of Cardiff Road with Clytha Square. This building had been constructed in the 19th century and can be seen on the Ordnance Map of 1902 (Map 2 and ref. p.26/9) at the corner between Cardiff Road and Clytha Square. Conveyancing documents held by The Gwent Healthcare N.H.S. Trust indicate that this building had been acquired by the Trustees of The Royal Gwent Hospital on 28th January 1925 *(information from Mrs. Gill Winstanley, Facilities Department)*. Previously, it had been three houses, and these were numbered 16, 17 and 18 Cardiff Road. In 1933, the administrative offices of The Royal Gwent Hospital were located in Number 16, nurses were accommodated in Number 17 and Number 18 was a private residence of a Miss Minnie Hurley. The Hospital Secretary in 1933 had been Mr. J.K. Milward and his assistant had been Mr. S.G. Jones *(information from Mrs. Nesta Roberts aged 86 who had worked in Number 16 during those years)*. It is not known when these properties were fused into one with its present postal address but it is probable that with time the whole building was acquired by the hospital by 1948.

The Management Committee met in The Board Room of the Royal Gwent until the dissolution of the H.M.C. in 1974 and its membership at the beginning of the era under the N.H.S. (according to *The Second Annual Report of 1949/1950*) was :

Chairman: Alderman J.J. Panes OBE
Vice-Chairman: Alderman G.A. Gibbs JP

House Committees were set up for:

> The Royal Gwent Hospital
> St. Woolos & Allt-yr-yn Hospitals
> Pontypool, Cefn Ila & Snatchwood Hospitals
> County, Lydia Beynon & Llanfrechfa Hospitals
> Cefn Mably Hospital
> Chepstow & District, TB Annexe Chepstow

The Royal Gwent Hospital in 1948 (Editorial Review)

The immediate change for the Royal Gwent Hospital after 5th July 1948 was not only loss of its independent status as a voluntary hospital but also its independence of action as it became only one of the group of hospitals in the county controlled by The Newport & East Monmouthshire Hospital Management Committee. Although the status of the Royal Gwent Hospital would be that of the lead institution in the south of the county, its priorities, especially with budgeting, would have to be shared with the other hospitals in The Newport & East Monmouthshire Hospitals Group. From 5th July 1948, therefore, the work of The Royal Gwent Hospital overlapped and became integrated with several hospitals in the county because consultants on the staff of the Royal Gwent were contracted to visit outlying hospitals of the hospital group.

However, consultants from some specialties (eg. gynaecology and paediatrics) visited other outlying small hospitals elsewhere in the county, such as Aberbeeg Hospital and Tredegar Hospital which were administered from North Monmouthshire.

Furthermore, surgery and obstetrics, some gynaecology as well as general medicine was carried out at Woolaston House on Stow Hill which in 1948 functioned independently of The Royal Gwent Hospital. These services were inevitably part of an overall hospital service in Newport as on-call services and other aspects of health care became shared between the two institutions after inauguration of the National Health Service.

Pre-convalescent beds (medical and surgical) were available at Allt-yr-yn Hospital in Newport where an Isolation Unit for Infectious Diseases was also located. It is of interest that at that time, notices appeared daily in *The South Wales Argus* reporting the progress of patients under isolation at Allt-yr-yn Hospital. These were classified under the following categories: 'Progressing satisfactorily', 'Some Improvement', 'No Improvement', 'Not so well', 'Discharged cured' and each list was accompanied by a series of numbers each of which had been allocated to In-Patients on admission. In this way, relatives could keep a check on events of their loved-ones presumably because visiting was prohibited to a Fever Hospital.

From July 1948, the nominal roll of Consultant Staff of The Royal Gwent Hospital became:

General Medicine
    E. Grahame Jones MB BS MRCP   P. Edward Dipple MD BS MRCS MRCP

General Surgery
    R.R.S. Bowker MB BCh FRCS   J.T. Rice-Edwards FRCS (Edin.) MRCS LRCP
    J. Elgood MB BS LRCP FRCS   H.G. Roberts BSc M BCh DRCOG FRCS
    D. Ioan Jones FRCS *   A.C. Lysaght MRCS LRCP FRCS *

Ear, Nose & Throat
    D.B. Sutton MB BS MRCS LRCP DLO FRCS
    J.L.D. Williams MB ChB FRCS   P. Thorpe MB ChB MRCS LRCP DLO FRCS

Ophthalmology
    F.W. Robertson MA MD MB BCh BAO DOMS RCPS
    G.W. Hoare MA MB BChir DOMS RCPS FRCS
    R. Vaughan Jones MB ChB DOMS FRCS

Dermatology
    B.A. Thomas BSc MD BS MRCS LRCP DPH

Traumatic & Orthopaedic Surgery
    N. Rocyn Jones JP MA MD BCh FRCS (Edin.)

Oral Surgery
    D.J. Dalton LDSRCS   J. Gibson FDSRCS

Obstetrics & Gynaecology
    R. Glyn Morgan MC MB BS MRCS LRCP
    D.W. Bowen MB BCh MRCOG   N.L. Keevil MD MRCOG
    M.D. Arwyn Evans BSc MD MB BCh FRCS MRCOG*

Pathology
    J. Fine BSc MD DPH DTM

Neurology
    J.D. Spillane MD BSc MB BCh MRCP*

Radiology
    W.H. Hastings MA MB BCh DMRE
    T.J. Thomas MRCS LRCP CMRE

Allergy
    D. Brown MB MRCP

Psychiatry
    G.M. King MRCS LRCP   D. Ellis Jones MRCS LRCP DPM
    W.T. Wales MRCS LRCP DPM

Diseases of Chest
    M.I. Jackson MRCS LRCP

Plastic Surgery
    Emlyn Lewis FRCS

Anaesthetics
    Harvey Nichol MA MB DPH   K.S. Thom MB DA
    H. Middleton MRCS LRCP DA

* *visiting consultant from Cardiff Royal Infirmary*

Senior Hospital Medical Officers:
    H.M. Horan FRCS LAH *(General Surgery)*
    W.M. Parry-Jones MRCS LRCP *(General Medicine)*
    S.W. Beswick BSc MB BCh DRCOG *(Obs. & Gyn.)*
    D. Stern MRCS LRCP *(Pathology)*
    Jackson Partridge LDSRCS *(Oral Surgery)*
    H.A. Ross BSc MB ChB DPH *(Chest Diseases)*
    H. James MB ChB *(Chest Diseases)*
    F.G.D. Kerr MB ChB *(Anaesthetics)*
    C.P. Elgood *(Anaesthetics)*

General Medical Practitioners:

P.W.M. Martin MRCS LRCP
E.E. Brackenbury MB ChB
H. Lister Wilson MB ChB
J.C.H. Bird MB ChB
J.D. Buckner MRCS LRCP
H. Joste Smith MC MB BS
D. Walford Davies MB
J.L.B. Fleming MB ChB

S. Rosehill MB BCh BAO
C.B.F. Miller MB ChB
J. Alsop Davies MRCS LRCP
Owen T. Jones MRCS LRCP
E.W. Hardman MB ChB
J. Weir Crichton MB ChB
J.P.J. Jenkins MRCS LRCP
W. Mackay MB ChB

Some members of the Visiting Medical Consultant Staff (1948).
Standing (Back Rows); G.W. Hoare, K.S. Thom, S. Rosehill, B.A. Thomas, unidentified,
D.R. Brackenbury, unidentified. Standing (Middle Row): J.L.D. Williams, J. Fine, H. Nichol,
E. Grahame Jones, N. Rocyn Jones, P.W. Martin, Partridge Jackson. Seated: W.H. Hastings,
unidentified, R.R.S. Bowker, R. Glyn Morgan, R.T. Rice-Edwards, F.W. Robertson, J. Elgood.

However, it is evident from the above list of Professional Staff that The Royal Gwent Hospital started its existence within the National Health Service with a comprehensive range of specialties served by well-qualified consultant staff. It was therefore, a well established General Hospital from its first day under the new Administration.

The layout of The Royal Gwent Hospital in 1948 shown on page 26 demonstrates the relatively remote location of The Friars from the main hospital and illustrates the considerable area of Friars Field which would play an important part in future planning and development during the next fifty years.

The bed and Theatre complement of the hospital at that time was:

In-Patient beds: 259 (Total)

General Medicine	37	General Surgery	110
Obstetrics	2	Gynaecology	18
Paediatrics	9	Oral Surgery	4
Dermatology	4	Ear, Nose & Throat	22
Ophthalmology	8	Orthopaedics	36
V.D.	3	Convalescent	6

Operating Theatres: 2
1 (Fracture & Orthopaedic)
1 (Casualty Theatre)

All surgical disciplines shared use of the twin operating theatres whereas the F.O.U. theatre was dedicated to orthopaedic surgery. The Casualty Theatre continued as such in the original Theatre accommodation of the 1901 hospital.

In the year ending 31st December 1949, the statistical data of hospital activity at The Royal Gwent was:

Average In-Patient bed occupancy	221.2 (ie. 85.4%)
New Out-Patients seen	17,700
Out-Patient attendances at clinics	67,929
Casualty Department attendances	27,034
X-Ray Department attendances	18,825

Total Out-Patient attendances during 1949 were 170,739.

There were only 6 births during that year at The Royal Gwent.

The Physiotherapy Unit was a busy department with 56,951 attendances and 81,456 treatments given in 1949.

Waiting Lists at the hospital were:

Surgical	2,179
Medical	57
E.N.T.	388
Ophthalmic	132
Gynaecology	245
Dermatology	8
Others (dentistry)	19

It is evident from these data that The Royal Gwent was a busy General Hospital. It is also evident that even in those days, waiting lists for surgical specialties were a significant feature of the hospital's working requirements.

Chapter 4: Woolaston House Hospital
(1837 to 1948)

Cliff Knight, Anne Freeman FRCP, and Brian Peeling CBE FRCS

St. Woolos Hospital, still known locally as Woolaston House Hospital by older residents of Newport, gradually became involved in the work of The Royal Gwent Hospital after it was taken over by The National Health Service in 1948 and eventually became fully integrated with the Royal Gwent in 1997. However, historically, the Workhouse that preceded Woolaston House Hospital stems back to 1838 with its origin as the 'Poor House'. This incidentally, coincided with the start of The Royal Gwent Hospital in 1839 as The Newport Dispensary.

The Newport Poor House or Workhouse

In 1834, the Poor Law Amendment Act came into being and by this legislation commissioners were elected on to Boards of Guardians throughout the country to establish unions of parishes that would become responsible for local administration of poor relief in place of individual parishes and townships. Thus, on 2nd August 1836 the Newport Board of Guardians was formed and became responsible for poor relief and public health. The first Chairman was Sir Charles Morgan and the Board included Mr. Reginald Blewitt MP, who later became involved with the Newport Dispensary (p.3), Major Mackworth and John Frost.

On 12th November 1836, a meeting resolved that a new Workhouse should be built for two hundred paupers at an estimated cost of £3,000. Consequently, in 1838, the Newport Union 'Poor House' or 'Workhouse' (ref Map 1 area 324) was built off the Turnpike Road from Newport which is now a continuation of Stow Hill. It can be seen from the map that this was a considerable distance away from the Newport Dispensary that was established in 1839 at Llanarth Street (Map 1: site 1). It was referred to as the 'Newport Workhouse' in historical references to the Newport Chartist Insurrection in November of 1839.

It is likely that the Newport Workhouse was a substantial institution for, in 1839, part of the building was requisitioned as a barracks for the soldiers that took part in the Chartist Riots outside the Westgate. Indeed, it seems that the Newport Workhouse became a focal point for the demonstrators because of the presence of troops there. They were likely to have been directed to the Workhouse because Sir Edmund Head, the Assistant Poor Law Commissioner, had noted that the Workhouse had sufficient unoccupied accommodation for 120 troops of the 29th Regiment to be lodged there under the command of a Major Wrottesley. *(information from 'The Last Rising' by David J.V. Jones: University of Wales Press, Cardiff. 1999).*

The work and conditions of this institution have been extensively documented in records referred to in 'Guide to the Monmouthshire Record Office' by W.H. Baker, County Archivist, published in Newport in 1959. For example, there are Admission and Discharge Registers (1837 to 1950), Registers of Births and Deaths (1837 to 1925), Guardians' Minute Books (1836 to 1927), Finance Minute Books (1842 to 1930) but the most significant document summarising the events of the Poor House/Workhouse from its inception up to 1901 is 'Newport Union. A Retrospect' by Ithel Thomas. This is a chronological but unstructured résumé of records held by the Gwent Record Office and it is hoped to revisit this valuable source of information at a future date to examine a wider and more detailed account of Workhouse conditions and work in those days. For the purposes of this book, therefore, it is not possible to embark on an in-depth study largely due to restrictions of space.

It is reasonable to assume that in 1839 the workhouse may only have been partially filled which left enough unoccupied space to billet a considerable military force and it is known from the 1841 Census of the Workhouse that there was a probable total of 97 people registered, 48 males and 49 females. However, a recent search through other archives revealed that in 1861 the nominal roll of residents in the Newport Workhouse showed that one hundred and eighty-three individuals lived in the workhouse with seven staff members (a Master, a Matron, a porter, a nurse, a cook and two maids). In 1861, the institution was called 'The Workhouse of the Newport Union, Saint Woolos Newport, Mon.'. Of the residents, one hundred and fifty-four were registered as 'paupers', fifty-eight were widows or widowers, and sixty-seven were 'unmarried'. Fifty- three of the women were aged under 30 years of age, there were thirteen infants with mothers, one foundling and two children aged five and seven respectively. It has usually been assumed that the majority of residents cared for in a workhouse would have been elderly: however, in 1861, eighty-three residents (45%) were aged over 60 years and one hundred (55%) were aged less than 60 years.

A more detailed picture of the Newport Poor House comes from a Board of Health Trignometric Survey of the Stow Hill area thought to have been carried out in 1851 and which followed the Public Health Act of 1848.

This shows a layout that is essentially the same as that on the Tithe Map of the Parish of St. Woolos, Newport of 1841 (Map No.1) and names the main road as the Turnpike Road from Newport (which used to be the main route to Cardiff passing over Penylan Hill from Bassaleg).

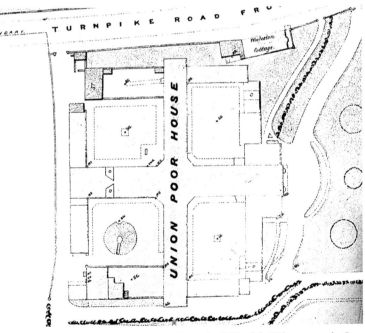

Floor Plan showing layout of the Poor House (Board of Health Trignometric Survey of Newport in 1851, with permission from Public Record Office, Crown Copyright). 'Wooleston Cottage', sited at the Turnpike Road boundary of the Poor House was purchased by the Guardians for £400 circa 1875 for use as a Clerk's Office. (ref. 'Newport Union. A Retrospect' by Ithel Thomas p.44). It is a reasonable deduction that previously Wooleston Cottage was a private dwelling and a similar building can be seen clearly on the Tithe Map of 1841 (Map 1). It is also present on the Ordnance Maps of 1882 and 1902 (Maps 2 & 3) and, according to the reference from Ithel Thomas was used in 1901 as temporary accommodation of the Master of the Workhouse (presumably during rebuilding - ref. pp.48-50).

(courtesy of Gwent Records Office)

An undated plan of the institution shows the layout of the accommodation in the Workhouse.

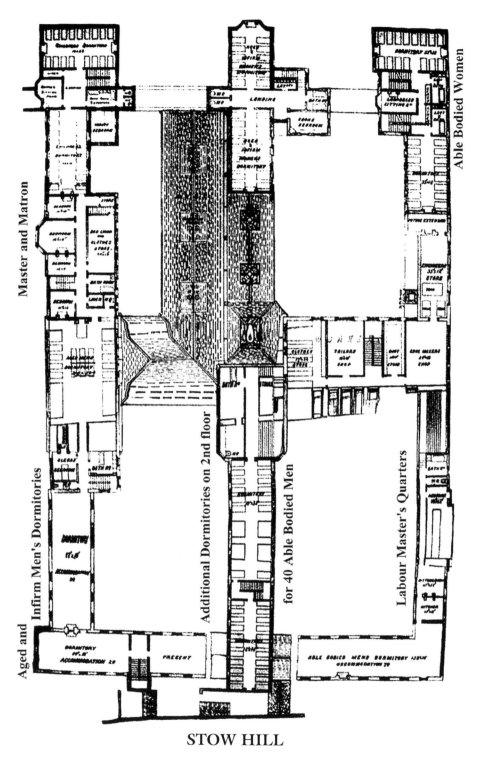

STOW HILL

Detail of the Ground Floor Plan of Newport Poor House (undated) - Scale 8 feet - 1 inch
(courtesy of Gwent Record Office County miscellaneous Plans No.18)

This shows segregation of sexes and division into able bodied, infirm and aged people, and separate accommodation for children. Residents slept in dormitories for about 20 individuals but in the case of able bodied men up to 70 men were put together. WCs were not plentiful and hand basins (called 'lavatories') were largely communal. There was social support on site in the form of tailors, bootmakers, and the Master and staff were resident.

The Workhouse was only one aspect of the appalling social conditions existing in Newport in those days. These led to fearful epidemics of cholera, typhus, smallpox and other infectious diseases which were then prevalent throughout urban areas in the land and it was not until the middle of the 19th Century that the first Medical Officers of Health were appointed primarily to deal with these situations. During the 19th century, a number of Acts of Parliament dealing with the prevention of disease had been passed, but the diagnosis and treatment of illness remained a personal matter between the patient and the doctor (for those who could afford it). It is true that the State made provision for destitute people under the Poor Law and some people subscribed to Clubs and Societies to cover the costs of medical treatment when they were ill, but it was not until the beginning of the 20th century that medical care for poor people was undertaken by the State.

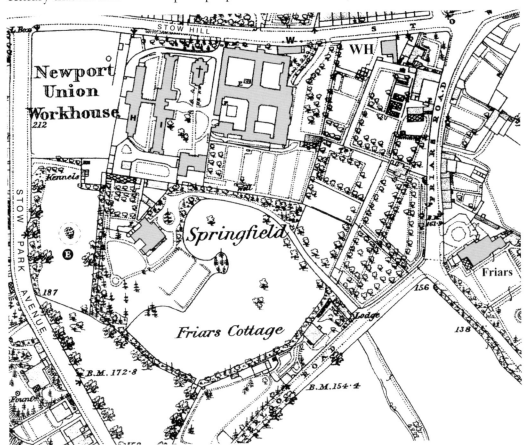

Map 3. Detail of Ordnance Survey Map, Monmouthshire, 1st Edition 1882 Sheet XXXIII.4, Scale 25 inches to a Mile. Showing the upper Stow Hill area and the Newport Union Workhouse. Note 1) addition of a Chapel (†), an Infirmary (I) and a hospital (H) 2) locations of Woolaston House (WH), Springfield House and the Friars 3) the continued presence of Wooleston Cottage (W) 4) an earthwork (E) in the field to the left of Springfield House, previously noted in Map 1. (For higher resolution see Pull-out Map 3).

(photographic copy Andrew Ponsford)

However, it is possible that attempts to reduce the prevalence of epidemics and to control infectious disease led, in the later part of the 19th century, to increased accommodation in Poor Houses and, by 1884 there had been considerable enlargement of the institution on Stow Hill which was then called the 'Newport Union Workhouse'. The principal additions were a Chapel, an Infirmary and a Hospital (ref. Map 3). The area surrounding the Workhouse would seem to have been given over to private gardens.

A few years later, in March 1897, minutes of a meeting of the Building Committee of The Guardians of the Newport Union Workhouse indicate that the facilities provided needed improvement. It is recorded in documents held at Gwent Records Office in Cwmbran that the members considered *'engaging an architect for carrying out alterations and additions to the Workhouse, including Board Room and Offices'*. In June of that year, *'Mr. Lawrence prepared a sketch plan for remodelling the Workhouse with a view of giving accommodation for 700 inmates'*. The committee also considered *'the possibility of obtaining additional space... of Woolaston House and grounds adjoining the Workhouse lately in possession of Mr. W. Downing Evans (deceased)'*. This was agreed and this property was bought for the sum of £1050. Its address was 'Woolaston House, Stow Hill' (ref. Map 3: building labelled 'WH').

As well as 'Woolaston House', the committee was interested in purchasing 'Springfield House' together with its land of about 5 acres (ref. Map 3). This was an extensive property immediately adjacent to the Workhouse but the idea was dropped because it was too expensive and the local Government Board refused a loan over 30 years of £31,000 for its purchase. However, in February 1898, negotiations were re-opened into the purchase of 'Springfield House' Estate which were concluded at a price of £10,450.

Dated 5th July 1898.

The Right Honourable G. C. Lord Tredegar and the Trustees of the Settlement of his Family Estates

to

The Guardians of the Poor of the Newport (Mon) Union

Conveyance

of a piece of land and premises known as Woolaston House, situate at Stow Hill in the County Borough of Newport.

Part of Deed of Conveyance for the purchase of Woolaston House 1898.

(courtesy of Mrs. Gill Winstanley, Gwent Healthcare N.H.S. Trust)

In February 1898, the local Government Board sanctioned the plans to rebuild and alter the Workhouse. This entailed *'the whole of the existing buildings to be taken down with the exception of the Infirmary, the Hospital and the Chapel and utilisation of Woolaston House'*. The estimated cost by the architect was £30,000. However, the plan excluded premises for a Board Room and Offices but the local Government Board consented for these to be developed in a building at Queen's Hill at a cost of £5,000, away from Stow Hill.

Tenders were sought by The Guardians of the Newport Union on 26th May 1898 for *'erection of New Buildings in separate blocks and sections with sundry Alterations and Additions to existing buildings at their Workhouse, Stow Hill'*. Nine bids were received varying from £29,100 to £34,990. The contract was awarded to David Rickards for £29,100: it is of interest that the firm that eventually built the new Newport & Monmouthshire Hospital (Messrs. A.S. Morgan) also entered a tender which was £34,990.

Reference to the Ordnance Survey Map dated 1902 (Map 4) suggests that building developments had taken place by that time to link the recent purchases of Springfield and Woolaston House to outbuildings separate from the main part of the Workhouse which remained in outline unchanged from the layout shown in the map of 1882 (Map 2).

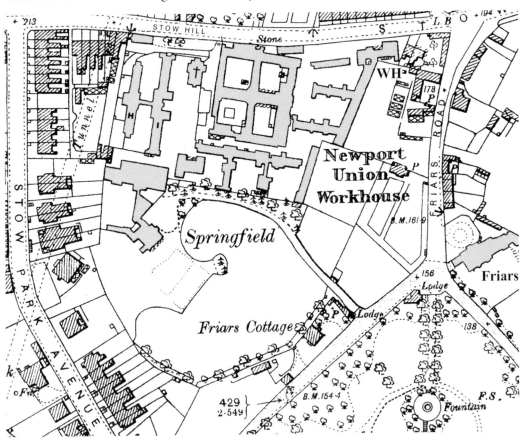

Map 4. *Detail of Ordnance Survey map, Monmouthshire, 2nd Edition 1902, Sheet XXXIII.4, Scale 1/2500 being 25.344 Inches to a Mile showing the Estate of the Newport Union Workhouse after purchases of Woolaston House (WH) and Springfield. Note: 1) the link of buildings with Woolaston House (WH). 2) the land acquired with Springfield extending to Friars Road. 3) houses of Stow Park Avenue (built circa 1880s) covering the site of the earthwork (E)- see Pull-out Maps 1 & 3. 4) the route of Stow Hill Railway Tunnel. (For higher resolution see Pull-out Map 4).*

However, on 18th August 1903, the minutes of the Building Committee confirmed that the contract for rebuilding had been completed and among details the Committee *'recommended that the quotation of Messrs. Pocock Brothers, London for fitting up the padded room at the sum of £95 be accepted subject to the padding being carried to 7 feet 6 inches high'*. Details of the new construction are shown by original drawings of the Architect's Site Plan (dated 1904) made available by courtesy of Terry Gale (Plan 1 see p.50). Comparison of this plan with the Ordnance Survey Map of 1884 shows that there had been considerable re-design of the central buildings especially creation of a Dining Hall, a new main entrance together with addition of significant buildings along the periphery of the site, in particular a Laundry and Wash House, extra wards, workshops.

A minute recorded on 3rd March 1904 stated that *'the committee consider that the time has now arrived when the new Workhouses should be formally opened. The main blocks have been occupied as they were completed. The whole of the Buildings should be formally opened by the Chairman on Sat. 26th instant'*.

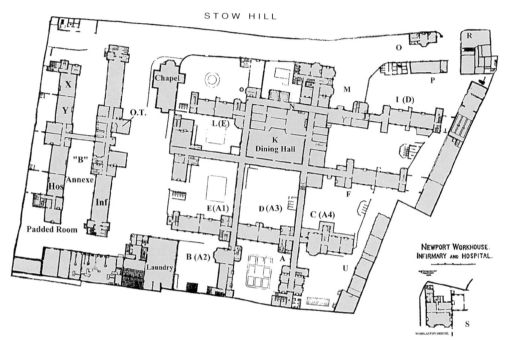

Plan 1. *Original Drawing of Architect's Site Plan. Comparison of this plan with the Ordnance Survey Map of 1882 (Map 3) reveals the extent of the peripherally placed additions of buildings. A new Porters' Lodge was built in August 1901 (point 'O'), and an 'electric bell be installed at the Main Gate £1.13s.0d'. Wooleston Cottage had disappeared. The Hospital/Infirmary complex was designated as 'B' Annexe - a title which persists to this day as 'B' Block. A single Operating Theatre ('OT') was created at ground floor level. The floor plan of Woolaston House (section S) is displayed separately in the lower right hand corner of the plan due to lack of space but should be attached to the building labelled 'WH' as shown by Map 4. Note the title of the institution as 'Newport Workhouse Infirmary & Hospital'. Numerical labels within parentheses indicate ward blocks for patients. These were: 'A' Block buildings labelled A1, A2 etc; 'B' Annexe; 'D' Block and 'E' Block. Individual arabic labels specify sections of the establishment designated by the architect.*
(For higher resolution see Pull-out Plan 1.)

Associated with the Workhouse, the hospital and infirmary had been built in the 19th Century as separate buildings. These buildings are indicated in the Architect's Plan of 1904 labelled as 'B' Annexe (ref. Plan 1) and presumably were included in the updating work carried out. In the Infirmary there was a single Operating Room which continued to be used for surgery into the early 1950s even after the appointment of Mr. Hywel Roberts in 1948. Elsewhere, there was a Padded Room and a Detention Room. Also in 1912, an electric lift was installed at a cost of £455.

These changes and new building at the Workhouse site in 1902 are only shown on the Ordnance Survey Map dated 1921 (Map 5). In effect, this layout has persisted in overall general design to the present day.

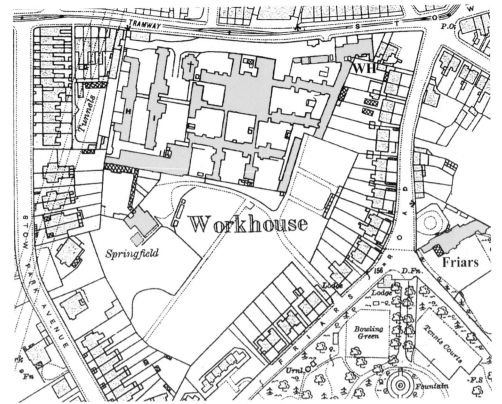

Map 5. Detail of Ordnance Survey map, Monmouthshire, Edition of 1921, Sheet XXXIII.4, Scale 25 Inches to a Mile (1/2500). Final layout of the Newport Workhouse off Stow Hill (compare with Maps of 1882 and 1902).

Aerial view of Woolaston site showing the buildings which can be related to the Architect's Plan and Map 5, and in particular the presence of Springfield House and its land. It is thought that it was taken in the 1930s.

(photograph courtesy of Cliff Knight)

51

'Springfield' has another aspect to its history prior to its ownership by The Newport Union. It is known that the Normans invaded Gwent within a few years of their victory at Hastings in 1066 under the leadership of William fitzOsbern who died in 1071. The Conqueror sent his son, Prince William (later William II) on a punitive expedition to Gwent in 1072 and a motte-and-bailey castle was constructed possibly by him in 1075. This was on Stow Hill close to the church of St. Gwynllyw (St. Woolos Church). These forts were high mounds of earth surrounded by a ditch. A wooden tower would have sat on the flatenned top of the mound. Later, the motte-and-bailey became the power base for Robert de la Haye who came to south-east Wales with Robert fitzHamon in 1093. It remained the principal power base for the Normans until 1126 when the construction of a new castle began under the Earl of Gloucester at Usk ford. This is the site of the present ruins of Newport castle.

At that time, the motte-and-bailey at Stow Hill went out of use but remained evident as a mound and was known locally as Twyn Gwynllyw ('Gwynllyw's Tump'). It is highly probable that the 'lofty tumulus' standing by St. Gwynllyw's Church described by William Harris in 1772 and the moated mound drawn in the Index to the Tithe Survey (circa 1812) refer to the motte. Furthermore, in area 274 of the Tithe Map of St. Woolos Parish (Map 1) a possible earthwork is evident (labelled 'E') and this artefact again appears in an equivalent position on the Ordnance Survey Map of 1882 (Map 3). This mound survived until 1848 when it was mostly covered by spoil removed from the new railway tunnel that was being constructed under Stow Hill. Soil and stones were lifted from the tunnel up a fifteen foot shaft alongside the mound leaving exposed only its summit which was fifty feet in diameter. The motte was evidently a considerable construction. Later, 'Springfield House' was built nearby and its large garden included the site of the motte and bailey. Mr. Octavius Morgan lived at 'The Friars' across the road from the entrance drive to 'Springfield' off Friars Road, and he asked his neighbour at 'Springfield', Mr. Gething, to mark the site of the motte and bailey, which he did with a cairn of stones. Unfortunately, when the houses of Stow Park Avenue were built in the 1880s (see Map 4), the parcel of land containing the cairn was obliterated under the houses numbered 27 to 29 Stow Park Avenue *(information from 'Gwent Local History' No.85, 1998. Ed. Tony Hopkins, Gwent Record Office).*

It is of interest that the present driveway from Friars Road to the rear of St. Woolos Hospital follows the route of the original driveway to Mr. Gething's house. The large area of land acquired with the purchase of the Springfield Estate would become an important asset in future development of the Royal Gwent/St. Woolos Hospital complex in the 1970s and later, and the site of the motte would become a car park for the hospital.

(Footnote: the Editor acknowledges the extensive assistance and advice concerning sources of information about The Newport Workhouse and 'Springfield House' that was generously made by Dr. Luned Davies MA DPhil DAA, Mr. David J. Rimmer BA DAA and Mr. Colin Gibson MA of the Gwent Record Office and of Dr. Howard E.F. Davies BSc MD FRCP, retired Consultant Physician of St. Woolos Hospital).

Woolaston House Hospital up to 1948

In the time of the Newport Workhouse, the more able residents were expected to supplement their keep and this workhouse philosophy spilled over into the 20th century and was much feared. Despite the availability of old age pensions from 1909, the allowance given in those early days did not keep pace with rising costs of living so that many preferred poverty to the stigma of applying for public assistance with its taint of the Poor Law.

In 1911, three quarters of poor provision beds in England and Wales were either in workhouse accommodation or wards of Workhouse Infirmaries, such as the Newport Union Workhouse. The remainder were in Voluntary Hospitals, some of which were long-standing but most, like The Royal Gwent Hospital, had only been recently established to look after these people. Sometime during these years, the Newport Workhouse must have become known locally as Woolaston House, presumably by adapting the name of the building purchased in by The Guardians in 1898. This must have been preferable to the taint of the Workhouse title for this name persisted.

The Poor Law as such ended in 1929 after Acts of Parliament swept away the Unions of Guardians and transferred responsibility for the poor law to County and County Borough Councils that had previously been established under the Local Government Act of 1888. Nevertheless, the dichotomy in status between Voluntary Hospitals and Poor Law Infirmaries continued even though the Infirmaries became Municipal General Hospitals. These provided comprehensive clinical services, as in Woolaston House which is likely to have become Woolaston House Hospital at about that time. These differences of apparent status prevailed even after the advent of the National Health Service in 1948 and the buildings at St. Woolos Hospital are still a reminder of their Poor Law origins. In fact, some older people in Newport, even in the 1990s, might still refer to St. Woolos Hospital as 'Woolaston House'.

Following an Act of Parliament in 1928, a Medical Superintendent was appointed to take over Woolaston House Hospital and in 1947 was still known as the Master of the institution (who with the Mistress was still resident as he had quarters in the hospital). The Master was responsible for residents cared for by the Local Authority.

In the Second World War, as in The Great War of 1914-18, Woolaston House was used as an Emergency Centre for the treatment of members of the Armed Forces injured while on active service, many of whom had been wounded at Dunkirk (ref. p.25). At one time, there were as many as 750 beds in use!

However, the buildings outlined by the Architect's Plan of 1904 did not change in general layout up to the takeover by The National Health Service. Therefore, up to 1948, structurally, the hospital had remained mainly unchanged for nearly fifty years and in 1948 housed accommodation for general surgical, general medical, gynaecological and obstetric beds and some E.N.T. beds so that the unit functioned as a general Municipal Hospital.

After the Second World War, Woolaston House still catered for residents supported by the Local Authority. In addition, acute hospital facilities were provided with general surgical services, which were as before supervised by Dr. McMahon MA MD, and obstetric as well as some gynaecological services under the care of Dr. S. Beswick. Medical cases were accommodated in 'B' Block and the Chest Clinic, which had previously been the original 'Woolaston House'.

After the death of Dr. McMahon in 1947, general surgical services were taken over by Mr. Hywel G. Roberts FRCS who was appointed Consultant Surgeon in 1948.

Woolaston House Hospital in 1948

In 1948, after The National Health Service Act had been empowered, the Newport & East Monmouthshire Hospital Management Committee assumed management of the acute part of Woolaston House Hospital (equivalent to The Infirmary of earlier times).

The bed and Theatre complement was:

In-Patient beds:	379	
Operating Theatre:	1 (for all specialties)	

Some residents within the hospital continued to receive care supervised by the Local Authority until 1968, when the remaining residents were transferred to Social Service Homes for the Elderly in the area.

Beds provided services for general surgery, general medicine and a Chest Clinic, E.N.T., gynaecology and obstetrics, ophthalmic surgery, dermatology, tuberculosis and children's nursing. The wards were served by auxiliary departments which included radiology, physiotherapy and pathology. There was a general Out-Patients department and specialist Out-Patient departments and treatment units for ophthalmics and dermatology.

The hospital was renamed St. Woolos General Hospital in 1949 at the request of Mr. Hywel G. Roberts FRCSE who worked for the whole of his professional life at the hospital as a general surgeon with an interest in urology.

A modern Nurse Training Unit had been set up previously giving a three-year course for the State Registered Nurse Diploma of The General Nursing Council (the Principal Tutor was Miss O. Doherty SRN RFN).

Nurses (and the Matron) were accommodated in 'Springfield House' located in the precincts of the hospital. The Nurse Training Unit was eventually amalgamated with Nurse Training at The Royal Gwent so that nurses were accommodated elsewhere and 'Springfield House' remained unoccupied for several years. In 1979 it was replaced by a purpose-built unit for geriatric and psycho-geriatric patients on the site of 'Springfield House' and hence called 'The Springfield Hospital' (ref. p.116). A stained glass window from the house was incorporated in the new building.

Apart from Mr. H.G. Roberts and Drs. M. Jackson and K. Hilliard (chest physicians), consultants from The Royal Gwent undertook clinical sessions in the medical wards, gave anaesthetics and supervised the pathological and X-Ray services Technical, administrative, domestic, catering and other staff were on the St. Woolos Hospital payroll as the hospital had its own administrative structure under the direction of a Hospital Secretary, Mr. Bob Chissell.

In 1948, St. Woolos, therefore, functioned as a second General Hospital in Newport.

The work at St. Woolos Hospital from 1948 is reviewed in Chapter 6 (p.84).

Present-day photograph of the Main Entrance to St. Woolos Hospital: this was also the Main Entrance of the rebuilt Newport Workhouse and shows the date '1902' above the lintel.
(photograph Brian Peeling)

Chapter 5: Fundraising before
The National Health Service
Cliff Knight

It is appropriate at this stage of this history of hospital services in Newport to pause and review the role that had been played over many years by voluntary organisations. These had provided the life blood which had enabled an effective hospital service, especially The Royal Gwent Hospital, to develop and thrive in Newport up to 1948 when The National Health Service took over this responsibility *(Editor)*.

General Overview

It is clear from the preceding narrative covering the years from 1839, that efforts to enable The Royal Gwent Hospital to provide continuing care to the local population had been a constant struggle to find and to attract money to maintain medical and nursing care. It was the success of voluntary organisations during these years that maintained continuity of the hospital's work and also enabled it to expand and update its services. This was a truly remarkable achievement by local people. Retrospectively, it is difficult to appreciate after experiencing 50 years of the National Health Service the depth of the extraordinary generosity of local people, poor and well-off, that created funds to meet the hospital costs for over a hundred years. Much of the labour had been free as it had been given by volunteers but regularity of income under a voluntary system of funding had been unpredictable so that it is not surprising that the hospital had often been in debt. This had led on occasions during hard times to restriction of expenditure on food, drugs, equipment and other items for the hospital and its patients. Therefore, it is important for us today to look closely at the self-help fundraising achieved by local people that proved itself as the lifeblood of the hospital over so many years.

Fundraising for the voluntary hospital in Newport evidently occurred several years before the ideas leading up to The Royal Gwent had been born. For instance, 'Ye Olde English Fayre' was held as long ago as 1882 at the Albert Hall in Newport to support the Newport Infirmary & Dispensary on Stow Hill.

Mention has already been made that donations made by local churches had also been an important source of revenue - as much as four per cent of the hospital's income - as well as the

unusual source of intermittent but welcome income that had come from the shipbreaking yard of John Cashmore in Pill.

However, over the years the main means of voluntary support was derived eventually from the ordinary people of the town and area through the Workingmen's Fund and from carnivals and fêtes organised by the hospital.

The Workmen's Hospital Fund

The forerunner of the Workmen's Hospital Fund started shortly after the opening of the Dispensary in Llanarth Street in 1839. The 'ordinary citizen' was encouraged to make a contribution to the Dispensary to help with its upkeep - while they were in good health! This meant in practice that support came mainly from 'better off' citizens with little interest from the 'working classes'. The poorer people in those days had no money to contribute.

In 1860, the *Monmouthshire Merlin* reported details of a penny-a-week health benefit scheme at Bristol Royal Infirmary subscribed by work-people employed by Derham Brothers and observed that a similar scheme might operate well in Newport.

This idea took a few years to take root in Newport but by 1870 groups of workmen started making donations to the Newport Infirmary & Dispensary and these were not regarded as a special item of receipt in the Infirmary's Annual Report until 1875. Although it is possible to mark that year as the date of birth of the Workmen's Hospital Fund, the idea of the Fund must have started earlier because the first subscription to the hospital came from Batchelor's Timber Yard in Pillgwenlly in 1870, and the concept of a Fund had originated amongst active trade unionists who were members of the Newport Trades Council. They had a vision to help the hospital and at the same time protect their members in times of sickness. In those early days, men working in the shipyards, timber yards, docks, railways, wharves and industrial works made donations and the regularity of these must surely have been an important factor for developments to be planned at the Infirmary.

However, little is known of its early days probably because its first secretary, Mr. Frank Gillman, was an engineer at the hospital who kept his records in his office near the boiler house. When he died, his successor tidied up the office and stoked the boiler with the records.

In 1893, the Workmen's Fund was officially formed and firms agreed to co-operate with the Fund by deducting one penny from the wages of employees who wished to take part, paying their contributions in bulk to the hospital. As the years went by more and more firms joined the scheme, the contributions rising from £159 in 1893 to £1,490 in 1903. In return, workmen's representatives were given votes on certain hospital committees and were allowed to nominate patients whom G.P.s found suitable for hospital treatment. At first, the scheme was confined to Newport but it eventually spread to the whole of the county area and later to those not on the payrolls of large firms who wished to share the responsibilities and privileges of the Fund. So people in small businesses, policemen, teachers, shop assistants, clerks etc. were brought into the scheme.

With time, the number of subscribers increased to join the Fund and to give some idea of its progress and the growth of its contribution to finances of The Royal Gwent Hospital, the following published income figures tell a remarkable story:

1898:	£1,000	1920:	£9,000
1908:	£2,000	1929:	£14,000
1915:	£3,000	1939:	£20,000

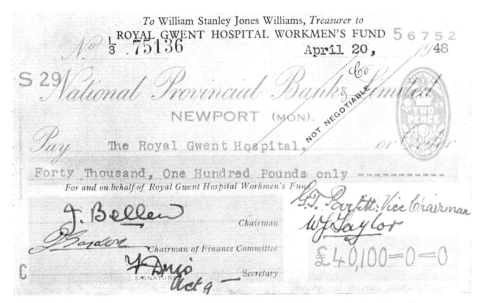

The record and last cheque from the Workmen's Hospital Fund.

(*photographic copy Andrew Ponsford*)

In fact, in the year of 'nationalisation' of the Royal Gwent, the amount donated to the hospital was £40,100 which was the figure on the last cheque to be made out to the Directors dated 20 April 1948. This was a record amount.

Much support for the Workmen's Fund came from Newport Council. Each year, the incoming Mayor would become President of the Fund, not just in name but also in active participation. One Mayor who gave the most devoted and loyal service was the eloquent Councillor Peter Wright who was Mayor in 1919. He travelled hundreds of miles, made hundreds of speeches and by his enthusiasm and persuasiveness secured the willing support of many workmen and the co-operation of their employers.

The Workmen's Fund not only supported the work of the hospital financially. It continually looked ahead, always debating how the services of the hospital could be expanded and improved. In 1935, for example, it was the Executive Committee of the Fund that persuaded the Directors that an Orthopaedic Surgeon and an Orthopaedic Department were necessary in Newport and they prepared the ground to raise £100,000 towards this project. When the first £50,000 had been realised, the Committee asked their members to subscribe an extra penny from their wages; this brought in another £25,000 towards the outstanding target. Members of the Fund also suggested an appointments system for patients to be seen, a canteen at the Out-Patients Department and a waiting room near the entrance to the hospital so that visitors need not wait in the cold and the rain. In 1920 the Minutes of the Executive Committee showed that they were the first to suggest a hostel for the nurses, and in 1930 they encouraged the Directors to open a new ward. Other matters like the endowment of beds came from the initiative of the Workmen's Fund and to recognise their work, the Directors decided to place in the hospital a record of their outstanding achievements. This plaque, and others, were placed in the entrance hall of The Royal Gwent, and they are in safe keeping (in St. Woolos Hospital) following demolition of the old hospital in 1991. Whenever there was something helpful to be done, one could be sure that the workmen had their share in it. At one time, sixty per cent of the hospital's income came via the Workmen's Fund and one wonders if the hospital would have survived without them.

This is, indeed, a most remarkable story of dedication and forward vision by a community starting with small beginnings that grew into a major venture that latterly was entitled 'The Royal Gwent Hospital Workmen's Contributory Fund'. The Royal Gwent Hospital became a major hospital in Wales largely as a result of the energy, vision and also demands of the Workmen's Fund for a top-grade medical institution to be in Newport and their role in the community expanded in 1939 when the Workmen's committee co-operated with the Newport Welfare Committee, Woolaston House Hospital and other hospitals so that fund contributors became entitled to receive free treatment at County Hospital, Griffithstown and any voluntary hospital in the county. The Fund, therefore, transformed into the 'Gwent Hospitals Contributory Fund'.

Fêtes and Carnivals

Another important source of income came from the Fêtes and Carnivals that were held every August Bank Holiday week. The Workmen's Fund gave considerable help in organising these.

The first of these Fêtes was in 1906 and was held in the nearby Belle Vue Park twelve years after the park had been opened (ref. Map 2 for location). It was a modest affair that raised £80. A further Fête was held there in 1907 and the following year the Workmen's Hospital Fund organised a Carnival as well as a Fête when £200 was raised.

After 'The Friars', with its 14 acres of land, had been given to the hospital in 1913, the Fêtes were held in Friar's Field on the ground that is now occupied by residential buildings, administration offices and parking spaces for staff of the hospital. The first Fête in 1914 raised £479 but during the First World War (1914-18) the Fêtes were suspended.

As soon as the War was over, Fêtes and Carnivals recommenced but on a much grander scale. The whole of the area between the Friars and the main hospital buildings were crammed with stalls and entertainments of all descriptions run by voluntary organisations such as the Round Table, the Scouts, local business people, churches, the local press, hospital staff, Y.M.C.A., St. John Ambulance, Rotary Club, the Armed Forces, Women's Institutes, political and sports associations, Trades Unions, British Legion - indeed every conceivable organisation in the county. There were roundabouts, shooting galleries, bandstands, tents for dancing and concerts, Morris Dancers, parade of beauties, fantastic characters in costume and indeed there was every imaginable activity that could raise money.

Fêtes opened at 2.30pm daily and, whilst all the sideshows and other activities were taking place, road races, tug-o'-war competitions and ambulance displays proceeded inside and outside the grounds. Fêtes were opened each day by either a civic dignitary or a prominent local businessman who was expected to make a generous gift to the hospital.

The highlight of the week of the hospital Fête occurred on the Thursday when what was billed as 'Britain's One Great Carnival' took place. Thousands of people came from near and far to line the pavements four-deep as the mile-long Carnival wound its way through the main street of the town led by bands, always ending up with the vehicles of the Fire Service bringing up the rear of the procession. Such was the national prestige of the Carnival that in 1929 permission was obtained to borrow the Royal Stage Coach to carry the Mayor and Mayoress in the procession and it was described as 'a Pageant of Splendour when the County spent and laughed.'

The main feature of the Carnival was the Carnival Queen chosen for her good looks and deportment with her four Court Ladies seated high up on a tastefully decorated vehicle.

Royal Gwent Hospital Fête Grounds

1 - The Friars	12 - Round-abouts	34 - Concert Tent
2 - Cloak Room	13 - Showmen's	35 - Putting Green
3 - Refreshments	Side Shows	36 - Starting point
4 - Dancing	14 - Hospital Side	Road Races
5 - Fairy Glade	Shows	38 - Whist
7 - Tobacco	15 - Fruit	Competitions
8 - Sweets	16 - Spinner	Daily
9 - Secretary and	17 - Chepstow	41 - Tug-of-War
Public Phone	Mike	42 - Skittles
10 - Shooting	18 - American Bar	43 - Reserved
Range	19 - Fortune	44 - Shows
11 - Showmen's	Tellers	45 - Gent's
Side Show	20 - Utility Stall	Lavatory
	21 - Cake Stall	46 - Wood
	22 - Flowers	47 - Fireworks
	23 - Ballet	48 - Red Indian
	24 - Miscellaneous	Show
	25 - Refreshments	49 - Tennis Court
	26 - Showmen's	50 - Ambulance
	Side Shows	Competitions
	27 - Showmen's	51 - Rover & Boy
	Side Shows	Scouts' Camp
	28 - Swinging	52 - Car Park
	Chairs	53 - Laundry
	29 - Concert	54 - Boiler House
	Pavilion	55 - Casualty
	30 - Orchestra	Department
	31 - Ladies	56 - Male Block
	32 - Show	57 - Administration
	33 - Hospital Side	Block
	Shows	58 - Female &
		Children's
		Block
		59 - Outpatients'
		Dispensary
		60 - Outpatients'
		Department
		61 - Old
		Outpatients'
		Department

Site Plan of stalls etc. of a Hospital Fête held on Friars Field (circa 1930) showing Royal Gwent Hospital and The Friars illustrating the wide range of activities.

Onlookers were expected to throw coins onto the moving vehicles or deposit their gifts in a bucket carried by walking entrants. Prizes were given for the best displays in various categories.

Everyone was expected to wear a mascot on Carnival Day as an emblem of continued good luck and fortune for the hospital and anyone not wearing one in his coat lapel was looked upon with disdain. A special mascot committee was set up each year and many hundreds of pounds were raised by their sale.

General View of Newport Carnival and Fête on Friars Field (circa 1930s).

At 9.30pm on the final night, there was a grand firework display given by Brocks of Crystal Palace ending at 10.30pm with the words 'Goodnight' in brilliantly illuminated colours on a large framework at the bottom of the field.

During the years of the Fêtes and Carnivals, much money was raised, the last one in 1947 realising £5,023 - a considerable sum in those days.

Since 1947, and after the arrival of The National Health Service, attempts were made to continue the spirit of the Royal Gwent Carnival but despite valiant attempts, none has come up to the standards of previous events.

The Needlework Guild

The Needlework and Linen Guild was another major supporter of the hospital during its difficult days. The women of the Guild not only supplied garments, linen, blankets and other necessities to the hospital but helped to support it financially. Its membership consisted mainly of well known dignitaries of the town whose husbands were equally renowned as local businessmen, solicitors, doctors and wives of consultants.

(It is sad to record that The Needlework Guild ceased to function after 1948 as it was informed by the authorities that its work was no longer necessary for, under the new National Health Service, the hospital was deemed to be self-sufficient - Private information to Editor).

Other Subscribers

Other subscribers to funds for the hospital during its time as a Voluntary Hospital had included The United Services Fund, The Merchant Navy Comforts Fund, Stewarts & Lloyds Limited and Girling Limited, Cwmbran.

Newport Carnival 1929. Mayor and Mayoress riding in the Royal Stage Coach on loan from Buckingham Palace. (photograph courtesy of Newport Museum)

The Carnival Queen and her court ladies passing the Town Hall in Commercial Street 1939.
(photograph courtesy of Newport Museum)

Chapter 6: The Years of Change
(1948 to 2003)

The years immediately following the start of The National Health Service in Gwent presented a time of re-adjustment and stabilisation within the new regime for all concerned with the hospitals. However, the half century since 1948 will be remembered as years in which the structure and delivery of Health Care changed radically in every respect.

These were concerned with:
1) Modernisation of the Royal Gwent Hospital from 1964
2) Changes at St. Woolos Hospital
3) Changes at other hospitals in South Gwent
4) Re-structuring of Organisation and Management
5) Advances and expansion of Professional services

This chapter is intended as a historical record of the changes that occurred at the Royal Gwent Hospital, mainly from 1964 onwards, and the secondary effect that these had on hospital services elsewhere in the south of the county especially St. Woolos Hospital. A review will follow of organisational and management changes during these years that have inevitably shaped the delivery of health care in Gwent as it moved into the 21st century.

Changes of professional services will be reviewed in Chapters 7,8, 9 and 10.
(Editorial Introduction)

1) The Royal Gwent Hospital - Re-development and Modernisation

Background to Re-development (Editor's Review)

For the first twenty-five years under The National Health Service, there were three major structural additions to the main building of The Royal Gwent Hospital. These were
1) a new purpose-built Casualty Department built in the early 1960s to replace the Casualty Unit established on the ground floor of the extension of the hospital opened in 1916,
2) a 24-hour Short-Stay Unit built in 1974 as a branch of the Casualty Department,
3) a Post-graduate Lecture Hall opened in 1968. (see p.26 for the location of these units).

The new Casualty and Accident Department was built on the ground floor attached to the front of the east wing added to the hospital in 1916. It had been designed by Mr. R. Vernon Jones, Consultant Casualty Surgeon, and incorporated two Emergency Resuscitation Rooms as well as examinations room, treatment rooms, consultation rooms and the usual waiting areas. It is said that the incentive behind this development had been a Question in the House of Commons by a powerful local Member of Parliament whose father had had to wait for several hours before examination following an accident!

The Short-Stay Unit was built on space at the front of the hospital alongside the eastern ward block. Emergency admission with head injuries, abdominal pain and other conditions requiring a period of observation were kept under overnight surveillance in this ward. This unit gave some relief to the long-standing problem to both medical and surgical units of beds for emergency admissions primarily requiring observation. In those days it was the policy of the hospital that, if necessary, extra beds were put up in the centres of wards (and even in corridors on occasions) which could happen on certain festive nights such as one St. Patrick's night in the early 1970s when the surgical emergency intake reached forty-five individuals! *(personal recollection of Editor)*.

View of the new Casualty Unit in the foreground with the East Wing alongside and the windows of the Operating Theatres overlooking.

A typical ward.

Elsewhere, the internal design of the hospital was little changed from the 1920s with wards still of the 'Nightingale' pattern. These had advantages in that all patients were within the view of nursing staff but personal privacy was limited.

However, The Royal Gwent Hospital was nearly fifty years old in 1948 when it was taken over by The National Health Service and thoughts towards re-development of the hospital began soon afterwards. Consequently, plans were put in hand as early as 1957/58 for a first stage re-development programme to take place.

A proposal was put forward for re-development of the hospital to be in a green field site at Tredegar Park adjacent to Tredegar House. This plan would have provided ample space for new buildings and expansion of the hospital as well as other needs, especially for parking space. In particular, constructional work on a green field site could have been undertaken independently of the normal daily activities of the hospital and would not have disrupted its day to day work. Furthermore, it would have been an ideal site for access from the town via the A48 from Newport and eventually from the valleys and areas east of Newport via the M4 Motorway. However, it is not on record whether a long-term vision of these possibilities was available to the authorities at that time. In particular, no-one was predicting the density of motor vehicles of modern times which has contributed so much to the overwhelming problem of lack of parking space at the present time on the Royal Gwent site, as well as in Newport.

According to the late Mr. Hywel Roberts, previously Consultant Surgeon at St. Woolos Hospital, an alternative location considered for re-development of The Royal Gwent had been another green field site to the west side of the Malpas Road. This land still exists untouched and is adjacent to the angle between the Malpas Road with Junction 26 of the M4 motorway. It was viewed in 1957 by Mr. Roberts with Dr. Arthur Culley, who was Chief Medical Officer of The Welsh Board of Health at that time, from a vantage point off The Ridgeway known locally as 'Little Switzerland'. The idea was not taken forward. *(Personal communication from Hywel Roberts to the Editor)*.

However, it is evident from Dr. Gareth Jones' recent history of Nevill Hall Hospital (*The Aneurin Bevan Inheritance: the story of the Nevill Hall and District N.H.S. Trust*. Old Bakehouse Publications, Abertillery. 1998. ISBN 1 874538 17 4) that there was another view in the late 1950s that a single County Hospital for the whole of Monmouthshire should be developed. This was supported by Dr. Maldwyn Jackson and Mr. Hywel Roberts, consultants at St. Woolos Hospital, and Mr. J.S. McConnachie, consultant surgeon in the North of the county at Tredegar Hospital, but was opposed by Mr. Trevor Rice-Edwards, who was consultant surgeon at The Royal Gwent as well as Chairman of the Newport and East Monmouthshire Hospital Management Committee. To quote Dr. Jackson from Dr. Jones' book: *'There was St. Woolos, the old workhouse hospital, very badly built and not fit to be a hospital but it provided a good, kindly hospital service. The Gwent was on a slope; Rice-Edwards insisted on the hospital going up. While Howell Roberts and I and one or two others wanted to build further up the valley up towards Llantarnam: a thousand beds there for the whole of the county. But Trevor was a real Gwent man.'* Mr. McConnachie also wrote: *'In Newport, they had the old Gwent Hospital. It was a terrible place and it couldn't expand. And the surgeon there Hywel Roberts had the best idea that they should build a hospital to the north of Newport with access to all the valleys. And I think that would have been the best thing. But the Gwent was so embedded in the hearts of Newport people and they were so keen to get a new hospital in Newport. If they could only have agreed there would have been only one hospital for Monmouthshire somewhere north of the M4 with access to everywhere'*. Other views are said to have prevailed on the grounds that use of the Tredegar Park site in Newport would have removed the hospital from a central location in the town with its convenience of access for the local people. It was also feared that the hospital's 'Royal' status might have been compromised by a move away from Cardiff Road. It is

64

now evident that the hospital's 'Royal' status would never have been affected by re-development at Tredegar Park for many hospitals with 'Royal' status elsewhere in the country have been re-built away from their original locations without a change of their Royal title.

Another obstacle to agreement about a single hospital for the county was that each of the Hospital Management Committees in the county (Newport and East Monmouthshire, North Monmouthshire, and Rhymney and Sirhowy Valleys) wanted to have new hospitals in their own areas.

However, the decision for re-development of the Royal Gwent at the Cardiff Road site was taken centrally at The Welsh Hospital Board. Furthermore, as capital money was only available from central sources such a decision was probably outside the final authority of the Newport & East Monmouthshire Hospitals Management Committee. Retrospectively, it is now agreed that this decision was unfortunate as experience during the past forty years has demonstrated the practical difficulty, poor economics and severe limitations of long-term strategy from rebuilding The Royal Gwent Hospital on its own footprint. This will be discussed later in this chapter. In fact, the site at Tredegar Park that was rejected so many years ago now houses the Business Statistics and Patents Offices of the government and nowadays is widely regarded by many in retrospect as a lost opportunity of the greatest magnitude.

On the 1st September 1960 a headline of the *South Wales Argus* read 'The new Royal Gwent.' The article went on to say that the old hospital was to be pulled down and replaced by eleven-storey buildings with beds for 800 patients, over three times as many were accommodated at that time.

The article further reported that a start would be made in 1962 beginning with a Maternity and Gynaecology Unit with 156 beds to replace the Maternity Unit which existed at St. Woolos Hospital at that time. In addition, an antenatal clinic and four operating theatres would be built as well as a new kitchen to serve the whole of the hospital. The first stage was expected to take 2^1/$_2$ years to complete.

The ultimate intention of a re-building programme was to replace with modern new buildings all the existing old accommodation on the site: at a later stage, in the 1980s, it was intended that all major clinical services in South Gwent would be centralised on the Royal Gwent site.

After 40 years of re-development, complete rebuilding of the hospital has yet to be achieved. However, this situation has had an unexpected advantage in that the present Royal Gwent can be regarded as a more modern institution in its design and delivery of care than would have resulted from a *de novo* total construction on a green field site. Since 1957, when the original hospital development plan was drafted, plans for each new stage (or 'phase') were amended and upgraded to reflect current thinking and needs at the time of construction. Therefore, it has been possible to incorporate up-to-date design and, especially include current technological and clinical advances into new building in each phase of the rebuild. Some hospitals in Wales built in their entirety 40 years ago are now showing signs of age requiring upgrading and even replacement.

While the story of rebuilding The Royal Gwent Hospital will undoubtedly have its critics, the following account of the re-development is a record of the work done and of the process of organisation of a difficult job carried out under unfavourable conditions. There was a limit to the amount of Capital Money available for this project which had to be planned to proceed in stages. But these were not carried out chronologically in the sequence of Scheme numbers designated to the original plan.

Re-development: The Royal Gwent Hospital (*main contributors: Noel Bellamy & Terry Gale JP*)

The sequence of re-development programmes has been colour-coded on the Pull-out Plan 2. These indicate the location and dates of the various building programmes that took place and are intended to accompany the text covering each phase of the overall project. Labelling of individual sites indicates the final designations of buildings and/or locations of departments in the hospital at 2004 - Editor).

1963 to 1966: Scheme 1

The first phase of re-development planned to create a dedicated, modern obstetric and gynaecological unit, modern operating theatres with central sterile supply services as well as new kitchens for the hospital and dining facilities for staff.

It was fortunate that, for the first stage of the programme, an area of ground was available between Belle Vue Lane and the existing buildings of the old hospital, and below the Nurses' Home. This gave sufficient space on which to construct the first stage of re-building (see page 26).

Consequently, construction work began on site for Scheme 1 in July 1963 for a new building at the west end of the hospital. There were six floors in a main block to provide for new Obstetric and Gynaecological Wards with an Antenatal Unit attached and two Operating Theatres dedicated for gynaecological surgery, two Delivery Rooms as well as a Special Care Baby Unit. Instead of a 'Nightingale' ward design, accommodation for patients was based on four-bedded units and some single rooms with en-suite facilities.

General view in 1966 of the Scheme 1 development with the Antenatal Clinic in the foreground, and the six floor Obstetric and Gynaecology Ward building adjacent. The lower corner of Belle Vue Lane at its junction with Cardiff Road can also be seen with a gate into Belle Vue Park.

(photograph Cliff Knight)

A separate building containing new Main Operating Theatres for General Surgery was included in this Scheme. Four Operating Theatres were opened in 1967 leaving a void for provision of additional theatres in the future. These theatres were situated above a new Central Sterile Supply Department (C.S.S.D.) which had direct access to the Theatre Suites above. In 1967, it was anticipated that the void would accommodate three additional operating theatres.

A new Dining Room with kitchens and stores were also included in the development. Also, a new hospital switchboard was installed.

The Scheme 1 buildings were constructed to the West and the northern aspects of the old 1901 hospital. The cost of this part of the re-development programme was £1.365m and the main contractor was McAlpine Limited.

H.M. Queen Elizabeth The Queen Mother arriving to open the first phase of the redevelopment of The Royal Gwent Hospital in 1966. To the right behind her is Mr. George Thomas later to become Speaker of The House of Commons and to be Lord Tonypandy.

(photograph courtesy of The South Wales Argus)

In 1966, the maternity unit in St. Woolos Hospital moved to this new building in The Royal Gwent. It was opened on 8th June 1966 by Her Majesty Queen Elizabeth the Queen Mother, Patron of The Royal Gwent Hospital. This was a memorable occasion when consultants paraded in university gowns and degree hoods, a colourful sight not seen at the hospital since, and the town came to watch and cheer this popular and lovely lady.

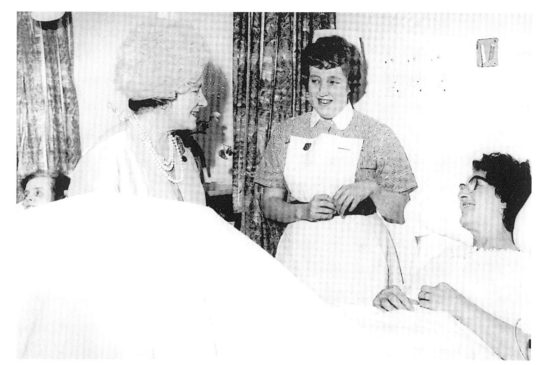

The Queen Mother touring one of the new wards in the Maternity Unit.

(photograph courtesy of The South Wales Argus)

Scheme 1 of the redevelopment programme increased the bed capacity of The Royal Gwent Hospital from 247 to 427 beds.

However, this development was not without its teething problems.

The four new Operating Theatres were opened specially for the visit of The Welsh Surgical Society in July 1966, for in those days it was the custom for local surgeons acting as hosts to the Society to demonstrate surgical procedures to their visiting colleagues. This was supplemented for the first time with a closed-circuit television system inserted in the theatre lamps that was used to demonstrate the operations to the visitors. The demonstrations went well but the consultants noticed large gaps between ceiling tiles in the new theatres through which debris and dust could fall into the operating area. The surgeons declared these conditions to be unhygienic and closed the theatres for further use until the ceilings had been made safe. Surgery, therefore, continued in the old twin theatres in the East Wing.

Rectification of these matters took one year to resolve before General Surgery moved into two theatres of the new facility and the orthopaedic surgeons also moved into the remaining two theatres which became dedicated to their specialty. The old theatres were taken over full-time by the E.N.T. surgeons who had previously shared these with the General Surgeons. The single Operating theatre that had been commissioned in 1943 in the Fracture and Orthopaedic unit on the ground floor of the old hospital was re-designed as a Plaster Room.

1966 to 1967: Scheme 2

The second development provided additional staff residential accommodation to support nursing staff increases needed to service the increased number of beds that had occurred with the arrival of the new wards and building for gynaecology and obstetrics.

Construction work began in March 1966 to build two nurses' residential blocks in Friar's Field (now known as Blocks 9 and 10). This was completed in March 1967 and cost £147,000. The main contractor was John Laing Construction Limited.

Aerial view of Royal Gwent Hospital site after completion of Schemes 1 & 2 redevelopment projects. This shows Cardiff Road and the old hospital in the foreground with the stack of the Boiler House at the rear. From left to right are: the Antenatal Unit, the Gynaecological ward block with a link to a six-floor building containing Operating Theatres for gynaecology (top floor) and Engineering services (ground floor). A bridge built to link the Nurses' Hostel with the new buildings is clearly visible. To the right is a lower building that housed new residential quarters and behind the Boiler House the new Operating Theatre/C.S.S.D. complex can be seen joined to the main hospital by a bridge. Further up the hill is the new residential accommodation for nurses (Scheme 2) and The Friars. The extent of the vacant area of Friars Field is clearly evident, In the distance is St. Woolos Hospital with a chimney stack visible of the Boiler House that came to serve both hospitals after the Boiler House of the old hospital had been demolished to make way for Scheme 5 and 'C' Block.

1971 to 1972: Scheme 4

In the third development (known as Scheme 4), a new (but temporary) Radiology Department was built and over the following years was regularly expanded to incorporate new imaging processes and technology as the hospital developed. To enable this to occur, the Medical Staff Dining Room in the Western end of the old hospital was removed to increase radiological facilities and doctors' residential quarters were transferred to a new location in the Scheme 1 building. The doctors subsequently fed in the main Dining

Room. Apart from abolition of the perceived elitism of a dining room dedicated to medical staff, this development had some logistic drawbacks in that the ease of internal communication previously possible between medical staff for business matters, disappeared. Inter-departmental referrals for clinical opinion and action became more difficult and slower. (*This was generally regarded as a disadvantage to clinical care by professional staff but not by management - Editorial comment*).

This Scheme also included a Training Unit for Midwifery.

The Scheme 4 programme began in January 1971 and was completed in July 1972 at a cost of £215,000. The contractors were Hinkin & Frewin (Newport) Limited.

Extension to the Gynaecology and Obstetrics building

Additional Out-Patient accommodation (for paediatrics and diabetes patients) was gained by an extension at ground floor level to the lobby of the new Obstetric Block. This was named The Belle Vue Out-Patients as it was adjacent to Belle Vue Lane. A Short-Stay Unit of 11 beds was also provided. (See Pull-out Plan 2 - Site 4)

1972 to 1977: Scheme 5

The next major development (Scheme 5) was planned to provide a new Pathology department, to complete the Operating Theatre Suite, and to build the first of two Tower Blocks for additional beds and some service departments. Scheme 5 occurred in two Phases.

In Phase 1, a new Pathology Department was built and five Operating Theatres constructed in the void that had been mothballed since 1967 from Scheme 1. The completed Operating Theatre Suite therefore consisted of nine Theatres which housed operating accommodation for 4 General Surgical Units, 2 Orthopaedic Units, 2 Theatres for E.N.T. (which vacated the Theatres in the old building) and one Theatre for Emergency use.

This development opened in 1977 and cost £470,000. The main contractor was Costain Construction Limited.

In Phase 2, the first of two tower blocks of the redeveloping hospital was built. This was a 7-floor building which provided 218 additional beds in surgical and orthopaedic wards. To make way for this development, the Boiler House of the old hospital had to be demolished with a new Boiler House being built at St. Woolos Hospital taking over to serve both hospitals. The boiler unit was oil-fired and for several years, local residents were troubled by oil smuts falling from its tall chimney.

On completion of the new tower block, surgical beds were moved from wards in the old hospital that had been in use for surgery since 1901 and orthopaedic beds left the Fracture and Orthopaedic Unit that had opened in 1943 to move into the new wards. This gave the opportunity to transfer Children's Wards in St. Woolos Hospital into the orthopaedic adult wards vacated in the old Fracture & Orthopaedic Unit as well as some adjacent converted accommodation (ref. p.129). These wards became known as 'The Lydia Beynon Unit'.

Service departments to support both the existing hospital and future developments were also included in the new tower block such as Medical Illustration which moved from its original quarters opposite the Main Dining Room and Pharmacy which had been in the old hospital near the Out-Patient building. Also, an extended Multi-disciplinary Training Unit was constructed in the new building as well as accommodation for stores and a centralised staff changing facility.

1975 to 1977: Scheme 3

To keep pace with the enlargement of clinical accommodation created by re-development of the hospital, additional staff residential accommodation was put up in Friar's Field (Blocks 1 to 7 in Friar's Field) to support further increase of In-Patient beds created by Scheme 5 of the development plan.

The work on Scheme 3 started in June 1975 following Phase 1 of Scheme 5 and was completed in July 1977. It cost £790,000 and the main contractor was Mears Construction Limited.

View of some of Residential Accommodation on Friars' Field taken from area outside Pathology Department.

Re-designation of nomenclature for Units built in the Re-development (1978)

At this stage of re-development in 1978, it was abundantly obvious that clarification of the titles for the several parts of the old and the new hospital was needed.

Scheme 1, when completed in 1966 was known as 'The New Hospital'. As completion of Scheme 5 approached in 1977, it was realised that Scheme 5 should receive an individual title for identification within the overall re-development of the Royal Gwent.

Hence, the buildings constructed in Scheme 5 became known as 'C' Block and Scheme 1 buildings housing gynaecological, obstetric units and catering became known as 'B' Block. The old hospital buildings were named 'A' Block and the future Scheme 6 buildings would become 'D' Block on completion (ref. Pull-out Plan 2).

It was intended that new buildings planned for Schemes 7 & 8 of the re-development that would replace the residual buildings of the old hospital buildings would retain the label 'A' Block. These were never completed so that those buildings dating from the old hospital became designated as 'A Block'.

Scheme 5 was opened in 1979 and cost £3.77m. The main contractor was P.G. Trentham Limited.

1979: Sale of Lydia Beynon Maternity Hospital

Lydia Beynon Hospital had been a general practitioner obstetric unit situated near The Coldra in the western outskirts of Newport.

This 19th century house had been the home of Sir John Beynon Bart. CBE and had been built about 1860. It was called 'The Coldra'. On 30th November 1924 it was given with seven and a half acres of land to The Monmouthshire County Council by Sir John in memory of his mother. He specified that it was for use as a Maternity Hospital especially for expectant mothers with difficult or complicated labour. Consequently, the house was renamed 'The Lydia Beynon Maternity Hospital' by The County Council. The house was altered and adapted as a Maternity Hospital at a cost of £12,000. It was also intended that, after further facilities had been installed, to treat women with gynaecological disabilities and damage following confinement.

Lydia Beynon Hospital in the early 1960s. On the first floor, rooms were used (from left to right) as a general ward, the sluice room (with spectators at the window), a labour ward and the operating theatre. At the front of the hospital were extensive gardens.

(photograph courtesy of Mrs. Ray Morgan)

It was anticipated that the running costs would be about £5,000 each year and Professor Gilbert Strachan from Cardiff was appointed as Consultant Obstetrician and supervisor of the Antenatal Clinic which received cases from sixteen Antenatal Clinics in other areas of the County.

It was not until 1940 that the hospital finally opened due to difficulty with adaptation of the existing drainage system for hospital purposes (*South Wales Argus: 16th March 1976.*)

With the arrival of the National Health Service, the Hospital and its land became vested in the Ministry of Health in 1948 and under the control of The Newport and East Monmouthshire Hospital Management Committee. The clinical control of the unit was under the care of Dr. Nora Keevil who is remembered for her preference for carrying out caesarian sections under local analgesia rather than general anaesthetic which was usual elsewhere. She also preferred to run the hospital with female staff and apparently it was most unusual for male colleagues to be involved with clinical management at Lydia Beynon Hospital.

In 1974, the newly established Gwent Health Authority assumed control of the hospital but moves to close it because of low bed occupancy (5.5% to 7.6% in 1975) arose soon after. These aroused vigorous local opposition from The League of Friends of the hospital, the Community Health Councils of both South and North Gwent, and numerous individuals many of whom had been mothers whose children had been born there. There was an underlying feeling that the reasons for closure had been deliberately engineered by doctors for 'empire building' reasons and by management for financial reasons. Indeed, one document from a local public body asked the question *'that if the cost of the unit is causing concern there could be greater attention to halting the growth of the number of administrators in the Health Service and to items of waste occurring in Lydia Beynon Hospital'.*

In 1979 it was closed and its beds transferred to 'B' Block at The Royal Gwent where 11 Maternity beds were set up in a ward named 'Coldra Ward' presumably to preserve the original name of the house. Dr. Keevil retired from practice by choice at that time. The building was boarded up for several years until it was bought by Mr. Terry Matthews (now Sir Terry Matthews). He originated from Newbridge and studied electronics at Swansea University and had created a leading semi-conductor business in Canada *(Mitel Telecom)*. However, he had been born in Lydia Beynon Hospital and wished to preserve the house. Thus, started the rise behind the old house of The Celtic Manor Resort which now has worldwide fame and has been chosen to host the Ryder Cup in 2010. *(Editor - information about the hospital from Mrs. Ray Morgan, previous midwife-sister at Lydia Beynon Hospital.)*

1986 to 1994: Scheme 6

The main objective of Scheme 6 was construction of a second Tower building ('D' Block) to be in parallel with 'C' Block with an adjoining 'link' block to connect the two towers which would complete the Scheme 5 project.

However, from 1986 several small enabling schemes were carried out to clear the intended area for the construction of Scheme 6. These included engineering workshops, accommodation for resident staff, offices, a chapel, part of the Accident & Emergency Department (X-Ray) in its connecting corridors.

Also, a new hospital switchboard was needed in the mid 1980s. The funding of this development was made possible by proceeds from the sale of Lydia Beynon Hospital.

To make room for the switchboard and its hardware, the Medical Staff Coffee Lounge situated opposite the Dining Room was closed. *(This removed the last 'privilege' of medical staff, for this room had been used not only for relaxation but also for staff meetings and especially for referral of requests between specialties and consultants about In-Patients in the hospital - Editorial comment).*

The main Scheme 6 project started in 1987 with completion of the 'link' building so that the final building would be H-shaped.

Construction of 'D' Block provided a further 348 beds for medical, E.N.T. and paediatric patients as well as Short Stay and Day Case beds. Other components of this new building were 1) at ground floor level, an Accident & Emergency Unit and 2) in the undercroft, three Operating Theatres.

When 'D' Block had been completed and occupied, the number of beds in The Royal Gwent Hospital totalled 750.

'D' Block opened in November 1990 although earlier temporary commissioning was established to provide stand-by medical facilities in the Accident & Emergency and Short Stay Units for casualties from the Gulf War. At the end of hostilities it was decommissioned and thankfully not put into active service.

The cost of this part of the redevelopment of the hospital was £9.7m and the main contractor was Wimpey Construction Limited.

The Royal Gwent Hospital in 1991: In the foreground is the Casualty Unit standing in front of the old hospital with newly built Blocks C and D behind. To the left of the tower of the East Wing of the old hospital the white roof of the Short Stay Unit is visible (see p.26/b) and in front of the West Wing block is an angled white fascia of the roof of the Postgraduate hut (see p.26/c).

(photograph Cliff Knight)

1992: Consequences of Scheme 6

Several schemes were needed to use space vacated in the old building by departments that had moved into 'D' Block.

The largest programme was conversion of the first of two Children's wards from above the Out-Patients Department previously known as Ward 9 to create a custom-designed Cardiology Unit and to move the department from its inadequate site in a hut near the front gate of the hospital. New homes were also made on this site for departments of Occupational Therapy, Dietetics, and Surgical Appliances. (see Pull-Out Plan 2 - Site 8)

These works cost £750,000 and were carried out by White Bros. & Speed Limited.

'D' Block, when built, was located immediately behind the old hospital. In fact, a gap of about six feet separated the two buildings. This meant that daylight did not penetrate directly into the lower three floors of 'D' Block so that the outlook from these wards was a brick wall and permanent lighting was needed to dispel the semi-darkness within. These conditions created complaints from patients and some health problems such as headaches and stress illnesses among nursing staff.

It had always been the plan to demolish the old hospital on completion of 'D' Block to make way for Schemes 7 & 8 that were intended to complete the re-development of The Royal Gwent Hospital. However, there was some delay pending adequate funding for the work to be carried out but the situation suddenly assumed extreme urgency when the tower of wards at the Eastern end of the old building moved 20 mm in one week. This situation appeared virtually overnight and was rapidly controlled by scaffolding. However, emergency action was required to cope with increasing movement of the building and several tons of patients, staff and equipment were moved elsewhere in a rapid evacuation of these wards that started during an International Match at Cardiff Arms Park (with inevitable recall of reluctant senior engineering managers). However, there was great consternation in the Works Department a few days later when other managers saw an opportunity to move seventy tons of files and paperwork for storage into this apparently unoccupied area! They were removed with the utmost speed.

Therefore, the demolition went ahead without further delay and was carried out very expeditiously with great skill bearing in mind the closeness of 'D' Block to the old building. There was sadness among the older members of the community in Newport when the old Royal Gwent disappeared for ever, leaving as evidence of the old hospital only those buildings that had been put up later than 1901. These are the Out-Patient Hall and Children's Wards opened in 1924, and the Fracture and Orthopaedic Unit opened in 1943. Thus, the hospital built in 1901 to commemorate the Golden Jubilee of Queen Victoria was no more.

The cost of demolition was £270,000 and the main contractor was Cardiff Demolition Company Limited.

Demolition of the East Wing of the old hospital showing scaffolding to shore up the tower and cupola. The roof of the Short Stay Unit is visible to the left of the picture.

(photograph Cliff Knight)

Three important projects were undertaken to complete the revised functional content of the Scheme 6 programme of development to build 'D' Block.

The first was to accommodate the Department of Urology for its long planned move from St. Woolos Hospital where it had been set up and developed from 1974. It had been agreed that this department should maintain its functional integrity as a single working unit when transplanted to the Royal Gwent. To achieve this, the second of the former children's wards in the old Fracture and Orthopaedic Unit (in 'A' Block) was re-modelled into an integrated unit consisting of Out-Patient Department, urological ultrasound and urodynamic units and offices for consultants and medical staff, secretarial staff and research staff as well as a library and teaching area. This required an extension to the first floor of the original building to make room for consulting rooms. (see Pull-Out Plan 2 - Site 9)

The ground floor of this building continued as an Out-Patient Department and Plaster Room for the Orthopaedic Unit.

The work began in August 1991, was completed in June 1992 and cost £550,000. It was carried out by Wallis Western Limited.

The Urological Department moved from St. Woolos Hospital to this new accommodation in October 1992.

Simultaneously, two wards in 'D' Block were designated for 40 urological patients as well as the three Operating Theatres in the undercroft of 'D' Block to be used for urological surgery.

The second additional Scheme was to re-furbish and extend further the 'temporary' Radiology Department that had been established in 1971 as part of the Scheme 4 development to add additional General Rooms and include gamma camera, C.T. and M.R.I. services. These developments were necessary to cope with the additional investigative demands that followed establishment of urology on the Royal Gwent site and in practice, converted the 'temporary' nature of the improvements of radiological services made in 1971 into a 'permanent' situation.

Allied to this work was full upgrading of kitchens and the hospital Dining Room from the Scheme 1 development of 1966: this opened on 14th December and was re-named 'The Belle Vue Restaurant' (see Hotel Services Chapter 11). It is open to members of the general public.

The work was completed in 1994 at a cost of £6.34m and the main contractor was Shepherd Construction Limited.

The third additional scheme was construction of Day Surgery & Endoscopy Units (1990 & 1993). A combined centre for Day Surgery and Endoscopy was constructed adjacent to the main Operating Theatre Suite in 1990. This work displaced the Female Staff Changing Rooms. It opened in January 1991 and the unit consisted of one suite for Endoscopy, one theatre for Day Surgical procedures and there were curtained-off spaces for 13 trolleys and a sitting area of 10 reclining chairs for endoscopy patients (see Pull-Out Plan 2 - Site 10).

By 1993, the demand for Day Surgery and Endoscopy had outstripped the capacity of the Unit so that a dedicated Endoscopy Unit was built alongside the previous one to cope with increased demand. This was opened in 1994 and consisted of two Endoscopy Rooms and 8 beds. (see Chapters 7 & 8).

The cost of this development was £350,000 and the main contractor was White Bros. & Speed Limited.

1991: Open Day for 'D' Block

In April 1991 hundreds of people and the general public were invited to view the new million pound development in 'D Block' before they were brought into use to see the new Accident and Emergency Department and the Children and Young People's Unit where, for the first time, teenagers were able to stay in a ward with people of their own age, and mothers were able to stay with their sick children. The old fashioned multi-bedded wards were replaced with smaller four and two-bedded ones, and even single-bed wards with en-suite toilet facilities were made available.

1991: Conversion of Blocks 9 & 10 in Friar's Field)

With increased centralisation of services to the Royal Gwent site and administrative reorganisation to form The Glan Hafren N.H.S. Trust, accommodation for an administrative centre was needed.

For this to be achieved, the two buildings originally built for nurses' accommodation in Friars Field in Scheme 2 in 1967 (Blocks 9 & 10) became unoccupied and were converted into offices so that administrative staff could move from the main hospital to create extra space for clinical uses. Some facilities were transferred to St. Woolos Hospital. Offices in 64 Cardiff Road were vacated permanently (see Pull-Out Plan 2 - Site 3).

Construction work for this development began in April 1996 and was completed in July 1996 at a cost of £465,000. The main contractor was W.H. Development Limited.

1994 to 2003: Post-Scheme 6 - Rationalisation for the future

Plans to complete the re-building of The Royal Gwent Hospital with a final development on the site of the former original hospital building were shelved in favour of a Rationalisation Programme. This would support a series of works that had been undertaken throughout the hospital over a number of years to provide purpose-designed facilities as the service had expanded. The cost would be in the region of £13m. However, during this time, refurbishment and upgrading works that were unconnected to the Rationalisation Programme would continue.

1994 to 1995: Maxillo-Facial & Oral Surgery Department

This development took place between June 1994 and February 1995 in a new purpose-built ground floor extension of previous premises in 'B' Block. It was opened in July 1995 and combined services transferred from St. Woolos Hospital and St. Lawrence Hospital, Chepstow following the move of the Burns and Reconstructive Surgery Unit to Morriston Hospital, Swansea.

The cost was £1.6m and the main contractor was Wallis Western Limited.

1996 to 1997: Medical Day Case Unit

There had been an increase in medical treatment on a day-case basis, such as chemotherapy, so that a Medical Day Care Unit was needed. A new unit was built between 1996 and 1997 by internal refurbishment of rooms opposite The Belle Vue Restaurant (see Pull-Out Plan 2 - Site 5). This was opened by The Prime Minister, The Rt. Hon Tony Blair.

Its cost was £1.2m and the main contractor was Davlan Construction Limited.

The Prime Minister, The Rt. Hon. Tony Blair meeting Sen. Nurse Sue Morgan during his visit to open the Medical Day Care Unit. He was accompanied by Mr. Gwilym Griffith, Medical Director and Mrs. Lindsey Davies, Director of Nursing.

(photograph Nigel Pearce, Medical Illustration)

1997 to 1998: Entrance Concourse, Children's Out-Patient Clinics

With demolition of the old hospital buildings, the main entrance to the hospital had disappeared. It had been originally envisaged that a new main entrance and Concourse would be built as part of the Scheme 7 development attached to 'D' Block and located on the footprint of the old hospital buildings. As has been noted earlier in this review, plans for Scheme 7 were shelved.

Therefore, an alternative scheme to provide the new hospital with an entrance Concourse was commenced in January 1997. This was located at the undercroft level of 'D' Block where a Welcoming Desk for visitors and patients was present. On the first floor, a Main Reception Desk for admissions was built next to a Café (Beechwood Café) for snacks and light meals for staff and visitors (see Chapter 11).

This project was completed with a dedicated Children's Out-Patient Department, Accident & Emergency Unit and Clinics adjacent to the Accident Department on the first floor of 'D' Block (see Pull-Out Plan 2 - Site 6).

The development was carried out at a cost of £1.134m and the main contractor was Ballast Wiltshier Limited.

1997 to 1999: Ophthalmic Unit and E.N.T. Out-Patients

To complete transfer of specialist surgical services from St. Woolos to the Royal Gwent, the former Nurses' Home of 1933 was demolished to make way for a new building in January 1997. This provided accommodation for the Department of Ophthalmic Surgery which was moved down from its previous home at St. Woolos Hospital. There are two Operating Theatres and one Theatre for Minor Procedures which are serviced from 8 adult beds and 3 beds for children.

Also this building provided new facilities for an Out-Patient Clinic for the E.N.T. Department which included a Hearing and Balance Unit which moved to this building.

The new building (known as 'E' Block) opened in April 2000 at a cost of £4.5m and the main contractor was Wallis Western Limited.

View of the new 'E' Block that replaced the Nurses' Home.

(photograph Cliff Knight)

1997 to 1998: Main Out-Patient, Fracture & Orthopaedic Clinic/Physiotherapy

The Main Out-Patient Department of the hospital has remained in its original building built in 1924. However, the interior of the Department was extensively upgraded and refurbished between February 1998 and April 1999. The League of Friends of The Royal Gwent Hospital has its centre and Snack Bar for patients in the Out-Patients concourse.

Similarly, the Fracture and Orthopaedic Clinic has remained in its original location from 1943 and, as with the adjacent Physiotherapy Unit, has also been refurbished and extended (see Pull-Out Plan 2 - Sites 9 & 12).

The cost for this work was £2.4m. The main contractor was Balfour Beatty Limited.

1999: Other Programmes

The School of Nursing moved off-site with the introduction of Project 2000 so that the former Multi-disciplinary Training Unit could be converted into a Medical Ward of 30 beds.(Cost: £750,000: contractor Davlan Construction Limited).

Additional Car Parking spaces were made (cost: £145,000).

A Departmental Centre for the Division of Anaesthesia was created in the former Midwifery Training Unit (cost: £300,000).

Alterations and extensions to The Department of Pathology (cost: £400,000).

During 1998, a scheme to improve and extend the facilities within C.S.S.D. was undertaken at a cost of about £1m. The actual works costs were £700,000 and the main contractors were White Brothers & Speed Limited.

Various other works were to transfer some services to St. Woolos Hospital away from an increasingly congested site at The Royal Gwent Hospital.

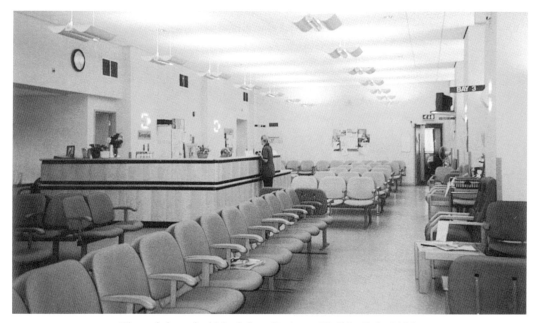

View of the refurbished Out-Patients Hall in July 2001.

(photograph Cliff Knight)

2003: Medical Assessment Unit

In October 2003, a new Medical Assessment Unit was opened at The Royal Gwent Hospital (see Pull-Out Plan 2 - Site 14). This was designed to provide a new approach

View of the interior of the new Medical Assessment Unit with some of the staff. Left to right are Chris Teague, Joanne Porter, Joanne Hughes, Toni Derby and Julie Smith.

(photograph Brian Peeling)

to admissions. It is open for twenty-four hours each day and is supported by specialist health professionals including Acute Care Consultant Physicians, Advanced Nurse Practitioners, Anticoagulant Nurses and many support staff. The intention is to achieve rapid assessment of the condition of patients, a prompt diagnosis and stabilisation and quick decision for subsequent management.

Overall Review of Re-Development: 1964 to 2003

The end result of the re-development programme is shown by the aerial photograph below.

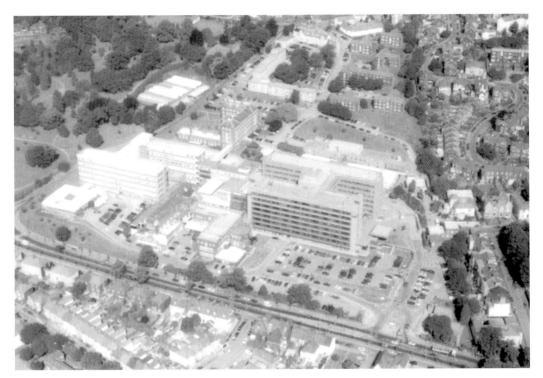

Aerial view of The Royal Gwent Hospital complex taken in 2003. Compare with Pull-out Plan 2.

(photograph courtesy of Gwent Healthcare N.H.S. Trust)

This was achieved by phased removal of most of the old hospital and replacement with new buildings to provide an expanded and extended service on the Royal Gwent Hospital site. Services from St. Woolos and some outlying hospitals moved into the Royal Gwent and the entire extent of Friars Field was developed for staff residences, administration accommodation and teaching facilities. Coordination of these moves was a major problem that, in general, was achieved successfully but the preceding account illustrates clearly the complexity of a major rebuild on the same site as the old hospital.

However, it is generally considered that the density of development on the present site of the institution may be approaching maximum saturation and, apart from a Health Science Institute to be built on the site of 64 Cardiff Road (see Chapter 10), further building and expansion could result in functional strangulation of the work of the hospital. Historically, this situation was predicted many years ago by Mr. Hywel Roberts and Mr. McConnachie (page 64) and others but it was not anticipated that the major factor underlying present overcrowding has been the need to keep up with ever accelerating advances of medical progress as will be reviewed in Chapters 7 to 10.

The re-development of The Royal Gwent Hospital has been maintained at a cost of many millions of pounds. It has also been achieved by a series of complex manoeuvres successfully carried out, as the preceeding narrative has recorded.

The Royal Gwent Hospital in 2003 (Editorial review)

After so many re-building developments over a period of forty years, the external appearance of The Royal Gwent Hospital presents a mixture of architectural styles. The red brick and white painted facia of the squared design of the Gynaecology and Obstetrics building opened in 1966 contrasts markedly with the pre-fabricated face of 'C' Block opened in the 1970s. 'D' Block opened in 1991, while impressive in appearance, presented a third style whereas the oldest buildings of 'A' Block remind us of the hospital buildings put up in the first half of the twentieth century which contrasts noticeably with the newer parts of the hospital. Nevertheless, the old hospital of 1901 was an elegant example of late Victorian architecture and it is clearly evident from the preceding chapters in this book that the vision of the founders of the hospital at that time has been carried through the intervening hundred years to the modern institution that exists now.

General view of The Royal Gwent Hospital from Cardiff Road. The car park and forecourt are the site of much of the old hospital. 'D' Block (1990) and 'C' Block (1977) are in the centre and to the right of the picture and 'B' Block (1966) can be seen in the distance to the left. 'A' Block (the remaining old hospital) appears in the mid-distance to the left. The picture is remarkable for the total absence of motor vehicles and traffic!

(photograph Cliff Knight 2001)

Throughout its history, the hospital has had to face up to steadily increasing demands for greater and more up-to-date clinical performance which have always been met. Data are only available in detail since 1974 but the details of clinical throughput since 1974, shown by Table 1 indicates clearly the constant increase of workload that has been undertaken with increased load from In-Patients (+184%), new Out-Patients (+257%), total Out-Patients (+122%) and new A & E attendances (+78%) in nearly 30 years. However, the startling statistic that Day Case work had increased from 385 procedures in the Royal Gwent in 1984 to 27,517 (+7147%) nearly twenty years later in 2003 highlights the effect of technological and other advances on clinical practice and staffing levels needed to advance with the time.

Table 1 - Clinical Throughput since 1974 *(from Information Services, Welsh Assembly courtesy of Sonia Stevens)*

Period	In-Patient D&Ds	Day Case Procedures	New Out-Patients	Total Out-Patients	New A & E
1974	15867	Not Available	24198	98095	39613
1984/85	29003	385	34265	138035	54841
1994/95	41224	16360	47848	176414	63048
2002/03	45109	27517	64524	217325	70554

To cope with increased demand and increasingly advanced technology in all departments, there has been an increase of personnel in The Royal Gwent Hospital as indicated by the following data shown by Table 2 *(by courtesy of Kate Davies, Workforce Information Manager, Gwent Healthcare N.H.S. Trust)*:

Staff Group	1991	1995	1999	2003	Overall % change
Ancillary	145	361	478	478	+230%
Maintenance	26	27	21	21	-19%
Admin. & Clerical	243	362	586	802	+230%
Medical	58	130	461	430	+641%
Dental	1	2	18	15	+1400%
Nurses-qualified	663	813	1102	1112	+68%
Nurses-unqualified	212	278	419	523	+147%
Professions allied to medicine	52	86	133	145	+179%
Scientific & Professional	19	23	35	56	+195%
Technicians	134	183	263	295	+120%
Works	12	13	29	27	+125%
TOTALS	1565	2278	3545	3904	+149%

To provide facilities and accommodation to cope with extra clinical demand, the redevelopment of the hospital since 1964 has resulted in the following complement in the year 2003:

In-Patient beds:		755
Day-case: Main Unit		3 beds
		35 trolleys
Urology		10 trolleys
Operating Theatres:	Main Theatre Complex	9
	Urology	3 (Lithotripter1)
	Gynaecology	2
	Obstetric	1
	Accident & Emergency	2
	Ophthalmic Surgery	2
	Maxillo-Facial	1
	Day-case Surgery	2
	Endoscopy	2
	(Total)	24

Contrast these data with the hospital statistics at approximately 50-year intervals:

	1901	1948	2003
In-Patients beds	96	259	755
Operating Theatres	1	4	24

These figures illustrate the response that had to come to react to the rapid march of technology in healthcare, the policy of centralisation of acute services to The Royal Gwent and the expansion of Day Care facilities that will be referred to in Chapters 7 to 10. These changes have been achieved by transfer of clinical services from other hospitals in the county some of which have closed or been replaced by new developments but the end result has maintained the high standard of service to the community that has been a constant theme in the historical chapters covering the years from 1838 to the present day.

Further demands of the scope and capacity of The Royal Gwent can be expected in the next ten and more years and it will be of more than academic interest to 'watch this space'.

2) St. Woolos Hospital - New Building and Changes of Use
Anne Freeman FRCP & Brian Peeling CBE FRCS

It has been noted earlier that St. Woolos Hospital acquired its modern name shortly after it had been taken over by The National Health Service at the request of Mr. Hywel Roberts, its consultant surgeon. He felt at that time that it was necessary to get away from the earlier title of Woolaston House because of the stigma of its Workhouse/Poor House history and that, as part of the new National Health Service the hospital should assume its rightful place alongside The Royal Gwent as a General Hospital (personal comments to 'BP'). In fact, St. Woolos potentially was a major player as at that time there were 402 beds in the hospital, many of which were providing acute medical services although a significant number were still designated for people cared for by the local authority (Part 3 Accommodation). The acute services functioned, therefore, as a General Hospital and were mainly medical, surgical, obstetric and gynaecological. With time, other specialties moved in such as paediatrics, dermatology, some E.N.T. and ophthalmics as those under local care reduced in numbers presumably largely due to death from old age or infirmity. However, even as recently as the early 1960s, local authority patients were still resident in wards such as Buckley Ward (shown as Sections I and J on Pull-Out Plan 1). At the time it was said that unless a resident could walk, he or she would only leave the ward in a box as there were no lifts to the wards. Nevertheless, they were well cared for and the local authority commitment ended in 1968.

This allowed development of the old, vacated accommodation into acute units shown on Plan 1 as follows:

paediatrics (sections D and E also known as Wards A3 and A1)
dermatology (Section L)
ophthalmics (Section F) where ward accommodation and an operating theatre were set up. These continued in full use for many years and, apart from dermatology, moved in 2000 into the re-developed Royal Gwent Hospital.

The previous facilities in the 1950s must have been very poor judging from reminiscences in a recent letter from Hywel Roberts to Sr. Bridie O'Connor (who worked in the theatre at St. Woolos for many years). He commented that

1) Half the buildings were still used by the Local Authority as accommodation for the *'able bodied destitute'*.

2) Dressing drums were sterilised in the Blanket Disinfector by the main gate and the drums were carried to the wards in an open truck in all weathers. All dressings were prepared in the theatre and all instruments and syringes were boiled - *'had steam pressure sterilisation only just been invented?'*.

3) Until the mid-1950s, there was only one operating theatre. This had been set up in a room of the 'B' Annexe in the 19th century (marked 'OT' on Plan 1) and continued in full-time use until the mid-1950s when Hywel Roberts arranged for a purpose-built twin theatre unit to be set up in two connecting rooms of the 'B' Annexe (marked 'X' and 'Y' on Plan 1). However, for this to happen it took seven years *'to house the physiotherapists on the site of the old garage near the main road so that the twin theatre could be concocted from the ward block that they had occupied'*.

4) Out-Patients at first were seen *'anywhere we could use a room, later a wooden partition of 'B' Block ground floor and later a prefab'*.

5) *'The Pharmacy making our intravenous fluids and all ampoules of drugs made up on site. Mr. Buckley of Santon's fitting an immersion heater in the autoclave to reduce the time for each distillation'*.

6) *'Autoclaves in the theatres for dressings and instruments. Autoclaves with recorded temp and pressure in the 'waiting room near the theatre''*.

Later in his letter Mr. Roberts recalls the arrival of the Image Intensifier for per-operative X-Rays in contrast with the first X-Ray which *'was a 1 valve affair'*.

Also, he mentioned fibreoptic instruments, resectoscopes for urology in the 1970s and the benefits of having a pathologist and his technicians on the hospital site. Even so, much of the pathological material needed to be sent down the hill to the Royal Gwent.

These comments from a hugely respected surgeon who started with very little and gradually built up the unit at St. Woolos into a modern concern are in reality a

*Out-Patient Department, St. Woolos Hospital. This prefab, referred to in Hywel Roberts' letter,
continued as an Out-Patient unit for another thirty years until the mid-1980s when a
purpose-built department was constructed near the front gate. Clinics in General Surgery,
Urology, General Medicine and Geriatrics, Cytology, Family Planning were held there. When
it closed, the Neuro-physiology Department took over until transfer to 'B' Annexe building.*

(photograph Brian Peeling)

commentary on the change of hospital practice within one working lifetime. Similar
changes and developments took place at St. Woolos in other disciplines as will be noted in
later chapters.

Recovery after surgery was carried out in the corridor outside the theatre; there were
only two oxygen and suction points in the corridor and it was not unusual with short
term day cases to have as many as six people recovering simultaneously each with a
ward nurse ensuring a clear airway. Clearly, this was not 'best practice' so in the mid-1970s
the Gwent Health Authority was induced to construct a new ward alongside the entrance
to the operating theatres to function as a recovery ward and dedicated Day Case and a
Short-Stay Ward. This had ten cubicles and trolleys, a Treatment Area and a Waiting
Area. After Hywel Roberts' retirement in 1979, it was named 'The Hywel Roberts
Ward'.

Similarly, the facilities of the Ophthalmic Department, especially for surgery, were
condemned as will be noted in accounts from that unit and a portable Operating Theatre
was installed alongside their ward block.

However, gradually St. Woolos Hospital was transformed away from being a General
Hospital due to centralisation of specialties in the Royal Gwent, apart from dermatology,
so that the main part of the hospital has little clinical commitment at the present time
and the clinical area now centres on The Springfield Unit (see Chapter 7 for Care of the
Elderly).

Consequently, the present clinical capacity of St. Woolos Hospital (2003) is;

1) The Springfield Unit (also known as The Casnewydd Unit):
     i) Day Unit   average 25 patients daily
     ii) Wards   Rehabilitation (Neurology/chest)   28 beds
                                                (Stroke/general)   28
                                                (Vascular/General)   30
                                                (Orthopaedic)   26
                           Psychiatric Assessment   16
                           Functional psychiatric care (elderly)   18
                           Dermatology   14
                           Ward closed-for Orthopaedic use   18
     iii) Morgan Therapy Unit: Occupational Therapy
                                    : Speech Therapy
                                    : Physiotherapy
                                    : Dietetics
                                    : Orthopaedic clinics
                                    : Clinical Psychology
     iv) Radiology Unit

2) 'A' Block   Pharmacy

3) 'B' Block   Cardiac Rehabilitation
                            Neurophysiology
                            G.P. Physiotherapy

4) Chest Clinic

3) Other hospitals in South Gwent - Final Years

Allt-yr-yn Hospital (Editor's Review)

Allt-yr-yn Hospital was built in the mid-1890s and located in a residential part of Newport about a mile away from The Royal Gwent and St. Woolos Hospitals. It consisted mainly of three buildings - an administration/residential block, a block of two wards and an Isolation Unit.

When it was taken over by the National Health Service, there were 57 beds overall in the hospital of which 17 were in the Isolation Block.

Its main function was to provide pre-convalescent and some rehabilitation services in the ward block which had equal numbers of beds for males and for females. These patients usually transferred from the Royal Gwent and St. Woolos after a period of In-Patient care and while in Allt-yr-yn remained under the care of the same consultant but were visited regularly by a registrar from the consultant's clinical team.

The Isolation Block was run by two General Practitioners, Drs. Sidney Rosehill and Ken Crowther, but with time and the diminution of infectious diseases requiring isolation, its activity decreased.

In the 1980s, a branch of the Pathology Department was set up at Allt-yr-yn Hospital to develop techniques using radio-active tracer elements.

The hospital closed in 1995 and has been replaced by housing development.

Photograph of main building of Allt-yr-yn Hospital taken about 1905.

(photograph courtesy of Dr. Anne Freeman)

St. Lawrence Hospital, Chepstow *(Editor's Review)*

St. Lawrence Hospital in Chepstow was originally a Military Hospital and, as with many wartime military establishments, was built as a series of huts linked by corridors. This was its basic design throughout until it was demolished in 1999 to make way for a large housing development. In 1949, the Plastic Surgery Unit attached to the Gloucester General Hospital was transferred to St. Lawrence Hospital to provide a Plastic Surgery and Burns Centre for Wales. Mr. J.R.V.B. Gibson was the dental surgeon who accompanied the unit from Gloucester; he had worked earlier in his career with Sir Harold Gillies. The founding Senior Surgeon was Mr. Emlyn Lewis. The first patients were admitted on 11th September 1950 and over the following years patients were referred to this unit from the entire Principality.

The hospital had accommodation for 201 patients in ten wards. These were designated as:

for men	plastic or orthopaedic surgery	(2 wards)
	convalescent and short stay	(1 ward)
for women	plastic or orthopaedic surgery	(2 wards)
for children	plastic and/or orthopaedic surgery	(2 wards)
	burns (cubicles in 2 wards)	
	post-operative recovery (1 ward)	

The hospital employed 400 staff (medical, nurses, physiotherapists, technicians, occupational therapists, administration and clerical, catering, porters, gardeners, engineering and works department).

The services of medical auxiliary departments were available for Occupational and Diversional Therapy, Pathology, Pharmacy, Medical Photography, Physiotherapy, Speech Therapy and Radiology.

Orthopaedic surgery was carried out by surgeons from The Royal Gwent Hospital many of whom were long-stay patients. An innovation ahead of its time was the establishment of a full-time hospital school staffed by 3 teachers and paid for by The Gwent Health Authority.

Later appointments of consultant plastic surgeons were Mr. Schofield (1976), Mr. Philip Sykes (1976), Michael Tempest who joined the staff as Senior Registrar in 1952, Stewart Watson, Martin Milling, Adrian Sugar and Michael Early. *(Michael Tempest waited longer than his contemporaries as a senior registrar before promotion to consultancy largely because of a conception among some influential senior plastic surgeons of his political views thought to be communist. This was refuted by Ian McGregor in his Obituary of Mike Tempest in The British Journal of Plastic Surgery (49, 254 1996) who confirmed that he had never supported that political group at any time as his views were wholly in accord with the Labour Party - Editor).*

In 1997, the Regional Plastics and Burns Unit transferred to Morriston Hospital, Swansea and these specialties closed at St. Lawrence Hospital. The decision for this move was greeted with some dismay in Gwent as it was felt that the Unit had been moved away from a part of South Wales in which the population had been in the majority.

The new Burns Unit is named after Michael Tempest, as is one road in the new housing estate that has been built on the site of St. Lawrence Hospital. His name became synonymous with Plastic Surgery in South Wales until his retirement in 1986.

Pontypool & District General Hospital *(Editor's Review)*

As in Newport, in the latter years of the nineteenth century the people of Pontypool decided to support a proposal to build a General Hospital to serve their part of Monmouthshire. Social conditions had been appalling, as in Newport, with recurring outbreaks of diseases like typhoid, cholera, smallpox, and other serious infections and there were no facilities for isolation of these potential killers. In Abersychan as recently as 1892, fifty-nine deaths had been attributed to measles, typhoid, scarlet fever, whooping cough, dysentery and diphtheria. Furthermore, there were only rudimentary facilities to treat accidents and fractures. Underlying all this, the population of the area had increased from 20,974 in 1861 to 32,000 by 1903.

Pontypool & District Hospital (1903) before construction of Hospital Road
(photograph courtesy of William Warren Lewis)

View of Main Entrance of Pontypool & District Hospital from Leigh Road (1903).

(photograph courtesy of William Warren Lewis)

The first move towards a hospital service was made in 1896, to consider an Isolation Hospital for the whole district. This was not universally supported and much of the objection came from members of the local medical fraternity. However, it was generally regarded, because of the growth of the population and its medical needs, that something had to be done and at a meeting on 6th December 1900 under the chairmanship of Mr. John Capel Hanbury, a committee of twelve persons resolved to draw up a scheme for a General Hospital.

Following public subscription and several acts of benefaction, a hospital was built off Leigh Road at an estimated cost of £8,000. The main contractors for construction of Pontypool & District Hospital were Messrs. Bailey Bros. of Pontnewynydd, whose family had originated in Newport and the sanitary work, lighting and telephones were carried out by Mr. E. Perman of Dock Street, Newport whose company was until recently still in business in Newport. The electricity for lighting came from an old oil generator with backup from gas lights and storage batteries for emergencies.

The new hospital was opened formally on 19th October 1903 by Mrs. Hanbury in the presence of Lord Tredegar, Mr. Capel Hanbury and Mr. Alfred Addams-Williams JP, Chairman of the Hospital Committee.

The completed hospital had accommodation for eight males and eight females, two beds for hernia cases, and one bed in the accident and emergency ward making a total of nineteen beds. There was one operating room.

The hospital existed by donations from many local workers of a penny each week from their paypackets, donations from churches (as in Newport) and a new wing (The Capel Wing) was finally opened in December 1910. In later years, Carnivals became an important source of revenue and after the arrival of The National Health Service in 1948, The League of Friends of the hospital frequently contributed items for patients' benefits as well as medical equipment.

Over the years, the hospital expanded its scope with a Children's Ward and a Nurses' Home (1916), a Dental Department (1924), a new Operating Theatre and Out-Patient

Department (1928) and an extension for three new wards and a Staff Dining Room (1931).

In 1931, there were 78 beds in the hospital, eighteen Honorary Medical Staff, thirty-nine nurses, four domestic staff and three out-door staff. In 1940, there were one hundred and fifteen beds in the hospital and with the addition of Snatchwood and Sunnybank Hospitals taken over as wartime annexes, the total bed complement came to one hundred and forty.

A mortuary in the hospital was largely used by the police and the Coroner. The post-mortems were carried out by Dr. Lister Wilson, who was on the Honorary Staff and was also a part-time local general practitioner. He had a varied career firstly as a general practitioner in the Pontypool area from the pre-N.H.S. years combined with his Honorary Staff appointment and later, became Consultant Anaesthetist with sessions at Pontypool as well as St. Woolos (Ophthalmic Unit) and The Royal Gwent Hospitals until retirement in the late 1970s. He is still remembered with affection by some surviving patients especially for his appalling timekeeping for appointments. Frequently, he would return from the hospital for an evening surgery at his house at 8pm or 9pm but his patients would wait for him without complaint. Nevertheless, by the time that they had been seen, the last buses had gone so he would run his patients to their homes by car even as late as 11.30pm! Similarly, he would arrive at the hospital at 10.30am or 11am for a 9am operating list but his charm and gentlemanly aura usually, but not always, calmed the frustrations of the waiting surgeon.

In the pre-N.H.S. days, visiting Honorary Consultant Staff, mostly from Cardiff, included such illustrious names as Dr. Strachan (gynaecology), Mr. R.A. Mogg (urology), and Mr. 'Jimmy' Wade (general surgery).

After 1948, consultants from The Royal Gwent Hospital held contracted sessions to the hospital. For surgery, two general surgeons shared forty-five beds for their patients with two operating sessions and one Out-Patient clinic each week. After 1948, these were Mr. R. Bowker (until retirement in 1961), Mr. R.D. Richards (1955 until his early death in 1968), Mr. L.P. Thomas (from 1961 until 1981), Mr. W.B. Peeling (1968 to 1974), Mr. G.H. Griffith (from 1974). Mr. Thomas and Mr. Griffith transferred their sessions to The Royal Gwent Hospital in 1981 when General Surgery centralised in Newport.

Similarly, the Consultant Physicians, Dr. J. Swithinbank and Dr. Owain Gibby also moved their sessions to Newport. Subsequently, Pontypool Hospital cared for geriatric patients until its closure in September 1993.

The hospital outlived its role towards the 1970s for the design and layout of the wards and the operating theatre became incompatible with the changes and requirements of hospital practice as well as the general trend towards centralisation of acute care. For instance, there were no changing facilities for surgeons and anaesthetists who were obliged to change into theatre garb in the office of the sister in charge of the operating theatre. This, naturally, raised difficulties and sometimes embarrassment especially for staff of Middle Eastern and Asiatic origin. Nor were there post-operative recovery facilities as patients were watched by a ward nurse either in the anaesthetic room of the operating theatre or in the corridor outside the theatre until they were considered fit to be returned to the ward. At least this arrangement had the merit that the anaesthetist was immediately available if required.

The activity of the hospital as an In-Patient Hospital declined after 1974 but Out-Patient Clinics continued and a Minor Casualty service was maintained until the hospital's closure.

Clinical Activity at Pontypool Hospital: *(from Information Services, Welsh Assembly courtesy of Sonia Stevens)*

Period	In-Patients	Day Cases	New Out-patients	Total Out-patients	New Minor Casualties
1974	1342	not available	3428	13167	5536
1984/85	197	0	3324	11318	4719
1994/95	0	0	0	0	0

(Editor - information (1896-1931) from 'The Penny Castle. A History of the Pontypool & District Hospital': Warren William Lewis. Marshall & Hicks Design & Print, Torfaen NP4 7AE by kind permission)

Monmouthshire County Hospital, Griffithstown *(Editor's Review)*
(Information concerning County Hospital from documents made available by Mr. David Hopkins, Chief Hospital Administrator - Editor)

In the early 19th century, the living conditions in Griffithstown were, as in Pontypool and in Newport, desperately poor, overcrowded and with inadequate sanitation and a contaminated water supply. Medical supervision was minimal and, as in Newport, a Board of Guardians Workhouse was established in Griffithstown in 1837.

The Workhouse was built at Coed-y-gric Road. The architect was Mr. Wilkinson of Oxford. The building was designed to accommodate 100 people and the Coed-y-gric site was chosen because it was near a railway and near a canal so that it was reasonably easy to bring materials to the site, especially by canal as the building was to be of river stone. The Workhouse was heated by coal fires instead of hot water as in many other Workhouses; this was much approved.

One office was designed to contain a Strongroom to protect records and valuables in case of fire. The walls of the strongroom were constructed with concrete reinforced by iron rods. It is of interest that the final cost of the buildings for the Workhouse was lower than the initial estimate.

A Master and Matron were appointed on 9th December 1837 with salaries of £25 and £15 respectively. The Master was required to be a good accountant and the Matron had to be competent as a Schoolmistress if required. Both were required to go *'security with a respectable surety in the sum of £50'*. Persons without family would be preferred.

Notices were put into *'The Monmouthshire Merlin'*, the local newspaper, inviting for contracts for three months tenders to supply the new Workhouse with the following provisions: bread, flour, cheese, salt, butter, milk, rice, split peas, oatmeal, beef, mutton legs, clothing, shoes, soda, soaps, candles, best coals (per ton). Also wanted were tenders for 20 rope mattresses and bedsteads.

In the grounds of the Workhouse was a building known as 'The Casuals Block'. This was for 'casuals' who were people who did not stay at the Workhouse but called in for a night's lodging. Only the destitute and infirm were allowed to be resident and *'the conditions were such as to discourage any but the destitute from seeking admission'*.

The Casuals Block had 8 cells, a big bath, a sterilising room and a room for meals. To gain admission, casuals had to go to the Town Hall in Pontypool, register with the Police who would give them a ticket for admission. Female casuals went to a different building.

On arrival at the Workhouse, only in the evening, men were taken to the cells, stripped, and their clothing would be fumigated. They were relieved of any money which was returned on discharge, and after bathing and supper (8ozs of bread, 1¹/₂ozs of cheese and a mug of cocoa), they went to bed.

Casuals were put to work next day depending on their fitness and if they refused to work their breakfasts would be stopped or the police called in, but if they were taken ill, the master would call a Medical Officer who, if convinced, would put them to bed in a cell. In later years, Infirmaries were built and sick casuals would be cared for and discharged when recovered. Fit and able casuals were only allowed to stay for one whole day and they were discharged after completing their tasks and breakfast.

Casuals were not allowed back in the same Workhouse within 28 days and they roamed the countryside going from one Workhouse to another.

Inmates had to work for their keep unless they were bedridden. Men attended to fires, gardens, kept the grounds neat and clean and the women cleaned the wards and restrooms, helped in the kitchens, the laundry, the sewing room. Children were put into children's homes.

Inmates had three meals a day and three times a week there was meat for dinner.

Married couples over 65 years of age were entitled to a room in the 'Married Quarters'.

After 1914 the Workhouse became a 'Poor Law Institution' and in 1930, boards of Guardians were abolished and care was continued by the County Council after which time medical care improved.

Between 1894 and 1897, an Infirmary was built at the Griffithstown Workhouse and this continued after the Workhouse was closed in 1911. There is little if any information about the Infirmary except that it was an Auxiliary Hospital during the war and after 1948 became The County Hospital in Griffithstown under the supervision of The Newport and East Monmouthshire Hospital Management Committee.

In the mid-1970s, the Operating Theatre was up-graded and a new twin Theatre suite was built. Some older staff recall the days when the weather was intemperately hot so that the temperature inside the old operating theatre was unbearable. On those occasions, the hospital gardener came to the rescue and hosed water over the skylight and windows hopefully trying to create some relief for those working in the theatre.

Also, a new Radiology suite was built alongside the Operating Theatre project.

At that time, consultants from the Royal Gwent Hospital visited the County Hospital - Mr. D.E. Sturdy (general surgery), Mr. Gwyn Daniel and Mr. Martin Stone (gynaecology).

From 1981, general surgical sessions were transferred to The Royal Gwent and in 1991, gynaecology followed.

In 1945 plans were drawn up to construct a temporary maternity unit in the grounds of County Hospital. Building began in 1947 and was completed in 1950 after the National Health Service had taken over the hospital. Initially it was a 'temporary' project to last 10 years: it lasted for 40 years.

At the present time in 2004, County Hospital has 95 clinical beds catering for Rehabilitation (5 wards), Strokes (1 ward), female orthopaedic recovery and rehabilitation (1 ward), and Continuing Care (1 ward). There is also a unit run by local general practitioners and a busy Minor Casualty unit. One Operating Theatre is used for minor surgery and the Radiology Unit is very active.

The hospital is also used by several charities such as Cancer Support, Crossroads and Alzheimers Support Group. A Day Case Palliative Care unit run by St. David's Foundation Hospice Care has been functioning at the hospital for five years.

The pattern of clinical activity at County Hospital has, therefore, changed during the past thirty years as is shown by the following table:

(from Information Services, Welsh Assembly courtesy of Sonia Stevens)

Period	In-Patients	Day Cases	New Out-patients	Total Out-patients	New Minor Casualties
1974	3760	not available	2285	9848	141
1984/85	4252	324	2446	11446	52
1994/95	663	1267	5988	16073	4525
2002/03	697	1896	5800	16109	7633

Aerial View of County Hospital, Griffithstown. The old buildings of Workhouse days can be seen to the left part of the site. Operating Theatre and Radiology unit (from mid-1970s) are centrally placed. Lower right is a Stroke Unit and a new rehabilitation ward while rows of huts extending to the upper part originated from the 1939 War for wounded servicemen: these have been fully used for clinical purposes until recently, mostly gynaecological services.

(photograph courtesy of John Jukes, Hospital Engineer)

4) Re-structuring of Management and Organisational Changes

Since 1948, changes of administrative influences on hospital services in Newport have taken place in three distinct periods of time which were:

- 1948 to 1974 when controlled by The Newport & East Monmouthshire H.M.C.
- 1974 to 1991 during centralisation of control under The Gwent Health Authority
- 1993 to 2001 from the introduction of N.H.S. Health Trusts

These changes have had immense influence on the infrastructure of the hospitals and the philosophy of care and management of the National Health Service in Newport and the surrounding areas.

• *1948 to 1974: The Newport & East Monmouthshire H.M.C. (Editor's Introduction)*

For twenty-six years after the foundation of The National Health Service, the two Newport Hospitals were managed by The Newport & East Monmouthshire Hospital Management Committee. The first Chairman of The Management Committee was Alderman J.J. Panes OBE. Mr. J. Trevor Rice-Edwards FRCS succeeded him in 1959 and the third Chairman appointed in 1969 was Mr. David Turnbull JP. The Secretaries of The Management Committee were Mr. Trevor A. Jones from 1948 followed by Mr. Alan S. Anderton until 1974 and Mr. R. Matthews acted as Treasurer from 1948 until 1974.

The Royal Gwent Hospital and St. Woolos Hospital were administratively separate as each institution had its own Hospital Secretary Officers of the Management Committee who were responsible to the Board of the H.M.C.. On the nursing side, there was a Hospital Matron of both the Royal Gwent and St. Woolos Hospitals but they had separate Nurse Training Schools and the nursing work was carried out independently of each other. The Matrons were all-powerful and made daily ward rounds to inspect the wards and woe betide any nurse, however senior, who was responsible for untidiness or poor routine in the wards. The Matrons commanded great respect from all, including consultants.

The Consultants of The Royal Gwent and St. Woolos Hospitals jointly formed the Senior Medical & Dental Staff Committee that met regularly in The Board Room of the hospital to discuss and decide on professional matters and organisational problems that could impinge on clinical services and patients. They would advise the Board of the H.M.C. accordingly when appropriate but were independent of the H.M.C. as they were responsible to The Welsh Hospital Board who held their contracts. This committee continued in this way until 1974 and was a very powerful force in the hospital. For much of this period, the Consultant Staff was represented on the H.M.C. Board by Mr. R. Vernon Jones, consultant in charge of the Casualty and Accident Department. His knowledge and expertise with administrative and political aspects concerned with hospital activity was much admired by all, especially by consultants who were indebted to him for representing the Consultant body in this way so that their role for the hospital could be wholly clinical. Relations between the consultants and the Board members were in general very good and this was enhanced by the fact that the Board Room was located in the Royal Gwent so that Board members and consultants frequently met each other and could exchange views about the hospital as well as other matters.

Further Commentary (Glyn Griffiths BPharm, MR PharmS)

However, despite this apparently stable balance between professional staff (medical and nursing) with administration which was probably typical of hospitals up and down the country, there had been increasing concern in the background by Governments about the costs of the service, even after its establishment in 1948 and continuing into the 1950s and 1960s. This was limited to two specific areas - funding levels and organisational structures. During the 1950s, the Treasury became increasingly desperate to find ways of reining in N.H.S. expenditure and anything came under review from hotel charges, ambulance charges, restriction of drugs to basic needs and even moving to an insurance-based system!

Finally, the Treasury insisted that a committee to assess the cost of the N.H.S. should be set up and appointed Claude Guillebaud, a Cambridge economist, to be its Chairman. His report, made in January 1956, proved a shock to the Government. He had shown that far from N.H.S. spending being out of control, it was, in fact, falling as a share of the overall 'wealth of the nation'. Inefficiency and extravagance had not accounted for the increased cost of the N.H.S.: this had been due to inflation and extra services.

The 1960s were no different. The revolution that had introduced modern medicine had effectively controlled the great infectious diseases that had been the scourge of earlier times, such as diphtheria, tuberculosis and poliomyelitis. Many of the drugs that are taken for granted today were introduced during this period of which antibiotics took pride of place, but their cost was spiralling. The cost of technological advances were adding to the pace of change such as renal dialysis, transplants particularly of kidneys, hip replacement and many other important developments in surgery in particular. And the twentieth Anniversary of the National Health Service was celebrated in 1968.

Consequently, the Government began a lengthy search for a more effective and affordable plan for the National Health Service. Sir Keith Joseph, Secretary of State for Social Services, appointed the management consultants, McKinseys, to examine the problem. They created a huge, multi-disciplinary study group which produced the 1974 re-organisation of the N.H.S. and a manual that defined the new organisation of the service - aptly named from its cover as 'the grey book'.

There was great tension about the idea that the ideal future planning of the N.H.S. lay in a merger of health and local government services. The medical profession, with its memories of pre-war local government medical services would never have agreed to work under local authority control. Similarly, local government was equally insistent that it would never agree to lose control of its social services and residential homes although some of its services might be transferred.

The ultimate solution at the end of four years work was, at best, an untidy compromise. It was decided to create fourteen Regional Health Authorities to replace the old Hospital Boards and ninety Area Health Authorities. Below these there would be two hundred District Authorities, each run by a Management Team consisting of administrators, doctors, nurses and treasurers. It was intended that these teams should operate on 'consensus management'.

In an attempt to give geographical links between Local Authorities and Health Authorities, 'Areas' ranged from those with a single District to those with five or even six Districts. To improve co-operation with Local Authorities, Local Authority members were given places on the new Health Authorities. The intention of this arrangement was to ensure that Local and Health Authorities could work together to create much needed improvements in Community Care. At the same time as local councillors became part of the Health Service, most of the remaining functions that had previously sat with Local Authorities were transferred into the National Health Service.

The presence of local councillors on Health Authorities was often helpful but since they had no direct responsibility for raising the funds to run their part of the National Health Service, they often added their voice to the critics of the system who called for more cash to be injected. Enoch Powell famously noted that one of the unique features, of the National Health Service was that everyone providing services as well as everyone using those services had a 'vested interest in denigrating it'.

The 1974 reorganisation also created Community Health Councils which were designed to give a voice for patients. Alongside all these changes there was a tortuous professional and advisory machinery associated with each separate tier.

The result of these changes, in the words of Sir Patrick Nairn, the Permanent Secretary of The Department of Social Services, proved to be 'tears about tiers'. The changes had been intended to improve planning and efficiency: in reality there were so many tiers between The Department of Health and the hospitals that delivered the service to people, that it took two years to get the plans for the new services to be discussed up and down the system.

In Wales, after reorganisation, the overall central control of the National Health Service was centralised in The Welsh Office. Thus, the new Gwent Health Authority came into existence in 1974 to be responsible to The Welsh Office, and the Newport & East Monmouthshire Hospital Management Committee was replaced by The South Gwent Health District which was responsible to the Gwent Health Authority.

1974 to 1993: The Gwent Health Authority (Editor's commentary)

On 1st April 1974 the Gwent Health Authority was created. Its offices were located half way between Newport and Abergavenny at Mamhilad Park, near Pontypool. Its function was to control and co-ordinate hospital services in Gwent between The South Gwent Hospital Group and The North Gwent Hospital Group. The Royal Gwent, St. Woolos and other hospitals previously of the Newport & East Monmouthshire H.M.C. made up the South Gwent Hospitals. Therefore, the siting of the Health Authority offices at Mamhilad was deemed to be equitably placed between the two groups of hospitals in the North and the South of the county. In practice, experience proved that this location created remoteness of the Administration from those delivering the service to the people - in the hospitals. In The Royal Gwent Hospital this was especially evident as the close contact previously enjoyed between members of management of the Newport & East Monmouthshire H.M.C. with professional and other staff was lost which, in the long run, proved to be a disadvantage.

The newly created Community Health Councils designed to provide a voice for patients and people in the community operated independently of the South Gwent Hospital Group.

The first Chairman of The Gwent Health Authority was Councillor Ron Evans from North Gwent with the Vice-Chairman as Mr. David Turnbull JP from South Gwent. This was regarded as an equitable sharing between the North and South of the county. The officers appointed to the new Gwent Health Authority were:

Area Administrator:	Mr. Gary Evans
Area Medical Officer:	Dr. Douglas Harrett
Area Treasurer:	Mr. D.S. Jones
Area Chief Nursing Officer:	Mr. Alun Giles

Mr. Evans, Dr. Harrett and Mr. Jones had moved from senior posts at The Welsh Hospital Board and Mr. Giles had previously been Nurse Tutor at the Royal Gwent Hospital when controlled by the Newport and East Monmouthshire Hospital Management Committee.

Membership of the Board of the Authority was made up from Local Authority members (4), local councillors (4), and one member representing each of the following staff groups - the consultant staff, the nursing profession of the hospitals in the county, the general practitioners in Gwent and the non-professional staff. Again there was a balance of representation between North and South Gwent.

The main effect of the new structure of the N.H.S. in Gwent was to do away with the old triumvirate of Senior Medical & Dental Consultant Staff Committee, the Hospital Matron and the Hospital Secretary that had previously run the Newport Hospitals. These disappeared in favour of a new South Gwent Health District Management Team whose operations were based on the new model of 'consensus management'. This sometimes worked well but, by definition, provided everyone on the Management Team with an opportunity to have a say which could make change difficult.

The District Management Team for South Gwent appointed in 1974 was:

District Administrator:	Mr. Alan Anderton
District Community Physician:	Dr. Margaret Salmon
District Nursing Officer:	Mr. David Thomas
District Finance Officer:	Mr. Chris Riley
Hospital Consultant:	Mr. Vernon Jones
General Practitioner:	?

The administrative infrastructure responsible to the District Administrator was:

Hospital Secretary (Royal Gwent Hospital):	Mr. Bryn Williams
Hospital Secretary (St. Woolos Hospital):	Mr. Ron Chissell
Hospital Secretary (County Hospital):	Mr. Simon Hodgson
Hospital Secretary (Pontypool & District Hospital):	Mr. S.O. Newick

The South Gwent Health District covered the same hospitals as the former Newport and East Monmouthshire H.M.C. with a total of 2,554 beds

Therefore, the 1974 re-organisation of the National Health Service removed from the consultants their previous central voice in the local management of the hospitals in South Gwent and did little to involve them in future planning and development of services.

Furthermore, a major change affecting professional medical influence occurred when the 'Cogwheel' concept was introduced at that time to create 'Divisions' of the various medical specialties. Each division elected (usually) a Chairman from consultants in the specialties of both The Royal Gwent and St. Woolos Hospitals and the remit of each division was to examine the needs of each specialty in terms of clinical demands, technical improvements and advances necessary to provide up-to-date delivery of care. Each division was expected to meet regularly so that its views and recommendations could be made through its Chairman to a Clinical Advisory Committee made up from all Divisional Chairmen. The Chairman of this committee represented the consultants on the Management Team of The South Gwent District Authority. This neat scheme had difficulty in competing with the many tiers of the new advisory machinery which had been set up by re-organisation and was ultimately by-passed as an advisory path. The overall result was that it gave the medical profession little if any opportunity to have a serious voice in planning and development of services. The line of communication was too convoluted and, at times, devious.

It is interesting that when the concept of 'Cogwheel' was first put forward in 1974, it was supported with great enthusiasm by younger consultants who saw it as a means of closer involvement with the future of the hospital although it has to be said that the previous relationship with the Hospital Management Committee had worked very well. The older generation of consultants were firmly opposed to 'Cogwheel' because it would destroy the unity of the consultants as a professional group through the Senior Medical Staff Committee. It was argued that the Senior Medical & Dental Staff Committee would still hold its previously important role as a powerful link with management but experience showed that the Senior Medical Staff Committee rapidly became irrelevant when priorities became competitive between specialties within the 'Cogwheel' Divisional structure. In other words, the Senior Medical & Dental Staff Committee as an advisory group fragmented so that interest from consultants waned and fell away. Indeed, at a higher level, priorities between the North and South Gwent District Authorities also became very competitive which added difficulties to the advisory role of medical staff to the Gwent Health Authority.

Further Commentary (Glyn Griffiths)

After re-structuring in 1974, the rest of the 1970s were beset, once again, by financial difficulties with complications coming from episodes of industrial action. Again, after 1974, there was an instant crisis about nurses' pay which led to creation of a special committee of enquiry, and fresh talks about contracts were started with consultants. These talks ground on inconclusively throughout the period of the government of the day which was also attempting to cope with the economic crisis generated by the oil price rises of 1973.

A couple of years of relative calm were followed by an explosion of industrial action in the 'Winter of Discontent' in 1978/79. Into this difficult time was dropped in July 1979 the report of 'The Royal Commission of the National Health Services'. The Commission argued that there were too many administrative tiers and that one of them, Areas, had to go.

Areas duly went, plunging The National Health Service into a second reorganisation within a decade. In Wales, it was Districts rather than 'Areas', that disappeared. With a sleight of hand which renamed each of the Welsh Area Health Authorities as a 'District', the title of the local Health Authority managing services delivered by the Royal Gwent Hospital changed imperceptibly from Gwent Area Health Authority to Gwent District Health Authority. In other words, in Wales the names changed rather than the organisation.

At a national level, finance for the National Health Service once again moved onto centre stage. The Treasury report showed some gloomy calculations predicting that public spending was on course to take an ever-rising share of national income. The report caused havoc among senior members of the government of the day and, once again, alternative options for funding the National Health Service began to be discussed. Among the many ideas that caused anxiety was replacement of the National Health Service with private health insurance and levying of charges by visiting general practitioners.

The financial problems did not go away, and in the 1980s the Government's search for ways to improve economic efficiency continued as hospital cleaning, catering and laundry services were subjected to competitive tendering. At the Royal Gwent and St. Woolos Hospitals, the in-house staff made their own bids within the tendering process and on all occasions were the successful bidders.

Financial controls at that time were especially harsh. Surplus land and properties were sold and the number of staff that the Health Authority could employ was capped.

The next major development was the report in 1983 by Roy Griffiths of Sainsbury's Supermarkets about the management of the National Health Service. In a 24-page document, which many consider to have been the most unusual in the history of the National Health Service, one sentence read 'if Florence Nightingale were carrying her lamp through the corridors of the N.H.S. today, she would almost certainly be looking for the people in charge'.

Griffiths said that
1) Administrators should be replaced by managers.
2) managers should be given clear performance targets and held to account.
3) consensus management had to go.
4) doctors needed to become involved in running the N.H.S..
5) treatment should be evaluated in terms of cost effectiveness and clinical effectiveness.

Thus, general management appeared and slowly advanced in responsibility and influence which led eventually to major re-structuring of The National Health Service from which, in Newport, was created the Glan Hafren N.H.S. Trust.

In the meantime, the 1986 financial settlement for the Health Service proved to be too tight. Health Authorities, in order to balance their books, closed beds and services throughout the country. In fact, the money involved was relatively small - perhaps £500m on a budget of £12 billion or more, but it needed to be recovered. Then came one major emotional crisis for the service.

A shortage of intensive care nurses actually unrelated to the financial crisis led to David Barber, a hole in the heart baby in Birmingham, having his operation cancelled five times in six weeks. The newspaper headlines were horrendous. David Barber's parents attempted to take legal action against the Health Authority in order to secure the much-needed operation and were unsuccessful. Tragically, David Barber's operation came too late and he died.

The Government though, could not withstand the endless waves of bad publicity and another review of the National Health Service was ordered.

Whilst the review was taking place, a committee was set up of a group of ministers who met, almost in secret, to discuss the future of the service. Since finance had caused the current crisis, it was finance to which the review first turned. Some of the members of the review team wanted more private financing of health care and some the imposition of charges for N.H.S. services. The debate on how to change the way the service was financed was deadlocked by the Chancellor who judged that any change in financing would be ineffective.

With no agreement on finance, the review turned to methods of delivery of the service to its patients. This led to the idea that an internal market of health services should be introduced. It was decided to create a purchaser/provider split within the National Health Service that would run the internal market.

Therefore, Health Authorities would cease to run hospitals directly but instead would become purchasers of care on behalf of their populations from either the public or private health care sectors. This idea has lived on to the present day. In this way, hospitals and community services would be allowed to become self-governing, created as free-standing organisations, but would remain firmly in the public sector. Family doctors would be offered budgets with which to buy a limited range of hospital and other care and also, as a small concession to the still ranging debate on finance, tax relief on private health insurance for the over 65s was introduced.

Eventually, in February 1989, the White Paper 'Working for Patients' was published. Cynics in the service immediately dubbed this document by a name which has often stuck - 'working for peanuts'.

The White Paper caused a furore and the British Medical Association spent more than £3m opposing the reforms but as the debates within the service raged, the Health Service in Gwent unwittingly moved centre stage in the discussions. The Labour Opposition claimed that the proposals outlined in 'Working for Patients' and creation of N.H.S. Trusts amounted to these hospitals leaving the N.H.S.. This had never been the intention of the government.

The debate around N.H.S. reforms was further complicated by proposals to reform contracts for general practitioners. This proposition was met with almost universal opposition from the medical world and meetings of G.P.s were attended on a scale not seen since the 1960s reforms. Repeated threats of resignation were offered. Whether these were over the new contract or the broader N.H.S. reforms or, perhaps both, was not clear and the idea grew up that somehow G.P.s would be protecting the N.H.S. by leaving it. Finally, after long negotiations, the Secretary of State and the B.M.A. leaders struck a deal - only for the doctors' conference to overturn it and demand a ballot. This ballot resulted in G.P.s voting against the deal by 4 to 3. An exasperated Secretary of State did what he threatened to do all along and simply imposed the reforms.

This, then, was the politically contentious background of the arrival of the Glan Hafren N.H.S. Trust in Gwent. All the turmoil around contracts and new proposals had obscured the fact that the review had been caused by a financial crisis, but did nothing to change the financing of the N.H.S..

In terms of the N.H.S. reforms as they affected The Royal Gwent and St. Woolos Hospitals in Newport and the other associated hospitals, it is important to realise that the pace of N.H.S. reform had been deliberately slowed down in Wales. Whilst the first N.H.S. Trusts in England had been established in 1991, it not until 1993 that the Glan Hafren N.H.S. Trust, of which the Royal Gwent Hospital was the largest part, was set up.

1993 to 1999: The Glan Hafren N.H.S. Trust (Glyn Griffiths)

The Glan Hafren N.H.S. Trust was formed on 1st April 1993 in accordance with Statutory Instrument (1992) 2733. The Trust's first Chairman was Mr. Colin Hughes-Davies who had been appointed by The Secretary of State for Wales, the Rt. Hon. David Hunt. The first Chief Executive was Mr. Martin Turner.

The Board of Directors was made up of Executive Directors appointed by the Chairman and Chief Executive and non-Executive Directors appointed by the Secretary of State.

The Executive Directors appointed in 1993 were:

Mr. Andrew Cottom	(Treasurer)
Mr. Gwilym H. Griffith FRCS	(Medical Director)
Mrs. Hazel Taylor JP RGN	(Director of Nursing Services)
Mr. Glyn Griffiths	(Service Development Director)

The non-Executive Directors were:
Professor Keith Griffiths DSc PhD.   (for The University of Wales)
Mrs. Pat White
Mr. Alf Gooding
Mr. Andrew Kilsby
Mr. Alan Carr

The headquarters of the Trust were set up in a former nurses' home on the Royal Gwent Hospital site in the lower part of Friars Field (known as Block 9 on Friars Field). (ref. Pull-out Plan 2)

The Board was responsible to the Secretary of State for Wales.

The Trust provided Health Care for 9 hospital sites in Aberbargoed, Caerphilly, Chepstow, Griffithstown, Oakdale, Redwood, The Royal Gwent and St. Woolos in Newport and Ystrad Mynach. In addition services were provided in a number of health centres, clinics, G.P. surgeries, schools and homes of patients. In the Rhymney Valley the Trust provided hospital, community and mental health services whereas in the remainder of South Gwent mainly hospital services were provided, although there were effective combinations in midwifery and children's services. Furthermore, a good working relationship was formed with the South Gwent and Caerphilly Community Health Council.

The Board of Glan Hafren N.H.S. Trust in 1997. Back row, left to right: Mr. G.H. Griffith, Mr. M.P. Turner, Mr. A.J. Cottom, Mr. G.E. Griffiths, Mr. A.J. Kilsby, Mr. B.J. Margrett. Front row: Mrs. H.M. Taylor, Mr. D.F. Jessopp, Mrs. P.A. White, Mrs. J.E. Child (inset) Professor K. Griffiths.

(photograph Nigel Pearce, Medical Illustration R.G.H.)

In 1996, Mr. Denis Jessopp MBE was appointed Chairman of the Trust to follow Mr. Hughes-Davies*.

* Mr. Hughes-Davies died tragically of a dissecting aortic aneurysm just a few months after retiring as Chairman. This had occurred while he was flying his private aircraft which he landed safely but was taken to The Royal Gwent Hospital shortly afterwards (Editor).

The following years brought significant change to the N.H.S. locally. Financing of the service for the early part of the 1990s was substantially better than in previous years and during its lifetime, the Glan Hafren N.H.S. Trust appointed an additional 25 consultants to work at the Royal Gwent Hospital. Another part of the reforms of the N.H.S. was introduction of G.P. fundholding and during the lifetime of the reforms, more than 70% of the population served by the Royal Gwent was registered with fundholding practices. Fundholding, combined with the introduction of 'The Citizen's Charter', had very significant effects on the waiting times for treatment and in 1996 the waiting times at the Royal Gwent Hospital were at their lowest ever with no one waiting more than 6 months for an Out-Patient appointment and no one waiting more than 18 months for In-Patient treatment.

Unfortunately, later in the 1990s, financial settlements for the N.H.S. grew tighter and the pressures created by increasing emergency medical admissions meant that funds needed to be diverted away from specialties with waiting lists into financial commitments to help The Royal Gwent Hospital to handle the increasingly crippling load of emergency admissions, which were mostly medical. This situation in due course had a devastating effect on surgical throughput as the extra load from medical emergencies could only be accommodated in surgical beds.

In 1998, yet another restructuring of the N.H.S. in Wales was announced. It had been determined that the number of N.H.S. Trusts in Wales was too large and a plan emerged to decrease the number of Welsh N.H.S. Trusts from more than thirty down to fifteen. This plan affected health services in Gwent by proposing that all three N.H.S. Trusts serving the population of Gwent should merge. These were The Glan Hafren, Nevill Hall and the Gwent Community N.H.S. Trusts which would result in a super-Trust that would oversee hospital services for the population in both south and north of the county and the borough of Caerphilly, as well as community and mental health services. Many arguments for and against the idea occurred as part of a major consultation exercise undertaken in 1998. The Secretary of State for Wales decided to unify Trusts in Gwent into one single provider for the population of Gwent and the new borough of Caerphilly.

On 1st April 1999 the Gwent Healthcare N.H.S. Trust was set up. The merger resulted in integration of health services across the county and the long held friendly rivalry between the Royal Gwent Hospital and Nevill Hall Hospital in Abergavenny began to turn to collaboration.

The Chairman appointed was Councillor Peter Law but he resigned after a short while due to his election as a Member of the new Welsh Assembly. Mr. Denis Jessopp MBE was invited to take over.

The Chief Executive appointed was Mr. Martin Turner.

Members of the Management Board were:

Executive Directors:	Mr. Andrew Cottom	(Finance Director)
	Dr. Stephen Hunter	(Medical Director)
	Mrs. Lorene Read	(Nursing Director)
	Mr. Glyn Griffiths	(Planning Director)
Non-Executive Directors:	Mr. Michael Badham	
	Dr. E. Coles	
	Mr. John Davy	
	Mr. Andrew Kilsby	
	Mrs. Beryl Melvin	
	Mrs. Carol Morgan	
	Ms. Pat Smail	

Mr. Jessopp retired in 2003 and was followed as Chairman by Dr. Brian Willott CB MA PhD.

As the Millennium came to an end, the Royal Gwent Hospital was part of one of the largest health care organisations in the United Kingdom.

From the point of view of managing the services that the hospital provides, there are many challenges yet to be faced. Waiting times for treatment have yet again grown and the hospital has experienced enormous pressures on its emergency services. When the original plans to develop the Royal Gwent on its current site in Newport were mooted in the late 1950s, it was impossible to have predicted the growth of need for health service delivery locally, the demand for services and in particular the exponential growth of skills arising from technological advance that was needed to give an up-to-date service. The hospital is left today on a constrained site with massive difficulties associated with car-parking on the site and enormous constraints around its ability to continue to expand clinical services. The current government is committed to increasing the numbers of medical and nursing staff available to treat the public, but creating extra space and accommodation for these increases to happen will be one of the major difficulties with which the hospital will face over the next few years.

The Millennium Year, 2000, was not a year of sudden revelation of the way forward into the 21st century. It marked the starting point of the third phase of the history of hospital care in Newport and readers of this book in fifty years time will be able to fill in the events that will have occurred in the meantime.

5) Professional Services 1948 to 2003 *(Editor's Review)*

When The Royal Gwent and Woolaston House Hospitals were taken over by The National Health Service in 1948, there was an existing specialty infrastructure in place which provided for general medicine, general surgery, E.N.T., ophthalmic surgery, gynaecology and obstetrics, management of fractures and orthopaedics: these services were supported by anaesthetists. There were also pathology services, a radiological department and specialist services in dermatology, venereal diseases, allergies, dental problems and psychiatric illnesses. At Woolaston House, there was a large department for Chest Diseases.

This infrastructure was the basis for the next fifty years of hospital practice in Newport from which the present-day hospital services have evolved.

For the first twenty years after 1948, the pattern of clinical practice and professional services changed little in Newport. For instance, of the general specialties, in the 1950s there were three physicians and three surgeons at The Royal Gwent Hospital and one surgeon and one (chest) physician at St. Woolos Hospital. Four consultant anaesthetists served both hospitals and each of these consultants covered clinics and operating sessions in Pontypool & District or County Hospitals outside Newport.

These numbers did not change for several years for in 1970 there were still four physicians (one with an interest in chest medicine), four general surgeons and four consultant anaesthetists responsible to The Newport & East Monmouthshire H.M.C.. Each of these consultants dealt with all aspects of each general specialty. In other specialties there was also no significant expansion. A similar pattern of clinical cover occurred in specialty units.

Since 1970, there has been an expansion of consultant posts based in Newport so that in the year 2004 for example, there are now nine general physicians, nine general surgeons and thirty-seven consultant anaesthetists: however, the modern role of most of these staff is to offer expertise in clinical subspecialties in addition to general cover. An increase of consultant numbers has also occurred in other specialist groups such as paediatrics, gynaecology, E.N.T., ophthalmic surgery and extra consultants have been needed to staff new specialties which have been created in to Newport such as geriatrics, pain relief, neonatology, urological surgery, facio-maxillary surgery.

Such extraordinary expansion of clinical and other services has occurred during a relatively short period of time and has been a direct consequence of the ever-accelerating and increasing range of technology that began in the 1960s. This has widened the range of possibilities of successful treatments which has resulted in increased expectation from the public and greater demand for services.

Until the 1970s, changes in clinical practice related mainly to introduction of better drugs which expanded the horizons of medical management and increased clinical possibilities in anaesthesia and of critical care. These in due course enabled surgeons to undertake operations with greater precision, ambition and safety. There was also a realisation that formal training and testing of trainees before appointment to consultant posts was an essential element to achieving high standards of clinical performance throughout hospitals in the country. Hence, increased emphasis on postgraduate education and research grew up in the 1960s in Newport and from the late 1960s, the Newport Hospitals became heavily involved with teaching undergraduate medical students mainly from Cardiff but also from other universities. In fact, there have always been outstanding opportunities in Newport for training of undergraduate, post-graduate medical and other staff as well as for research because of the large range of clinical material that comes to the Newport hospitals.

In the nursing profession, increased educational opportunities as well as new professional skills have enhanced their role in clinical care by creating academic levels of achievement as well as specialist responsibilities and in recent years, a new breed of nurse - the nurse specialist and nurse consultant is involved with aspects of clinical care of patients.

Also, other professional departments supporting clinical care, such as pharmacy and dietetics, have developed academic, educational and research programmes that run alongside technical and other advances within their skills.

Therefore, new dimensions to clinical practice have occurred which have posed considerable challenges to everyone in Newport, professional and management, to keep up with the times and ahead of it when possible.

As a result, clinical practice in Newport in the new Millennium is vastly different in scope and style from practices before the 1970s although the need to preserve diagnostic and therapeutic skills has always remained, and hopefully always will remain, the cornerstone of quality care.

However, looking back at these years of change, the enormous new possibilities of healthcare due to new drugs are probably overshadowed by two factors that have been responsible for change. The development and growth of microchip technology and computers from the 1960s has created the basis from which modern advanced equipment for investigation, treatment and information collection has come. Of similar importance have been developments in optical technology which have revolutionised the role of inspection of internal parts of the body that previously had never been accessible. As a result, new instruments have been designed to detect and to treat conditions that previously had required major surgery or had been untreatable so that it is now common-place in Newport for these to be done as day cases rather than as In-Patients, all of which has contributed to increased safety and decreased discomfort for patients but has created a radical shift in logistics of hospital management. They have also totally transformed the balance of clinical activity as is evident from the activity analyses of The Royal Gwent and other hospitals presented in the first section of this chapter.

Therefore, in Newport in the past twenty-five years, these specialist surgical, medical, investigative and therapeutic services have grown out of general services to provide expert, modern treatment in line with Teaching Hospitals and other major District General Hospitals elsewhere. For this to happen, the advances of technologies have been the key and to take advantage of technical change, new professional skills have been needed so that the range of therapeutic possibilities has expanded exponentially. Therefore, additional physicians, surgeons, radiologists, pathologists and others with the appropriate training have had to be appointed.

However, in recent years a major cloud over all aspects of clinical care, medical and surgical, has emerged from ill effects of development of bacterial resistance to antibiotics especially M.R.S.A. (Methicillin Resitant Staphylococcus). This has had serious effects on morbidity and mortality which required the need for specific facilities to be developed by both medical and surgical staff.

In the following chapters, accounts of changes of practice in all specialties have been presented to cover much of the spectrum of hospital care in Newport Hospitals and, where relevant, some of the important historical background has been included and could be of interest, especially to non-medical readers, as they illustrate the enormous shift in practice and changes of endeavour that has taken place within the professional lifetime of some, especially the older and more recently retired staff.

Chapter 7: Medical Specialties

General Medicine
Gerald Anderson MD FRCP

With the inception of the N.H.S. in 1948, Dr. E. Grahame Jones and Dr. P.E. Dipple were appointed as the first consultant general physicians to the Royal Gwent from their previous positions as Honorary Consulting Physicians. Both would have fulfilled functions as physicians, geriatricians and paediatricians - now requiring approximately 30 consultants.

At the time of changeover to the National Health Service, Dr. Bernard A. Thomas continued his previous status as Honorary Physician to become Consultant Physician to the Skin Department and the Department for Venereal Diseases.

A third general physician, Dr. John Swithinbank, was appointed in 1965 from a previous consultant post at Merthyr and Dr. Gerald Anderson was appointed in 1969 as a fourth general physician but with an interest in Chest Medicine. All these physicians visited other hospitals in the county and each was responsible for as many as 75 beds overall. Dr. Anderson, with a specialty interest in Chest Medicine, became primarily based at The Chest Clinic of St. Woolos Hospital.

In common with all other UK hospitals at that time, general physicians were expected to be experts in all medical specialties which was clearly unrealistic. Apart from the Chest Clinic which continued its work at St. Woolos Hospital, the first move towards sub-specialisation in General Medicine came with the appointment in 1961 of Dr. Morag Insley as the first consultant in Geriatric Medicine. She was based at St. Woolos Hospital.

Radical changes in clinical practice occurred. For instance, in the 1960s it was usual for patients admitted to The Royal Gwent with myocardial infarctions to be confined to bed for up to six weeks and the hospital would be filled with them. Dr. Anderson announced that his patients would get out of bed on day three and go home after two weeks. His colleagues confidently expected disaster but when nothing happened, they adopted the same procedure and the following year such patients were sent home after one week. Thus, shorter stay hospitalisation became a fact although it was to take some years before it became respectable. Another important change of practice has been the move towards day case procedures in place of In-Patient hospital admissions such as for biopsy, bronchoscopies and especially cancer chemotherapy. These will be noted further under specialty sections later in this chapter.

A fifth general physician, Dr. Brian Calcraft, was appointed in 1975. He had been born in Jamaica of missionary parents. He qualified from Cardiff and after some time at The Mayo Clinic came to Newport with a specialist interest in gastroenterology (see p.107). Dr. Calcraft collaborated with Mr. Keith Vellacott from the Department of General Surgery in setting up an Endoscopy Unit for investigation of gastroenterological diseases which, in some cases, had become treatable by non-surgical means. Consequently, medical and surgical specialties overlapped and worked together to treat many bowel conditions which had previously been treatable only by surgery. This had clear advantages for patients.

Sadly, Dr. Calcraft died in 1991 from colon cancer. He was succeeded by Dr. Miles Allison as gastroenterologist. He had graduated from St. George's Hospital, London and was later joined by Dr. E.D. Srivastava who had trained in gastroenterology in Cardiff, Newcastle and Amsterdam. In 2003, Dr. N. Balaratnam was appointed as the third consultant in gastroenterology after training as a specialist registrar on the All-Wales scheme during which worked for a while as a registrar in Newport. He is a graduate of Nottingham.

Dr. Dipple, who had served as consultant physician since the days of the Royal Gwent as a voluntary Hospital, retired in 1975. He was succeeded by Dr. Howell Lloyd whose sub-specialist interest was diabetes. He carried on Dr. Dipple's diabetic clinics as well as his work as General Physician. In 1983, he was joined by Dr. Owain Gibby to expand diabetic services.

Further sub-specialisation arrived in 1983, when a cardiological unit was established with the appointment of Dr. John Davies. Expansion of cardiological services inevitably followed due to the prevalence of cardiovascular problems in the community, especially of new investigative methods and more cardiologists were needed so that Dr. S. Ikram was appointed in 1996 followed by Dr. Nigel Brown in 2001.

Separate Departments have also been set up in recent years in rheumatology (Dr. Peter Williams), haematology (Dr. C. Hewlett, Dr. E. Moffatt and Dr. H. Jackson) and neurology (Dr. Gareth Llewellyn).

Over the past 30 years, the range of medical sub-specialties and treatments has increased exponentially but has done so without a corresponding increase in bed numbers although, as with other specialties, general medical beds were centralised at The Royal Gwent mainly with a move from St. Woolos Hospital in the late 1980s. This situation has been managed by increased turnover and greater use of Out-Patient and day case procedures but in recent years, the whole fabric of services in The Royal Gwent has become overwhelmed with emergency medical cases many of which have blocked beds causing stasis of routine admissions, especially for surgical admissions.

In the 1970s, the junior staff complement of the Department of General Medicine at The Royal Gwent was four house officers, three registrars and one senior registrar on rotation from Cardiff. At St. Woolos Hospital, there were three senior house officers.

In 2004, the hospital can provide all medical treatments except ultraspecialist procedures.

Chest Medicine
Gerald Anderson MD FRCP

Before 1948

The history of Chest Medicine in Newport began with the tuberculosis service. In 1915, a tuberculosis hospital for servicemen was opened at Beechwood House and Dr. Carveth Johnson was Tuberculosis Physician from 1917 to 1949. An Out-Patient service was provided at Palmyra Place adjacent to the The Royal Gwent Hospital and in 1924 it was considered that an X-Ray service was badly needed. In that year, Beechwood Hospital closed and was replaced by Cefn Mably Hospital located in the outskirts of Newport.

In 1927, the records note difficulty experienced in examining tuberculosis contacts because of a smallpox epidemic. The horrors of tuberculosis are difficult for us to imagine now but even as recently as 1929, there were 334 new cases in Newport of whom one third were dead within three months of first attendance. The report for 1929 states that there were no entries in the Complaints Book: how times have changed!!

By 1946, the X-Ray unit in the Chest Clinic (which had originally been 'Woolaston House') was derided in a local newspaper and compared to 'an old fashioned magic lantern'.

The Chest Clinic seen from Stow Hill in 2003. The main building (in white) was previously 'Woolaston House' (p.47). It now houses consulting rooms and administration. The remainder of the Chest Clinic is in buildings constructed in 1902 (see Map 4 and Plan 1) and the entrance to the department can be seen in the pre-fabricated structure alongside the main entrance to St. Woolos Hospital.

(photograph Brian Peeling)

After 1948

In 1949, Dr. Maldwyn Jackson was appointed as Chest Physician with In-Patient beds at St. Woolos Hospital. He had qualified in Cardiff in 1927 and had previously been Deputy Medical Superintendent in North Wales from 1938.

Patients from Newport with tuberculosis were also treated at Cefn Mably Hospital near Newport. The Medical Superintendent was Dr. Norman Williams who had been appointed in 1951 having graduated from Edinburgh in 1935. Dr. Williams was a Clinical Teacher in tuberculosis at The Welsh National School of Medicine in Cardiff and when Cefn Mably Hospital closed in 1983, he was re-designated as a Consultant Geriatrician at St. Woolos Hospital where he remained until retirement in 1988. For many years, Dr. Williams was Secretary of the Senior Medical and Dental Staff Committee of the Newport Hospitals and was renowned for his great attention to detail with the business of the Committee.

From 1956, the generality of chest diseases could be treated at St. Woolos Hospital when chest and cardiac surgery became available with the appointment of Mr. Tom Rosser, visiting consultant thoracic surgeon from Sully Hospital. Surgery for tuberculosis and also for lung cancer was a regular feature of Mr. Rosser's work but over the next fifteen years or so, these operations faded from the repertoire because of greater understanding and increased success from medical management of these conditions.

Maldwyn Jackson was succeeded in 1969 by Dr. Gerald Anderson who had trained at The Royal Free and Brompton Hospitals in London where he had been the first Senior

Registrar to Dr. Margaret Turner-Warwick, who later became a most distinguished Professor of Medicine and President of The Royal College of Physicians. *(She confided to the Editor recently that she when started as a consultant she had been in considerable awe of her senior registrar!)*. Dr. Anderson's post in Newport was as a Chest Physician and a General Physician. He was responsible for beds at St. Woolos and the Royal Gwent Hospitals as well as Mount Pleasant Hospital, Chepstow. Within a week of his appointment he was told that all the old tuberculosis physicians were about to retire and that he had been appointed in absentia as the new Secretary of The Welsh Thoracic Society and was to take over as Advisor in Thoracic Medicine to The Welsh Hospital Board. A dramatic start to a new life as a consultant.

After 1969, the surge of work rapidly developed and Dr. Susan Cotton was appointed to join Dr. Anderson: she was the first female General/Chest Physician in Wales and also came to Newport after training in Cardiff.

When Dr. Ian Petheram was appointed in 1979 as a third General/Chest Physician, he introduced fibre-optic bronchoscopy to Newport. He had trained at The Brompton Hospital in London. Previously, examination of the bronchial passages in the lungs had been the preserve of thoracic surgeons (Mr. Rosser) carried out under general anaesthetic. Fibre-optic bronchoscopy could be carried out under local anaesthetic as an Out-Patient and was yet another benefit for patients. Its introduction to Newport by Dr. Petheram was a first in Wales outside Cardiff where it had been in use for only a few months.

A chemotherapy service and the first joint radiotherapy service for lung cancer started in 1969 which involved all three Chest Physicians. These doctors have now retired and have been replaced by Drs. Ian Williamson, Alison Whittaker, Patrick Flood-Page and Melissa Hack (whose grandfather was Dr. Ken Thom, one of the two consultant anaesthetists appointed to The Royal Gwent Hospital when it was taken over by The National Health Service in 1948, see p.41).

Recent Developments

The latest developments have been a Sleep Laboratory and appointment of specialist nurses in tuberculosis, sleep, obstructive pulmonary disease, lung cancer and palliative care. Use of National Minimal standards for lung cancer management has resulted in great improvement in dealing with this condition and its treatment by a specialist team.

Medical Gastroenterology
Miles Allison MD FRCP

In Newport, there had been no physician with a specialist interest in medical gastroenterology until Dr. Brian Calcraft was appointed in 1975. Previously, medical aspects of bowel diseases had been managed by general physicians and many physicians would lack confidence to carry out sigmoidoscopy to inspect internally the lower bowel which was, in general, the preserve of general surgeons. Furthermore, internal examination of the upper gut (the oesophagus and stomach) was a skill that even most general surgeons referred to a suitably experienced specialist surgical colleague. The technical problem that limited the scope of endoscopy of the intestinal tract was the fact that endoscopes were rigid instruments which could be passed into the large bowel for a distance of only 30 cm above the anus. For passage into the upper gut, a general anaesthetic would be needed as well as skillful manoeuvering of the instrument to avoid internal damage.

Apart from cancers, treatment of many intestinal conditions including peptic ulcer and inflammatory bowel disease are initially medical in nature with surgery reserved as a second line management. Therefore, the arrival of fibre-optic instruments that were flexible, that could bend round corners and be guided under direct vision into hollow organs in the body that previously had been inaccessible to traditional rigid endoscopes, opened the gates for the medical sub-specialty of gastroenterology. These technological developments were not confined to medicine; for instance, fibre-optic endoscopes are used in industry to inspect difficult corners of aero engines and even for inspecting drains.

Medical Gastroenterology as a Specialty

Therefore, the arrival in Newport in 1975 of Dr. Calcraft as a specialist gastroenterological physician was a landmark for medical practice in The Royal Gwent to develop this sub-specialty using the new fibre-optic tools which enabled physicians, as well as surgeons, to inspect directly the entire interior of the lower intestinal tract as well the oesophagus, stomach and duodenum. Further advance in skills occurred with the technique of Endoscopic Retrograde Cholangiopancreatography (E.R.C.P.) which allows the endoscopist to remove biliary stones from the lower common bile and insert stents to relieve obstructive jaundice resulting from tumours. E.R.C.P. is now the first-line management for infection of the biliary tree (cholangitis), a potentially life-threatening condition.

With fibre-optic instruments clinical diagnoses became more precise, biopsies of suspicious areas could be taken safely and easily and certain treatments using laser therapy, ultrasound or diathermy excision of, for instance small polypoidal cancers, could be undertaken. These have been revolutionary steps in medical clinical practice because these investigations and treatments can be carried out under sedation as day cases and without recourse to open surgery under general anaesthesia as often had been previously needed. Although these developments were initially directed in Newport by surgeons, it was not long before they were taken up by other medical and non-surgical specialists in the hospital including radiologists. The practice of gastroenterology by physicians has evolved to overlap with similar work by surgeons and other disciplines so that gastroenterology in Newport is now a multi-disciplinary clinical practice.

Members of the Gastroenterology Team. Standing, left to right: Angela Merrett, Sarah Knight-Beardmore, Terry Perkins, 'Manny' Srivastava, Jill Carter, Elizabeth Williams, Keith Vellacott, Miles Allison, Sue Barker, Frederick Stacey. Kneeling: Karina Mitchell, Chrissie Smith, Pamela Clarke, Gini Joseph and Denise Jenkins. Note photograph of Dr. Calcraft in the background.

(*photograph Brian Peeling*)

During Dr. Calcraft's career and following his sad death in 1993, the gastroenterological service has developed to meet over 95% of the specialist need of the population in South Gwent and fulfills the Calman-Hine requirements for a Cancer Unit. The management of upper and lower gastrointestinal malignancy has been transformed by establishment of multi-disciplinary teams. With the exception of physiological studies of the oesophagus and specialist hepatobiliary and transplant services, all the facilities required for management of benign diseases are provided in Newport.

Developments since 1995

Endoscopic innovations since 1995 have been in line with other Centres of Excellence in the country. These have included treatments such as expansile mesh stenting for oesophageal and pancreatic cancers, argon beam palliation for cancer and for coagulation of vascular lesions that bleed into the intestinal tract, endoscopic balloon dilatation of strictures in the bowel and band ligation of oesophageal varices that can occur as a complication of liver cirrhosis.

Other innovations include biopsy of the liver as a day case (1996) and urea breath-testing for H. Pylori (on site since 1998).

In 2002, money from The League of Friends of The Royal Gwent Hospital purchased equipment to introduce Wireless Capsule Endoscopy (£22,000). This is a non-invasive method of endoscopic examination of the small intestine. This part of the bowel had never been accessible to examination by fibre-optic instruments. The new procedure involves swallowing a small capsule that emits radio-frequency signals that are detected by leads attached to the abdominal wall of the patient. As the capsule passes through the small bowel, the detector stores video-signals which are downloaded later to a PC to obtain a video recording. This process is particularly valuable for detection of sites of bleeding from the small bowel allowing targeted definitive treatment. This is another example of technological advance that has led to greatly improved clinical care for patients in the county. The establishment of Wireless Capsule Endoscopy in Newport
is the first of its kind in Wales.

Research Work

Research in progress at the present time includes studies on colo-rectal cancer supported by 'The Brian Calcraft Memorial Fund'. The Fund was set up after Dr. Calcraft's death to continue and expand research into his chosen field of gastroenterology, especially bowel cancer which in 1995 killed about 18,000 people in England and Wales. He also carried out research into inflammatory bowel disease, such as ulcerative colitis and Crohn's Disease. The objective of the Fund is to raise money to support research into bowel disease by young physicians at The Royal Gwent Hospital with especial encouragement towards Doctorates of Medicine (MD). The Fund is a Charity (No. 1054094): its Patron is Mr. Colin Jackson MBE and the Chairman is Dr. Miles Allison.

Further details of the development of the Gastroenterological Service are described on page 145.

Dr. Brian Calcraft (1940 to 1991).
(photograph courtesy of Ellis Photography, Newport)

Diabetes Services
Owain Gibby OBE FRCP

In Newport, there was a specialist interest in the management of diabetes even before 1948 due to Dr. P.E. ('Ted') Dipple who was honorary consultant physician to the hospital at the time of its transition from Voluntary Status to The National Health Service. During his time at The Royal Gwent he managed the majority of people seen at the hospital with diabetes and was, in many ways, a man ahead of his time. Notably, he managed insulin treatment of ketoacidosis by continuous insulin infusion long before that treatment regime had become the standard method of management for this potentially fatal condition. He also appointed a dietician to manage patients with diabetes. His colleague, Dr. John Swithinbank, also managed people with diabetes in his clinic at Pontypool & District Hospital, although Dr. Swithinbank's main interest had been cardiology and this was also, perhaps, in anticipation of the current interest in the cardiovascular complications of diabetes and the metabolic syndrome of insulin resistance associated with increased cardiovascular risk.

Dr. Howell Lloyd was appointed to follow Dr. Dipple at the Royal Gwent Hospital in 1975; he had received much of his training at St. George's Hospital, London. Whilst serving the population with diabetes from a total catchment of 300,000 people, Dr. Lloyd brought the diabetes services in the hospital into the modern era. During his time, patients with diabetes gave up the old method of self-administering insulin using glass syringes with large metal needles which needed to be sterilised by the patient, and started using disposable plastic syringes with fine needles. Urine testing in a test-tube with tablets and a mix of urine and water was changed to blood testing with disposable test strips. Insulin became highly purified. Dr. Lloyd provided a very high standard of care for his many patients and he set out to achieve the level of care advocated by centres of excellence (though this was not always achieved by those same centres).

He was joined in 1983 by Dr. Owain Gibby who came to Newport from The Royal Free Hospital in London. He took over Dr. Swithinbank's clinic at Pontypool & District Hospital. Most In-Patients with diabetes cared for by these two physicians were accommodated at The Royal Gwent Hospital with some at St. Woolos Hospital (Dr. Lloyd) and some at County Hospital, Griffithstown (Dr. Gibby). In 1998, Dr. Philip Evans was appointed as a third consultant with a specialty interest in diabetes. He moved to The Royal Glamorgan Hospital in 2002. Two new appointments were made in 2003, Dr. Kofi Asuobic and Dr. Peter Evans.

Over the years, Dr. Howell Lloyd and Owain Gibby have expanded and developed the diabetes services by creating specialist teams which have included dieticians, podiatists (chiropodists), diabetes specialist nurses as well as the doctors, and clinic and ward staff.

Consequently, the overall scope of diabetes services in Newport in 2004 consists of the following specialist aspects.

Specialist Diabetes Nurses. These nurses have improved the education and support for people with diabetes. Their work has proved to be a major advance in supervision and management of patients. The first Specialist Nurse was appointed in 1985 and was Gill Vaughan-Best who sadly died in 1990. The Diabetes Specialist Nursing Service now has teams at The Royal Gwent and also at County Hospital, Griffithstown.

2) Diabetes Centre: Richmond House was opened as a Diabetes Centre in 1992 by Sir Anthony Hopkins who had just won an Oscar for his part as the cannibal in the film 'Silence of the Lambs'. The Richmond House Diabetes Centre provides the diabetes team

Some members of the Diabetes Team photographed outside Richmond House. Left to right are Rachel Knowles, Dr. Basu, Dr. J. Phillips, Sr. Glenys Matthews, Ann Hunt, Dianne Hodson, Dr. N. Agarwal, Dr. O. Gibby, Dr. K. Obubie, Sr. Siân Fitzgerald and Sr. Siân Ward.

(photograph Andrew Ponsford)

with an area where patients can be seen in appropriate surroundings for education and review although it was not long before its capacity became inadequate for certain sessions such as the Diabetes Foot Clinic. In the Diabetes centre, patients are seen as new patients as well as for follow-up and annual review by consultants, junior doctors and by general practitioners, Dr. Steven Jarrett and Dr. David Millar-Jones. Dr. Millar-Jones continues a tradition of general practitioner help that was led at The Royal Gwent Hospital by Dr. Tony Gray and at The County Hospital by Dr. Barry Bowden who was followed by Dr. Mici Williams. Other expert assistance has come from Dr. Basu, a Staff Grade Physician who has a special interest in cardiological aspects of diabetes.

3) Diabetes in Pregnancy: Patients with diabetes in pregnancy, which is a time of critical importance for good control of their diabetes, were seen originally by Dr. Lloyd with Mr. Israel Rocker, Consultant Obstetrician. In 1983, Dr. Gibby took over Dr. Lloyd's role with this service and in 1996, a Combined Diabetic/Antenatal Clinic was set up with Mrs. Jo Wiener, Consultant Obstetrician and Diabetes Specialist Nurse Glenys Matthews who is also a qualified midwife. This service enhanced further care of diabetes in pregnancy and gestational diabetes. Since that time, this clinic has functioned well with great support from the midwives and Sister in the Antenatal Clinic and Staff of the Obstetric Wards. This team was strengthened by the addition of Miss Ann Wright, Consultant Obstetrician, in the late 1990s.

4) Foot Complications in Diabetes: Management of foot problems in patients with diabetes has been improved greatly by collaboration with Professor Keith Harding and his team of researchers, registrars and research nurses from the Department of Surgery at The University Hospital of Wales.

Therapeutic Footwear and orthoses are provided by Wendy Tyrell, Senior Lecturer in Podiatry at The University of Wales Institute, Cardiff. The Diabetes Foot Care team have worked closely with the vascular surgeons at The Royal Gwent Hospital, Messrs K. Shute, A. Shandall and I. Williams, and more recently with Mr. Hariharan, consultant orthopaedic surgeon. The Community Podiatry Service led by Roy Nuth is attached to a network of services with rotating senior staff attached to the Diabetes Centre, Clinics and In-Patient services.

5) *Ophthalmic Complications in Diabetes:* For ophthalmic problems related to diabetes, the Diabetes Team has always received much support from the consultants of the Ophthalmology Unit, notably Mr. A. Karseras, Mr. Khan and Mr. Blyth. For many years, there has been a service from the Department of Medical Illustration at The Royal Gwent (Mr. Nigel Pearce) ensuring that most people with diabetes have retinal photography before annual review.

6) *Nutritional and Dietary Advice to Diabetics:* It had been noted earlier that Dr. Dipple had appointed the first dietician with an interest in diabetes, a Miss Richards. That was in the 1950s and was a remarkably advanced, even visionary, course of action. Since then, this tradition has been followed by chief Dieticians to the hospital, currently Mrs. Eirlys Cawdery and in 1996 Elaine Hibbert-Jones was appointed Diabetes Specialist Dietician.

7) *Diabetes in Children:* A Paediatric Service for Diabetes was developed by Dr. John Cawdery and Dr. Robert Prosser, general paediatricians with a special interest in diabetes. Dr. Cawdery later set up in the mid-1980s a separate clinic for children with diabetes and a Paediatric Dietician, Gill Reagan, was appointed in 1982. She became very involved due to her sporting interests in activity weekends for children with diabetes: (this has been noted on p.204).

In 1993, Dr. John Barton was appointed as specialist Paediatric Endocrinologist. He has developed a service whereby insulin treatment for newly diagnosed children can be stabilised at home without hospital admission; he is also involved in the Endocrine Clinic at The University Hospital of Wales. Dr. Barton developed further the Teenage Clinic commenced by Dr. Cawdery and was anxious to create a Young Adult Clinic to ensure smooth transition for diabetics moving from adolescence into early adulthood which is a time when control of diabetes is often neglected. The Paediatric Diabetes Service has received enormous benefit from appointments of Specialist Paediatric Diabetic Nurses Jane Bramwell and Grace Parfitt.

In 2002, diabetes services in Newport were included into a Directorate of Diabetes and Endocrinology formed at the level of the Gwent Healthcare N.H.S. Trust. Its Director is Dr. John Saunders (Nevill Hall Hospital) and Mr. Craydon Proudman is Manager.

(The development and work of the Diabetes Multi-Disciplinary Team was recently recognised in the 2002 Honours List with the award of OBE to Dr. Gibby and of MBE to Sister Matthews - Editor).

Cardiology
John Davies MD FRCP

In 1983, a Cardiological Unit was established at The Royal Gwent Hospital by the appointment of Dr. John Davies as a Consultant Physician and Cardiologist. The location of the new department was very humble and insignificant in appearance as it had been set up in two unused huts in the yard opposite the Accident & Emergency Unit. These have now been demolished to make parking space. A Stress Laboratory was also set up in the old building in a small room off the ground floor corridor leading to the Out-Patient Department.

In February 1992, the department moved to its present site in Block 'A' (see Pull-out Plan 2 - Site 8). This area had previously been the Paediatric Ward sited above the Out-Patient Department built in 1924. The interior of the building was extensively re-furbished to provide accommodation for a new and updated dedicated stress laboratory, a room for echocardiograms, twenty-four hour tapes room as well as space for consultation, offices and waiting areas.

In 1996, a second cardiologist, Dr. Shahid Ikram, was appointed and a third cardiologist, Dr. Nigel Brown came in 2001.

Cardiological Services

Before 1983, cardiological work had been shared by the General Physicians in Newport, and until 1979 the main investigation available had been only electrocardiography (E.C.G.s). There were about seven staff who provided an E.C.G. service covering The Royal Gwent and St. Woolos Hospitals in Newport as well as County Hospital, Griffithstown and Pontypool & District Hospital.

With John Davies' arrival in 1983, investigation of cardiological problems was extended initially by addition of echocardiography (M-Mode and later 2D-Echo Machines). Treatment with permanent pacemaker implants started in 1983. Also, staffing levels improved with five cardiographers available daily as well as at evenings and weekends and nine technicians in the department.

Angiography became available in January 2000 and this service was provided in an X-Ray room. A cardiac pressure monitoring system was purchased from moneys made available from the Cardiology Fund (see next page).

Some members of the Cardiology Staff. Left to right Shahid Ikram, Sharon Williams, Kim Grant, Wendy Covell, Lynne Morgan, Linda Eddy, Maureen Edwards, Hayley Coakham, Amanda Donkin, Lesley Gosling, Helen Veysey, Elaine Stephens, Gethin Webb, Siân Westlake, Linda Davies, J.D., Nigel Brown.

(*photograph Andrew Ponsford*)

In April 2002, echocardiography became more sophisticated by acquisition of three machines with strategic archiving systems, transoesophageal probes and paediatric probes.

The range of investigations now offered by the department is as follows:
E.C.G., angiography, stress and stress echo testing, tilt table testing, 24-hour tapes, 24-hour ambulatory monitoring, 24-hour blood pressure monitoring, echocardiography for both adults and children, transoesophageal echography, pacemaker implants and follow-up clinics, full lung function tests and spirometry.

The current staffing of the cardiology department is 13.4 Whole-time Technicians, nine cardiographers, two clerical staff and one part-time worker.

Therefore, in 2004, the department is considered to be an up-to-date unit in line with other Centres of Excellence.

Training and Research

In addition to state of the art clinical facilities, the cardiological unit offers an on-going clinical training programme for trainee cardiologists which comes under the auspices of the Specialist Registrar (SpR) training based at The University Hospital of Wales. Currently, there is one full-time SpR attached to the Cardiology Department.

Since 1985, there has been an active research programme and there has been a small Clinical Trials Unit for sixteen years. This has been run mainly by Research Registrars with one Clinical Research Assistant, Wendy Covell and until two years ago, there was also a part-time Clinical Research Assistant, Elaine Bartlett, who retired at that time.

A number of national clinical studies have been carried out on the use of different thrombolytic therapies (ISIS 1,2 and 3). There have been various unfunded studies which have been paid through the department's clinical research unit and very many, indeed too many to list, funded clinical trials including large multi-national and international studies (ESSENCE, INTERCEPT, NETWORK, EMIAT, OPTIMAAL, VALIANT, EUROPA, SEARCH, IONA and many others).

Most of these trials have been published under the name of the principal international investigator rather than coming directly from the Royal Gwent Hospital. However, it is to the credit of the department to have been involved in such studies which, for statistical power and significance, necessarily require huge numbers of cases provided by collaboration of clinical units which have a track record for clinical excellence. Also, there have been several publications on open access echocardiography and the principal author for these has been Dr. Victor Sim.

The Cardiology Fund

With regard to fundraising, John Davies set up nearly twenty years ago 'The Royal Gwent and St. Woolos Hospitals Cardiology Fund' to raise money that went directly into the Cardiology Department to be used for heart patients. It was started by Dr. Davies with a group of volunteers, mainly heart patients and their families, and over the years more than three quarters of a million pounds has been collected through annual events such as the 'Fun Run', Bike Rides, a Christmas Bazaar, raffles, and donations in memory of loved ones in lieu of flowers. There is a hardworking local committee that organises these events and with the Spring Bank Holiday of 2003, John Davies ran in the 'Fun Run' for the twentieth time and aims to see a total of £1 million collected from this event by the time of his retirement.

Advertising the Cardiology Fun Run.

Many of the benefits from the Fund directed to the investigation and care of patients have been mentioned earlier in this account but in particular the Fund donated £172,000 towards specialised diagnostic equipment and a Cardiac Catheter Theatre together with running costs for the first twelve months. Computerisation of the appointment system to release technicians to carry out stress and echo tests also came from the Fund. A twenty-four hour Blood Pressure monitor and tilt beds used for treatment of patients have also been purchased from the Fund and a specialised Echo Couch was donated by a local family in memory of a relative. Furthermore, the Fund has bought eight Heart-Tel Monitors for £2,400: these recorders are taken home by heart patients for a month to record continuously any irregularities of heart rate. The recordings are then transferred by home telephone direct to the hospital where they are analysed by technicians. This has resulted in a reduction of the waiting list from twenty-six weeks to three to four weeks.

John Davies and his colleagues give a great deal of time to post graduate and undergraduate teaching as all are appointed clinical teachers of the University of Wales College of Medicine. Dr. Davies had been an Honorary Senior Lecturer at The Royal Brompton Hospital in London for the past fifteen years where he assists with their overseas teaching programme and organises three courses for the M.R.C.P. each year.

'(The initiative from within the department to create funds that have supplemented the technical and other requirements have been a major factor towards the considerable reputation of cardiology in Newport and in Wales - Editor)'

Geriatric Medicine and Care of the Elderly
Anne Freeman FRCP

The concept of Geriatric Medicine (Care of the Elderly) did not develop in Newport until the early 1960s although the foundations of this important aspect of medical care had been laid in the 1930s at the West Middlesex Hospital by a physician named Marjorie Warren, and The British Geriatric Society had been created in 1947.

from 1960

The first specialist in Geriatric Medicine in Newport was Dr. Morag Insley who was appointed Consultant at St. Woolos Hospital in 1960 although Dr. Geoffrey Salkeld, Medical Superintendent of The Ministry of Pensions long-stay unit at Mount Pleasant Hospital in Chepstow had made a start in this direction. Accommodation at St. Woolos was in the wards of the old 'Poor Law' part of the hospital. These were located in buildings labelled 'I' of the Architect's drawing of the Newport Workhouse in 1904

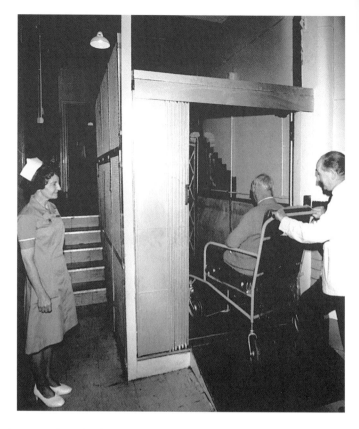

'Dr. Dipple's Lift' showing level differences indicated by the stairs on the left of the photograph and the method of handling trolleys and wheelchairs.

(photograph Nigel Pearce, Medical Illustration R.G.H.)

(see Pull-out Plan 1). The wards were the old-fashioned Nightingale design without a lift to the upper floors of the ward block. There was also a curious piece of design related to differences of level between the main hospital corridor and ground floor ward which was three feet lower (at Section J). There was therefore, great difficulty in man-handling patients on trolleys or in wheel chairs from one level to the next and transporting food trolleys to the ward. A solution was installation of a lift to bridge the levels. It was known locally in the hospital as 'Dr Dipple's lift' but it featured in The Guinness Book of Records as the lowest lift in the world! A consequence of this difference of levels meant that, unless patients could walk, those admitted to that ward stayed until they died.

Other long-stay geriatric patients were housed at Cefn Mably Hospital located just outside Newport when that hospital was no longer needed as a sanatorium for treatment of tuberculosis.

Springfield Unit

Dr. H.E.F. Davies was appointed as second Consultant Geriatrician in 1975 and with Dr. Insley pioneered a new custom-planned unit for care of the Elderly that was opened at St. Woolos Hospital in 1983. This was built on the site of the 'Springfield' Nurses' Home which had housed student and other nurses of St. Woolos Hospital in the days when the hospital had its own Training School and Matron (see p.51 and Pull-out Map 4).

The new unit was named as 'The Springfield Hospital'. There are 176 Geriatric beds, 42 day places and 70 beds for psychogeriatric patients. Patients from the wards in the old part of the hospital, as well as those from Cefn Mably Hospital were transferred over to the new building and the old wards at both hospitals then closed for ever. Also 'Dr. Dipple's lift' was removed.

Aerial view (2001) showing the modern Springfield Hospital in the lower right hand quadrant of the photograph. Stow Hill is seen towards the left with the older buildings of St. Woolos Hospital dating from 1902 (compare with Plan 1). The chimney stack near the Springfield Unit shows the location of the Boiler House that provides heat for both The Royal Gwent and St. Woolos Hospitals. The Royal Gwent site adjacent to Belle Vue Park appears in the upper right part of the picture. The houses of Stow Park Avenue can be seen running along the lower margin of the photograph.

(photograph courtesy of South Wales Argus)

Specialty Training for Geriatric Medicine

In the 1980s, a new era of geriatricians were appointed who had been trained as specialists in Geriatric Medicine at senior registrar level. These were Drs. Sarah Browne, David Sykes and John Toner. This coincided with a change of policy so that patients needing acute assessment were preferably housed at St. Woolos whereas those requiring rehabilitation, continuing care and day hospital provision underwent treatment in peripheral hospitals such as County Hospital, Griffithstown and Chepstow. It was shown that this was an effective way to keep patients in their home environments which reduced admissions to hospital.

Integration with General Medicine

In 1997, there was a major change of services by integrating geriatric medicine with general medicine. Acutely ill elderly patients were admitted directly to The Royal Gwent Hospital and only transferred to St. Woolos or other peripheral hospitals to receive rehabilitation. In other words, all patients irrespective of age were treated equally in an acute setting. The downside of this move has been reduction of geriatric medicine as a specialty in its own right so that only one quarter of elderly patients admitted with acute illness are assessed by a team headed by consultants specialising in Care of the Elderly. (For present-day facilities at the Springfield Unit see p.86)

Dermatological Services
M.D. Mishra BSc MD DDerm (Lond),
Cynthia Matthews FRCP and Alex Anstey MD FRCP

Before 1948

A department for treatment of Skin Diseases was first set up in Newport in 1921. There is no documentary information available to tell about its work and activities but presumably it was staffed by local general practitioners until the appointment as an Honorary Physician for Skin Diseases of Dr. Bernard Thomas in 1946. Before Bernard Thomas' appointment, Dr. Arthur Rook from Cardiff provided a notional consultant dermatology service.

From 1948 to 1974

In 1948, Dr. Bernard Thomas carried on as a consultant under the National Health Service and combined his work as dermatologist with venereology - a common pair of professional skills in those days. He became very well known throughout South Wales for his work with the British Medical Association and his interest in golf. He was also a great raconteur and was a popular after dinner speaker. His commitment to venereology stopped with the arrival of Dr. Joe Ribeiro as consultant venereologist but he continued to run the dermatological services single-handed until 1974 when he was joined by Dr. M.D. Mishra. Dr. Thomas retired in 1976.

Since 1948, he had been supported by two general practitioner clinical assistants, Dr. Sidney Rosehill (well known as a first class violinist and a magician belonging to The Magic Circle) and Dr. Paddy Martin. Later, Dr. Philip Thomas, a local general practitioner, also was appointed as clinical assistant. These doctors continued to support dermatology as clinical assistants until their retirements in the 1970s.

In the period 1948 to 1974, Out-Patients Clinics were held at St. Woolos Hospital, the Royal Gwent and Tredegar General Hospital and In-Patient beds were established at St. Woolos.

Although Dermatology was accepted as a specialty within the National Health Service, its establishment as a discrete department in Newport was non-existent at the time of Dr. Mishra's appointment. Shortly after taking up his post, Dr. Mishra considered that it was essential for the future of dermatology in Newport that a detailed evaluation concerning its strengths and shortcomings should be made for the authorities and insisted that a proper and more scientifically based dermatological service should be set up. To achieve this, he asked for allocation of special finance support and suitable accommodation for In-Patient care as well as a Day Treatment Centre. This request was fully supported by Cardiff colleagues at The University Hospital of Wales, Drs. G.A. Hodgson and Eric Waddington.

Consequently, Dr. Robin Peachey of Bristol was appointed by The Royal College of Physicians to inspect the dermatological facilities in Newport and to produce an official report. Various recommendations from the Royal College and The University Hospital Department went to Dr. Douglas Harrett, Chief Medical Officer of The Gwent Health Authority, which were accepted by him and a second dermatologist, Dr. Cynthia Matthews, was appointed in 1978 to add to the strength and formal implementation of a proper dermatological unit based at St. Woolos Hospital.

Dr. Bernard Thomas used to treat some skin disorders with the help of superficial X-Ray therapy which was located in the Out-Patient unit itself. The Grenze Rays came later on but this was provided at the Oncology-Radiotherapy at Velindre Hospital, Cardiff. The only medicaments available for treatment in those date were a variety of lotions, creams and ointments, a few antihistamines and ordinary antibiotics. This contrasts with the modern array of advanced therapeutic agents - corticosteroids, retinoids, powerful antibiotics, antihistamines and effective topical applications. Photochemotherapy, especially P.U.V.A., came after some time.

In due course, Dr. Mishra and Dr. Matthews achieved a modern integrated dermatological unit at St. Woolos with twenty beds at St. Woolos, consultants' personal rooms, a library, a conference area and a Day Treatment Centre. Photochemotherapy (PUVA) management of difficult psosiasis, leg ulcers, patch testing, minor skin surgery and microscopy was available in this Centre. Limitations of central funding was met with generous support from various organisations such as The Lions Club International of Newport (of which Dr. Mishra was President for some time) who donated £4,500 towards purchase of P.U.V.A. equipment for the Department. Further support came from The League of Friends of The Royal Gwent Hospital to purchase smaller instruments.

The consultants also promoted a full programme of undergraduate and postgraduate teaching and training in conjunction with general medical teaching programmes in Newport. There was also an increase of medical staffing including senior registrar training on rotation from Cardiff.

From 1994

Dr. Mishra retired in 1994 and was succeeded by Dr. Alex Anstey. However, the unit was moved to the Royal Gwent in 1994 but returned to St. Woolos Hospital in 2001 to be housed in a new specially designed unit with fourteen In-Patient beds (rather than twenty as previously) and an associated Day Treatment Centre for dressings, topical therapy, phototherapy, and minor surgery as well as improved facilities to investigate contact dermatitis.

Presentation of cheque of £4,500 by The Lions Club of Newport to the Dermatology Department (from Right to Left: Dr. Cynthia Matthews, Dr. M.D. Mishra, The Mayor of Newport Mrs. Rosemary Butler, The Chief Medical Officer of the Gwent Health Authority Dr. Douglas Harrett.

(photograph courtesy of Dr. Mishra)

Although most Out-Patient Clinics are now held at The Royal Gwent Hospital, the dermatological unit gives a wider service with clinics held throughout Gwent and the Rhymney Valley, Abergavenny, Pontypool, Ystrad Mynach, Chepstow, Caldicot and Brecon.

In line with developments in Dermatology nationally, clinics are offered in specialist areas such as laser therapy, skin surgery especially for skin cancers, occupational dermatology and vulval disease.

Since the mid-1970s, there has been an active educational programme for medical students from The University of Wales College of Medicine as well as Postgraduate teaching. There is also a Nursing Diploma in Dermatology which is run from St. Woolos Hospital in collaboration with the U.W.CM School of Nursing and Midwifery. This is the only full Dermatology Nursing Diploma Course in the United Kingdom and was launched in 1997. Nurses from many parts of The United Kingdom have combined in studying through distance learning courses.

The Department received the 'Hospital Doctor' Dermatology Team of the Year Award for Excellence in the year 2000.

More recent appointments to the consultant staff have been Drs. Natalie Stone, Richard Goodwin and Caroline Mills.

Genito-urinary Medicine
David Beckingham MA BSc MRCOG

Historical Review

Historically venereal diseases have been treated by a variety of medical practitioners, ranging from journeymen, apothecaries, surgeons and ships surgeons to general surgeons and physicians (for the upper classes) and finally dermatologists to venereologists who specialise in the treatment of this condition. In fact, in the European Union, the recognised term for this specialty is dermato-venereology.

It was during the Great War that it became apparent that syphilis and gonorrhoea were much commoner than had been realised. Clinics were set up by Act of Parliament for the treatment of these two diseases which would be free, confidential and anonymous. At that time, these were the only recognised venereal diseases. In Flanders, the army set up a 1,000 bedded hospital for the treatment of venereal diseases only and it was an offence to become infected. In fact it was considered to be a self-inflicted injury, albeit not officially, as this would have incurred the death penalty. However, it remained a military offence until well into the 1950s.

Venereology at The Royal Gwent Hospital

Therefore, between the two world wars clinics were set up in major hospitals, mostly the teaching hospitals, and the doyen of venereologists was Colonel Harrison who conducted affairs at St. Thomas's Hospital, London. Some more enlightened provincial hospitals opened clinics, one of these being The Royal Gwent Hospital's clinics in Newport. At first, the clinic was in the Out-Patient Department but later it was transferred to the old Out-Patients building which was at the main gate on Cardiff Road just by the bus stop. The top deck passengers and those standing waiting for a bus, must have had a good view of patients attending and it was only when a bus shelter was erected that there was any degree of privacy! It is not clear from 'The History of The Royal Gwent Hospital' published in 1948 how venereal services had been organised before the arrival of Dr. Bernard Thomas in 1946 whose appointment combined dermatology and venereology but it is probable that these had been run by general practitioners. However, there is a

The original Out-Patients department of 1901 later to become the V.D. Department.

photograph of the V.D. Department in 1948 in its original site in the Out-Patient building that was built in 1901.

After the Second World War Dr. Thomas was joined by Dr. Joe Ribeiro who was born in Trinidad and was a graduate of the Welsh National School of Medicine. He had learnt his speciality while in the army during the Italian campaign and later in India.

Dr. Ribeiro was actually appointed to Cardiff with sessions in Gwent. When he retired in 1976, Dr. David Beckingham replaced him having been a Surgeon Commander in the Royal Navy. His original contract had been, as with Dr. Ribiero, jointly between Cardiff and Newport. However, it became apparent that the Gwent clinic needed developing so he re-negotiated his contract to be virtually in Newport only.

Move to Clytha Square Site

In 1977, the building housing the Public Health Laboratory was vacated (for location see Plan 2 - Site 1). The building had been acquired in 1900 from the Trustees to Lord Tredegar's Estate. The G.U. Department moved into this accommodation in 1978 from the 'little box' at the front gate of the hospital. For the first time in Newport, access to this building gave some degree of privacy and anonymity for patients attending for advice (usually voluntarily) because its entrance was immediately off and only five yards from the Clytha Square entrance to the Royal Gwent. Therefore, potential patients could slip in and out quietly and unobserved from a side road. This was a far cry from the experience of some men serving during the Second World War. In some warships, for instance, a mess existed known as the D.C.A. (diseases caught ashore) mess whose members, all temporary, were those thought to have acquired infection while ashore: in fact, most infections were venereal although chicken pox was not unknown. However, these men were totally segregated even to their own plates and cutlery such was the stigma of venereal infection and this attitude to these diseases was prevalent among the public for many years afterwards. Therefore, to move the location of the G.U. Medicine Department from a site at the main gate of the hospital to Clytha Square for patients may have been fortuitous but was undoubtedly much appreciated by those who were paying a reluctant visit to the

Department. Even so, a senior nurse still at The Royal Gwent recalls that when she had been a junior staff nurse on Ward 2 in the 1960s, patients admitted as In-Patients to hospital under the care of the veneorologist were isolated in a side ward, forbidden to leave the room and ate from special crockery coloured yellow that was washed in the bathroom and was locked up after use in a special cupboard! The stigma lived on.

Therapeutic Developments

Originally the clinics were male only. The 'Nursing' staff were all male and not necessarily trained nurses in any guise. However, to be fair, they were very dedicated and good at their job. Before the days of antibiotics, various poisons such as mercury ointments, bismuth injections* and the oral administration of arsenicals in near lethal doses were the preferred treatment for syphilis. Irrigations of the urethra with carbolic solution and other irritants were the accepted treatment for gonorrhoea. These, as much as the disease itself, led to strictures of the urethra, which in turn was succeeded by frequent attendance at bougie clinics for dilatation. It must be presumed that this was the pattern of treatment in Newport as elsewhere and in those days dilatation of urethral strictures were often the prerogative of surgical housemen - or even medical students - in larger centres such as Teaching Hospitals especially in London. This tradition existed to some extent in Newport in the days before 1948 as 'stricture clinics' were run by junior surgical staff (information from Mr. L.P. Thomas who had been Resident Surgical Officer in 1945).

*An interesting piece of useless information. When examining veterans of the Great War and the pre-penicillin period, who flatly denied any history of V.D., an X-Ray of their buttocks frequently revealed the remnants of the Bismuth injections, thus confirming diagnostic suspicions!

Antibiotics were first used by the army during the Italian campaign and rendered treatment much less rigorous and time away from duty became unnecessary.

Non specific urethritis, genital warts, herpes, thrush, trichomonas and various female conditions entered the list of the recognised sexually transmitted diseases in the second V.D. Act of Parliament, which was passed during the Attlee government's time. To this list may be added certain forms of hepatitis and the fact that cancer of the cervix in women is now thought to be associated with chronic infection. These therapies became, therefore, part of the normal routines of the department.

For the benefit of the more sensitive section of the population, the term Sexually Transmitted Diseases (S.T.D.) was introduced. Linguistic correctness was achieved later when the speciality acquired the title of Genito-Urinary Medicine.

Latterly venereologists have joined the increasing number of medical specialities engaging in invasive investigative techniques, in this case colposcopy to examine the uterine cervix, formerly considered to be the prerogative of gynaecological surgeons. Curiously, urethroscopy to examine male urethras had been one of the routine skills of venereologists for a long time.

Dr. Beckingham retired in 1992 and was replaced by Dr. Robert Das, an alumnus of St. Thomas's Hospital, London.

Health Education

A most important function of today's clinic in Newport is health education, despite which the incidence of S.T.D. is again rising; mostly amongst the young. Most importantly, health education concentrates on contraception and 'safe' sex. The pill may be a good contraceptive, but it is no barrier to infection.

The recognition of AIDS in the late 1970s gave rise to a whole new culture within the speciality. It still is a major problem, most especially in the third world, where its incidence is more heterosexual than homosexual.

In the late 1980s, the department acquired a converted ambulance which the nursing staff would, during the early evenings, park in various town centres, where they would invite passers by in for coffee, condoms and conversation, which was essentially health education. This venture was most popular with the young, who were receptive and very appreciative. We like to think that this achieved some good.

Not the least of our functions of G.U. Medicine was screening of the 'at risk'. One of the more notable of Newport's 'Madams' used regularly to ring up for appointments for her girls: and all her new recruits were brought in for examination.

The Department of G.U. Medicine may give rise to all sorts of comment, but the one certain thing is that it is a highly rewarding - and entertaining - occupation for its practitioners.

The Childrens' Department and the Care of Children in the Newport Hospitals
John Cawdery FRCP FRCPCH

The Care of Children before 1948

The first recorded unit in Newport that catered specifically for children was in the Newport Infirmary and Dispensary at 34 Stow Hill. This institution had been re-named from The Newport Dispensary in 1867, and in that year two wards were opened, each with six beds. These were for adults but in 1887, to mark Queen Victoria's Golden Jubilee, a Children's Ward containing fourteen cots, was opened on the same site. It was called Victoria Children's Ward.

This institution at 34 Stow Hill was re-named The Newport & Monmouthshire Infirmary in 1888 and in 1901, moved to its new site at Cardiff Road in the new Newport & Monmouthshire Hospital which became The Royal Gwent Hospital in 1913.

It is probable that children were accommodated in the new hospital from its opening as records of endowments exist for individual cots and children's beds going back to 1901.

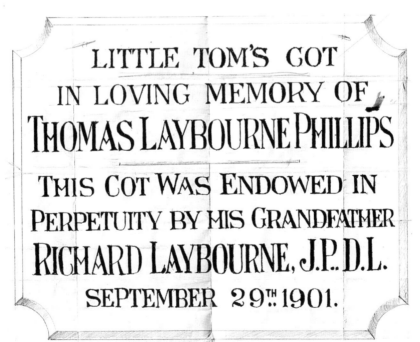

LITTLE TOM'S COT
IN LOVING MEMORY OF
THOMAS LAYBOURNE PHILLIPS
THIS COT WAS ENDOWED IN
PERPETUITY BY HIS GRANDFATHER
RICHARD LAYBOURNE, J.P., D.L.
SEPTEMBER 29TH 1901.

Photograph of Endowment Plaque from 1901.

(*photograph courtesy of Dr. Richard Harding*)

The plans of the original hospital labels wards in the West Wing for 'women and children' and a photograph taken at Christmas 1915 shows one of these wards with young children and women of various ages mixed together (p.27).

In 1919, when Lord Tredegar gifted the Friars and adjacent land (Friars Field) to the hospital, a condition of the gift was that The Friars should be used to accommodate women and children. Although, for a time, The Friars was used for this purpose, the majority of children were still cared for in the main hospital.

In 1926 there is a reference to toys being given to the Children's Ward for Christmas. However, at that time, there does not appear to have been a separate Children's Ward and it is most likely that children with medical and surgical disorders were still accommodated in adult wards, probably in the side rooms. This was certainly the case with E.N.T. children who were nursed on Ward A3W on the third floor of the west wing of the original hospital even until the 1970s. The side ward and/or treatment room in A3W were lined with white tiles and in order to make these rooms less clinical and cold, several picture tiles depicting scenes from nursery rhymes were set into the walls.

Tiles on the wall of the Children's Ward.

These tiles are said to date from the 1920s and as a result of the efforts of Sister Mair Jones and Mr. Marcus Brown (E.N.T. Consultant) they were preserved when the old wards were demolished in 1992. They were mounted in sets and can now be seen in parts of the new hospital including the Special Care Baby Unit (S.C.B.U.), Children's Out-Patients in 'D' Block as well as the new E.N.T. Department in 'E' Block. Children with orthopaedic problems were accommodated in the Trauma and Orthopaedic wards in the old building until this unit moved to 'C' block in 1977.

However, it would seem that from early in its establishment after 1901, it was appreciated that there was a need for a separate children's ward in the new Royal Gwent Hospital. In 1924, the new Out-Patient block was opened and the top floor of this building was designated as a Children's Ward (see p.26). However, at that time there was a serious shortage of space for the Nursing School and accommodation for nurses so that this floor was used as a Nurses' Home until 1933 when the new Nurses' Home in Friars Field was completed and the nurses moved there. When this ward was opened for children, it contained thirty-two beds and cots (called Ward 8). This ward was light and spacious with a glass partition dividing it transversely. The nearer portion had cubicles down the left hand side and beds for small children on the right. The further part (with balcony) contained beds only and in more recent times, usually accommodated older children.

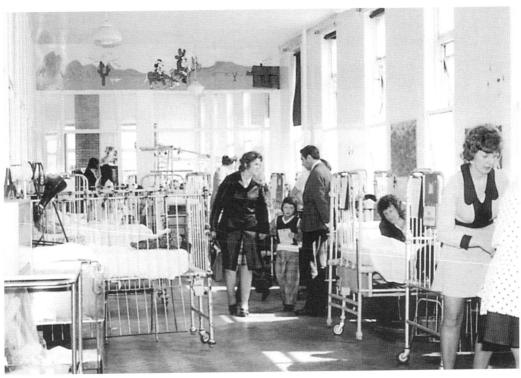

Children's Ward (Ward 8) The Royal Gwent Hospital.
(photograph courtesy of Nigel Pearce, Medical Illustration R.G.H.)

After 1948

By 1950, most children admitted to hospital in Monmouthshire were cared for in separate children's wards of which there were several throughout the county. In Newport, medical and surgical admissions were shared equally between St. Woolos Hospital and The Royal Gwent Hospital. Children with infectious diseases, including meningitis and gastroenteritis, were cared for in Allt-yr-yn Hospital.

It has already been noted that the two general physicians of that era, Dr. Grahame Jones and Dr. Ted Dipple, looked after children in the hospitals in Newport and the county as part of their overall remit as consultant physicians. Therefore, the appointment in 1950 of Dr. Terrence Brand as Consultant Paediatrician to The Royal Gwent Hospital marked the birth of Paediatric Medicine in Newport. His work was not confined to Newport and in fact, he covered children's services for the whole of Monmouthshire.

By the time that Dr. Brand had been appointed in 1950, the Children's Ward in St. Woolos Hospital was in 'A' Block (Christopher Robin Ward) which had previously been a male ward in the Workhouse era of the hospital.

At that time, 'A' Block had accommodated adult medical and geriatric patients as well (Sections D and E seen on Pull-out Plan 1). Christopher Robin Ward shared a ground floor with Lower Victoria Ward and there were two floors at higher levels for adult patients. However, the accommodation in this Block was very cramped and inconvenient, especially for adults as there were stairs everywhere and even rooms at different levels on the same floor. In the 1960s, adult beds were moved to 'B' Block (previously 'B' Annexe of The Infirmary) which gave an opportunity to expand paediatric space with conversion of Lower Victoria Ward into a Treatment and Admission Room for Christopher Robin Ward. During this period, care of children with meningitis and other infections was transferred from Allt-yr-yn Hospital to St. Woolos and The Royal Gwent Hospitals and in 1969, Hawthorn Ward (on the top floor of 'A' Block) was refurbished so that one half could be converted into a twelve-cot unit for babies with gastroenteritis. From 1972, no children were admitted to Allt-yr-yn Hospital.

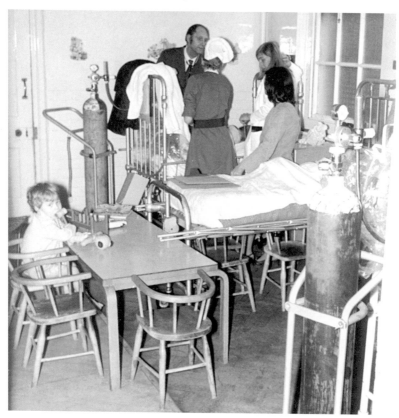

Christopher Robin Ward, St. Woolos Hospital (circa 1970) with the late Dr. Robert Prosser (consultant paediatrician) in the background.

(photograph Nigel Pearce, Medical Illustration R.G.H.)

These changes left empty space in 'A' Block in St. Woolos Hospital, so that proposals were made by the paediatricians to upgrade all wards to create a Centralised Children's Unit to accommodate all medical In-Patients from the south of the county and to include a number of surgical and E.N.T. children as well. Detailed plans were drawn up but the idea was abandoned at an early stage when it became apparent that the old adult wards in 'A' Block at St. Woolos Hospital were structurally unsuitable for upgrading. Apart from Hawthorn Ward, they were left unoccupied although parts of the ward on the first floor were adapted for use by parents wishing to stay with their children, and as a schoolroom.

Move to The Royal Gwent Hospital

Throughout the 1970s rebuilding of the Royal Gwent Hospital continued, and with the opening of 'C' Block in the new hospital in 1979, orthopaedic beds were vacated above the fracture and orthopaedic Out-Patient department. This created the opportunity to move all children's beds down from St. Woolos Hospital to make a centralised unit in the Royal Gwent Hospital. This was to include all the orthopaedic children from both the Royal Gwent Hospital and St. Lawrence Hospital, Chepstow and all E.N.T. children. A sloping corridor was constructed to link the paediatric wards (Wards 8 and 9) which had been in use since 1924 in the old building above the Out-Patient Department with the new accommodation in the orthopaedic wards that had been vacated. This link actually passed through part of the old Haematology laboratory, which was then used as a schoolroom. The new ward was refurbished for the use of older children (named A2 Paediatrics) and Ward 8 was re-designed for the use of babies and toddlers, the dividing partition being removed and the cubicles extended. This ward then became A3 Paediatrics. Ward 9 was also converted into a children's ward of 9 beds with a link into the adjacent playroom which had been built onto A3. At the end of these moves, there was a combined Paediatric Unit with total of approximately 80 beds: the move was completed by 1981.

Having all the children's beds on the same site was a great advance particularly as it allowed children to be nursed and cared for by children-trained nurses and made overall administration much easier and more efficient. But it was not ideal. Although since 1968 the department had had a policy of open visiting for parents with permission to stay with their children, accommodation for parents was still very limited and primitive, the cubicles in the ward being both very small and open to public view. On Ward A2, where there were several smaller areas, it was possible to segregate some children according to age and sex when necessary, but it was not wholly satisfactory and it was especially difficult to accommodate adolescents most of whom were still being treated on adult wards.

However, it was accepted that these wards were really temporary and that Children's Wards would be relocated to a final site in the Scheme 6 development to 'D' Block in the new hospital.

The new unit was, therefore, carefully planned to address these problems and 4 wards were set aside for children on the top two floors of the new building. These wards opened in the spring of 1990.

The Baby and Toddler Ward in the new building (D6W - named 'Bluebell') had cubicles throughout with 13 cots. All cubicles were large enough to allow a parent to stay with their child in some comfort. The other three wards each had three to four-bedded units and seven separate rooms for isolation or accommodation for parent and child.

But perhaps the most far-sighted innovation was the use of one of the wards (D7W - 'Emerald') for young people up to the age of nineteen years. This nineteen-bedded ward was the first purpose built adolescent In-Patient unit for young people with medical and

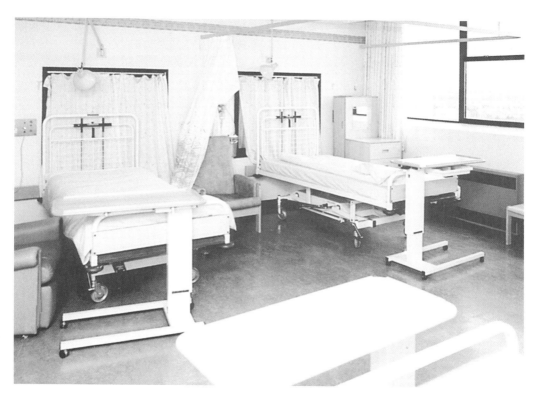

Children's Unit: four-bedded ward on Adolescent Unit.

Playroom Children's Ward 'D' Block.

surgical conditions in Wales and probably in the U.K. and remains pre-eminent. It has proved a great success and is very popular, not only with its 'clients' but also with the medical and nursing staff.

On both floors, accommodation for a playroom, schoolroom and teaching has also been provided.

In May 1998, when the new Children's Out-Patient, Casualty Unit and Day Unit was opened, D7E ward was given up for the use of adult patients and an extra seven cot/beds were added on to D6W by using the day room on this ward.

Neonatal Services (see Obstetric Services p.197)

Out-Patients

Out-Patient paediatric clinics in Newport between 1950 and 1972 were held in the Main Out-Patients Department in The Royal Gwent Hospital. Two rooms were used, one shared with Surgery and the other with the Dental (Oral Surgery) Department. The latter room housed a large dental chair, anaesthetic apparatus and other paraphernalia, sometimes but not always covered by a loose drape. This was not a very cheerful or relaxing environment for adults let alone for children.

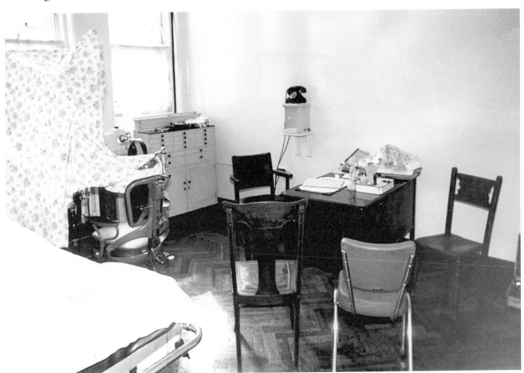

Paediatric/Dental consulting room, Old Out-Patients Department, The Royal Gwent Hospital.
(*photograph courtesy of Nigel Pearce, Medical Illustration R.G.H.*)

However, in 1971, building started on a 'temporary' Out-Patient department adjacent to the Belle Vue Entrance of the hospital which, from the curious layout of the building on a steep slope, was on the third floor and yet communicated directly with the outside at road level. This extension was completed in 1972 and was shared with adult medicine. The paediatric area was self-contained with separate waiting and play area for children in Belle Vue Clinic, as it was called, was a great improvement on the previous facilities and remained in full use for sixteen years until May 1998 when the Children's Out-Patients moved to the custom-designed Out-Patients, Children's Casualty and Children's Observation (Day) Unit built immediately adjacent to the main Accident and Emergency Department in 'D' Block (now renamed 'The Children's Assessment Day Unit'). The Day Unit is open daily from 10am to 2am the next day and children who are not seriously ill can be treated and observed in relaxed surroundings and not infrequently discharged home. The whole unit is staffed by children's trained nurses and play leaders.

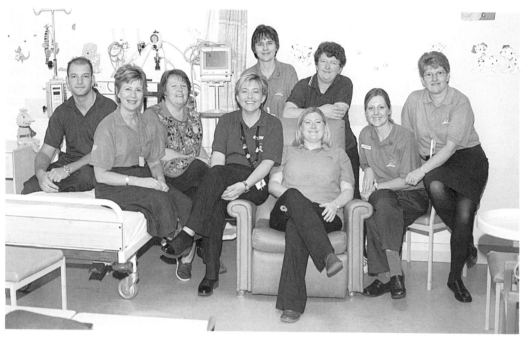

The Children's Assessment Day Unit and some members of staff. Left to right Phil Davey, Mandy Randall, Julie Harris, Marianne Scoble, Rachel Warner, Linda Barnard, Sharon Driscoll, Julie Meek and Kim Williams.

(photograph Andrew Ponsford)

Staffing

Before Dr. Brand's appointment in 1950, children were cared for by the general physicians, and children with infectious diseases admitted to Allt-yr-yn Hospital were looked after by two general practitioner clinical assistants, Dr. Sidney Rosehill and Dr. Ken Crowther.

From 1950, all children with medical disorders in St. Woolos and The Royal Gwent Hospitals became the responsibility of Dr. Brand and subsequent paediatricians. There was paediatric input at Allt-yr-yn Hospital from a weekly ward round by a paediatrician up to 1972 when the care of all children was transferred to St. Woolos and The Royal Gwent Hospitals. Children with surgical, orthopaedic or E.N.T. disorders were managed by the relevant surgical team and, with some modifications, this practice remains to this day.

Since children were accommodated in one unit in The Royal Gwent in 1981, their nursing care has been the responsibility of dedicated children's trained nurses. This has been complemented by other personnel specially trained in the care of children and their disorders such as teachers, play specialists, nursery nurses, dieticians and physiotherapists.

In 1964, the consultant establishment in Monmouthshire was increased to two with the appointment of Dr. Robert Prosser. Dr. Brand retired the following year and was replaced by Dr. Ralph Evans who moved to Cardiff in 1970. He was replaced by Dr. John Cawdery. Almost simultaneously, a paediatrician was appointed to the new Nevill Hall Hospital in Abergavenny and from that time, paediatric consultant services were divided between the north and the south of the county. Nevertheless, paediatricians from Newport continued to provide on-call cover to the single handed paediatrician at Nevill Hall until 1986 when a second paediatrician was appointed to that hospital. In Dr. David Ferguson was appointed as third consultant paediatrician to The Royal Gwent.

In the early 1950s, Dr. Brand's junior staff was one Senior House Officer (S.H.O.) at St. Woolos Hospital and one pre-registration House Officer at The Royal Gwent Hospital. In 1956, a paediatric registrar was appointed. In 1966, the junior staff complement covering both hospitals in Newport became one registrar, and three S.H.O.s. By 1986, with the planned centralisation of paediatric services at The Royal Gwent Hospital, the S.H.O. establishment had increased to six doctors. Thus, for the first time, it was possible to have dedicated S.H.O.s to the S.C.B.U. and children's wards working a 1 in 3 on call rota. Consultants and the registrar were on call on alternate nights and weekend until 1983 when it became a 1 in 3 rota. The consultants provided second on call to the S.H.O.s when the registrar was off duty.

The 1990s have seen a rapid increase of all grades of medical staff in the Paediatric Department. Incorporation of Rhymney Valley into the Glan Hafren N.H.S. Trust in 1995 provided the opportunity to create community consultant paediatric posts in that area, linked to the department in Newport. In 1999, merging of community and hospital services into one Trust has given further impetus to this programme of consultant-led community paediatric services. Increase of hospital-based paediatricians has allowed development of sub-specialisation to occur giving greater expertise in several areas of paediatrics.

At the same time as consultant expansion with the recent appointments of Drs. Sabine Maguire, Paul Buss, Ian Bowler, John Barton, Peter Dale, Hilary Lewis, Michelle Barber, Mario Schmidt and Siddhartha Sen there has been a big increase in the junior staff, particularly at middle grades. This has been partly to ensure skilled and experienced emergency cover (safety net) and consultant support, and partly to allow comprehensive training in the different areas of modern paediatrics.

Since its foundation in 1901, the care of children has been a very important part of the work of the Royal Gwent Hospital and many doctors, nurses and other staff have given dedicated service to the children of Newport and Gwent. The last hundred years have seen the service expand from a few beds for sick children scattered throughout in the wards of at least five hospitals in the county* into an integrated children's service providing, not only the most skilled and up to date care for sick children and babies within the hospital but also providing services to children with special needs, helping to protect children from harm and the prevention of disease and the promotion of good health in the community at large.

The next hundred years will continue to present problems for those caring for our children but there is no need to doubt that The Royal Gwent Hospital and the Children's Department can look forward to meeting those challenges with confidence.

Children's beds in The Royal Gwent and St. Woolos Hospitals, County and Pontypool Hospital, St. Lawrence Hospital and neonatal cover at Lydia Beynon, Cefn Ila Hospital and St. Joseph's Nursing Home.

Psychiatric Services
John Hughes TD OStJ BSc DPM FRCP FRC (Psych)

Before 1948

The background and development of Psychiatric Services are quite different from those of other medical services. Public attitudes also were different and for a long time there was little effective treatment available. This led to large 'County' hospitals being built in the mid-1880s in which mentally sick people could hopefully recover in pleasant environments, but these were remote from major centres of population. There was much social stigma associated towards residents of these institutions which were often called 'Lunatic Asylums' or just 'Asylums' - a term which persisted into the first half of the 20th Century.

These hospitals were run by local authorities with a mandate from the government. They were supervised initially by The Home Office and later by The Ministry of Health. In the first decade of the 20th Century, the newly independent County Boroughs of England and Wales were required to build Psychiatric Hospitals, which led to the opening of St. Cadoc's Hospital in Caerleon in 1906. It was a small hospital, by comparison with some similar hospitals, with about 350 beds but these were housed in buildings erected during a good period of hospital construction. It is of great interest locally that the architectural plans for St. Cadoc's were signed by none other than Winston Churchill, who was Home Secretary at that time.

Integration with other medical services started in Newport as long ago as 1935 with introduction of Out-Patients clinics in The Royal Gwent Hospital. This was an unusual development in a provincial hospital at that time. At about the same time, introduction of occupational therapy and other activities led to major improvements for patients in their lives and prospects for discharge.

After 1948

When the National Health Service was created, the psychiatric hospitals were integrated into the new service. Previously, such hospitals were directed by a Physician-Superintendent, who was the only doctor in the hospital recognised for administrative and legal reasons. These appointments gradually disappeared from the scene in the new system of the National Health Service especially as new consultants were appointed. The Welsh Hospital Board set up in 1948 continued to appoint Physician-Superintendents even after these posts had been given up in England and the final Physician-Superintendent appointed at St. Cadoc's Hospital in 1964 was the last of this distinguished group of public servants to be appointed in England and Wales. *(Editor - this was Dr. J.M. Hughes)*

After 1948, the catchment area of St. Cadoc's Hospital increased from serving the environs of Newport to cover the whole of South Gwent, a population of 250,000 people.

From 1950 onwards, major changes came from introduction of effective drug regimes to treat and prevent some mental illnesses. These methods became increasingly refined and led to a large drop in the number of long-term patients in St. Cadoc's Hospital, especially those with schizophrenia. The arrival of effective treatments also led to a major change in public attitudes to mental illness. The jokes about psychiatrists and their patients may all have been as good as ever but for a time psychiatry became a 'glamour' specialty in medicine and the media.

There followed increasingly effective treatments for some mental disorders outside hospitals or following a short period of In-Patient treatment. Consequently, a large and complex system of Out-Patient clinics and day hospitals was built up, many run in conjunction with Local Authority Social Services. This close co-operation led to many innovations. In the 1990s, Newport introduced 'Group Homes' - larger council houses in which five long-stay patients in each were successfully re-settled in the community. Eventually, there were six such homes in Newport alone. For this innovative service, Newport won a special Local Authority Award and the idea was soon copied widely throughout the United Kingdom.

The significance of these developments was not lost on colleagues in General Hospitals which led to increasing requests for help with treatment of patients with physical illnesses as colleagues became aware of the influence of psychological factors on the presentation and progress of physical conditions.

As the years went by, there was an increasing number of older elderly patients with physical and psychological complications of old age, and this led to the creation of a new sub-specialty of Psychogeriatrics. A new block of modern wards for this subspecialty was built in the Springfield Unit at St. Woolos Hospital with model facilities for managing this demanding clinical problem. This Unit opened in 1983.

In-Patient facilities for acutely ill psychiatric patients were never located at The Royal Gwent Hospital for a number of reasons. Firstly, facilities at St. Cadoc's Hospital were excellent with two post-war modern clinics. Secondly, space at The Royal Gwent was at a premium and there were no 'garden' surroundings that could help to create a therapeutic environment for patients with mental illness. Thirdly, a new consultant specialised in liaison work with medical and surgical colleagues and this improved co-operation across the clinical spectrum. And finally, consultant psychiatrists and their staff from St. Cadoc's Hospital have always been readily available to visit The Royal Gwent and St. Woolos Hospitals to advise about In-Patients in general and specialist clinical wards about urgent psychiatric problems.

Meanwhile, the widespread use of specially trained psychiatric nurses to work in the community was another major step forward. This contributed to early discharge of patients with acute mental disorders because the intensity of their treatments could be kept at almost the same level at home as in hospital. Such nurses played an increasingly important role in a specialty with a limited number of doctors. Regular team meetings to ensure close co-working of disparate professions inside and outside hospital also built up an environment in which all professionals spoke to patients and their families with one voice.

This principle is extremely important when treatments are likely to continue for years or even for a lifetime. For instance, long-term injection treatments for schizophrenia have been a great advance, enabling effective drug treatment with the equivalent of a minimal daily dose. Also, special drug clinics for the prevention of manic-depressive illness have been a great success, and have reduced the rate of recurrence dramatically.

It is evident, therefore, that the pattern of psychiatric treatment has changed comprehensively since 1950 with increasing emphasis on Out-Patient and community treatment and with increasing close co-operation with medical and nursing colleagues.

Llanfrechfa Grange Hospital

Equally dramatic changes took place in services for those unfortunates who were affected by low levels of intelligence. Before 1948, Gwent depended from other parts of Wales combined with Local Authority Support Services.

It was decided to build up Gwent services based on a brand new hospital built and developed on the site of a mid-nineteenth century manor house.

Coincidentally, big changes occurred in the way these handicapped people were categorised and treated. It was recognised that for the majority the needs were social and educational, with much emphasis on training for a more or less independent life. There was a minority who were severely handicapped with multiple physical and behavioural problems, which required considerable medical and nursing care.

For both groups, for two decades, the aim has been to place them in a variety of community settings with both residential and visiting specialist staff.

Llanfrechfa Grange Hospital.

(photograph Andrew Ponsford)

St. Cadocs Hospital.

(photograph Andrew Ponsford)

Chapter 8: Surgical Specialties

General Surgery

Lewis P. Thomas MCh FRCS & Brian Peeling CBE FRCS

Before the early 1970s, the four general surgeons in Newport were expected to undertake all aspects of surgical skills. This ranged from general abdominal conditions, urological problems, vascular disorders, endocrine states (thyroid and adrenal glands), cancers especially of breast, stomach and alimentary tract, as well as dealing with soft tissue injuries from accidents that also might need intra-thoracic or intra-cranial intervention. In addition, limb amputation, usually for ischaemic disease, was a frequent procedure undertaken. The surgeons were also required to offer surgical treatment of children usually with simpler procedures such as circumcision, orchidopexy, pyloromyotomy for pyloric stenosis in neonates (surprisingly common in Monmouthshire) but also would be called upon to treat intestinal obstruction in children especially when a hernia had obstructed. This pattern of General Surgical practice was usual in most District General Hospitals in Wales at that time and pure specialisation within any of the surgical subspecialties was usually confined in those days to Teaching Centres, with referrals sent sometimes to Cardiff, Bristol or more usually to London where specialist centres had been in existence for many years.

In 1948, three general surgeons in The Royal Gwent Hospital converted from Honorary status to Consultant Surgeons within the National Health Service (Messrs R.R.S. Bowker, J.T. Rice-Edwards and J. Elgood). At St. Woolos Hospital, there was one Consultant General Surgeon (Mr. Hywel G. Roberts).

Those early years of the National Health Service were the 'Sir Lancelot Spratt' days of general surgery when consultants held absolute authority (and responsibility) in hospitals and were usually held in considerable awe by junior staff, nurses and administrators. A very elderly ex-nurse trained at the Royal Gwent recalls those times in a recent letter to Mrs. Jeanette Dawes: *'Mr. Elgood (gen. surgeon) who we used to call Lord John God Almighty because he said you only run in the case of fire, haemorrhage and when he called. One morning running along the corridor to the lecture room, he shouted - Stop nurse, why are you running? Reply - for Mr. Glyn Morgan's lecture, sir - Elgood: Walk for his: run for mine'.*

Attitudes of patients were also, in general, very submissive to consultants. They rarely questioned advice given to them which was often regarded as infallible because it came from a consultant. There is the legendary tale that has been handed down in Newport for very many years of the following conversation during a surgical ward round: *'Surgeon - Good morning Mrs. Evans. We will do your operation tomorrow. Mrs. Evans - Thank you doctor. What will you do this time? Surgeon - Don't you worry my dear. When we get inside, we will find something to do'.*

The hospitals in Newport and the adjacent county were well served by the surgical consultants in the 1950s with more specialist back-up by some visiting surgeons from Cardiff (Mr. Ioan Jones and Mr. Lysaght). In due course, retirements introduced consultants trained with more formal, scientifically-based surgical backgrounds although Mr. Roberts, at St. Woolos, had received training at senior registrar level in Cardiff leading up to his appointment in 1948. The first change along these lines in the National Health Service era of the Royal Gwent Hospital occurred in 1953 when Mr. J.W. Bowker FRCS retired and was followed by Mr. R.D. Richards MCh FRCS who had trained in Cardiff and had previously held a consultant appointment in Merthyr Tydfil. In 1961, Mr. J. Elgood FRCS retired as Consultant Surgeon and was succeeded by Mr. L.P. Thomas MCh FRCS from a post as Senior Lecturer in Surgery at The Cardiff Royal Infirmary with Professor Lambert Rogers. Mr. Rice-Edwards retired in 1962 and was succeeded by Mr. D. Eric Sturdy MS FRCS, a Guy's graduate who had been senior registrar in Preston and Great Ormond Street Hospital, London.

Mr. Derek Richards tragically died in 1967 of a coronary thrombosis at the early age of 51 and was succeeded in 1968 by Mr. W.B. Peeling FRCS who was at that time Senior Registrar with Professor Forrest in Cardiff and had previously been Senior Registrar in Urology at The London Hospital and in General Surgery at Newport. The complement of three general surgeons at The Royal Gwent was increased by the appointment in 1972 of Mr. G.H. Griffith FRCS from his post as Senior Registrar with Mr. J.S.H. Wade in Cardiff. In 1974, with Mr. H.G. Roberts at St. Woolos, there was a team of five general surgeons in Newport.

Each of the general surgeons based at The Royal Gwent also undertook sessions either at Pontypool & District Hospital or County Hospital, Griffithstown as well as a monthly Out-Patient and operating session at Chepstow & District Hospital (until 1976). Each surgeon was responsible for about 25 designated beds at The Royal Gwent and about 20 beds at Pontypool or Griffithstown. Therefore, each general surgeon at The Royal Gwent cared for patients in about 40 to 45 beds across the county. At St. Woolos Hospital, Mr. Roberts was responsible for 62 beds. Mr. Richards had included a Saturday morning ward round at Pontypool Hospital as part of his normal weekly routine but his successor did not follow this schedule!

A monthly visit to Chepstow by each general surgeon was a vision of days gone by for this hospital had been converted in 1921 from a large private house called 'Gwy House' (pronounced 'Guy' House). It was expertly run by local general practitioners, in particular in more recent times by Dr. Eric Hardman, Dr. Bert Webb, Dr. Lyn Jones and Dr. Alec Davies and was, in effect, a Cottage Hospital. In the days before 1948 when the hospital was taken into The National Health Service, it was supported purely by the local community from fund-raising by fêtes, carnivals, donations from local organisations and businesses in the same pattern as The Royal Gwent and Pontypool Hospitals in other parts of the county.

Visiting consultant surgeons in the 1960s and 1970s would be welcomed on arrival by the Matron, sisters and nurses in the front hall and escorted into an Out-Patient room for consultation of about ten Out-Patients in the morning, followed by a three course lunch in the Matron's sitting room, and then an operating session at 2pm of a few minor cases such as hernia. There was no anaesthetic room but anaesthetics were administered by a local general practitioner on the landing at the top of a fine spiral staircase to the upper floor.

Operations were carried out in a large room converted from a bedroom in 1921 when the hospital had opened and, according to local rumour, the window of this room had been enlarged to increase the amount of daylight for surgeons carrying out operations! Understandably, some aspects of the conditions for surgery were limited and dated because of the structure of the building and its main function as a 'Cottage Hospital' but the standard of care and the results could not be faulted. Post-operatively, patients were looked after by their general practitioner and consultants' visits to Chepstow gave a probable insight into the personal character of medical care in smaller communities in the days before the N.H.S.. The hospital, albeit its old ways, deserves a special place in the history books of hospital care in Monmouthshire and Gwent. It is now the town Museum with a small exhibition of its work as a hospital. Its place in the community has been taken over by a new Chepstow Community Hospital built on the site of the old Mount Pleasant Hospital in Chepstow which for many years had been an institution for The Ministry of Pensions as well as a hospital to care for elderly people. The new Community Hospital was the first in the U.K. to be built through the Private Finance Initiative.

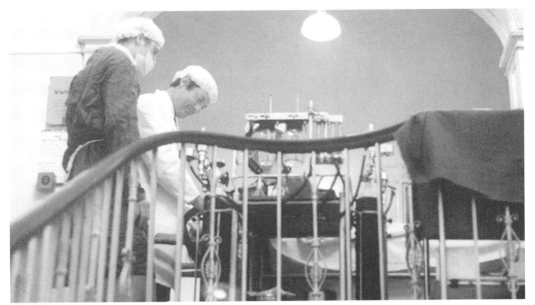

Chepstow and District Hospital 1974: Dr. Alec Davies anaesthetising a patient for surgery on the landing at the top of the main staircase. O.D.A. in attendance.

Operating Theatres 1901 to 1967

The original operating theatre of the Royal Gwent Hospital built in 1901 has been described in Chapter 2 and was a single operating room open off the main ground floor corridor of the hospital.

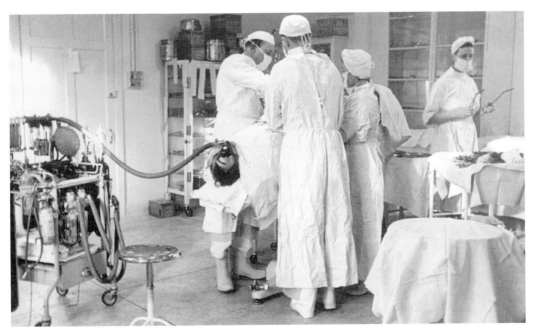

View of Mr. Glyn Morgan (consultant gynaecologist) and assistant operating in a Theatre of the East Wing of The Royal Gwent (circa 1950s) Note 1) patient anaesthetised with face mask (where is the anaesthetist?) 2) surgical instrument cupboards 3) sterilising drums in the background 4) surgical garb.

(photograph courtesy of H.H. Judge David Glyn Morgan)

139

This suite was in use for all surgical specialties until 1916 when an extension to the Royal Gwent was built at the East end of the hospital which included two operating theatres on the top floor. Until 1967, all the surgery for the hospital, with exception of orthopaedics, had been carried out in these two operating theatres located at the top of the East Wing of the hospital. They were presumably of up-to-date design when built, but inevitably became thoroughly old-fashioned with time especially with regard to open drainage channels for cleaning the floor and lack of air conditioning or climate control. In fact, ventilation during hot spells in summer could only be gained by opening the sash-windows high in the walls. Inevitably, an occasional sparrow would venture in but without any apparent disadvantage to anyone.

The Old Hospital in 1991 showing the 1901 Operating Theatre still in use for A & E (semi-circular roof) coming off lower corridor, Chapel and Meeting Room (straight roofs), rear of the Administration block, and storage huts.

(photograph courtesy of Terry Gale)

Therefore, the arrival of modern purpose-designed operating theatres opened in 1967 (for location see Pull-out Plan 2) as part of the Scheme 1 development was welcomed by the surgeons and nurses because the new environment and increased space for working was a new world from the old theatres. However, there were a few problems at the start. For instance, the climate control in the theatres offered by a modern ventilation system installed by the planners of The Welsh Hospital Board was often not as helpful as intended. Temperature control within the theatres depended upon a system that adjusted internal temperature to a preset level in relation to external conditions. While this worked reasonably well most of the time, the internal/external adjustment differential had its peculiarities in that during extremes of cold weather, theatre temperatures were definitely bracing whereas during heat waves temperature and humidity sometimes approached monsoon conditions. On these occasions, surgeons worked through a haze of dripping sweat and patients became over-heated while under anaesthesia so that occasionally, operations had to be hurried to a close and even postponed. It took a year or two to solve this problem.

Surgical Practice

Although the surgical practice of each general surgeon in the 1960s covered surgery in its generality, each individual surgeon developed areas of special interest in surgical subspecialties. For instance, Mr. Richards had an enormous experience of thyroid surgery, Mr. L.P. Thomas carried on his skills with vascular surgery which he had acquired in the United States as well as a special interest with breast cancer, Mr. Roberts and Mr. Peeling took a great interest in urology and Mr. Gwilym Griffith (from 1972) established a specialist service for thyroid and parotid surgery. However, the first specific subspecialist surgical work to be set up in Newport was paediatric surgery which was introduced by Mr. D.E. Sturdy from 1962 onwards. He had been trained at Great Ormond Street Hospital mostly by the great paediatric surgeon and urologist, David Innes Williams, so that for the first time and for some years the paediatricians in Newport had expert in-house surgical assistance for children and infants until a paediatric surgical unit was opened in Cardiff in the 1970s. Mr. Sturdy also had experience of urology to add an extra dimension to the urological work which all the general surgeons undertook in those days.

Surgical training

From 1964, Mr. L.P. Thomas arranged a rotational scheme between Newport and the Surgical Unit at Cardiff Royal Infirmary for training Senior Surgical Registrars. This entailed two years in Newport followed by two years with Professor A.P.M. Forrest in Cardiff. There were also three Surgical Registrars and one Senior House Officer appointed as assistant surgical staff but none of these was linked to any specific training programme. The normal tenure of appointment of registrars was one or even two years and all assistant surgical staff rotated between the Newport surgeons every 1st July. Therefore, it was possible for trainees to work under a consultant's supervision for one year at a time. This meant that trainees could acquire considerable knowledge and practical surgical skills from within one surgical team and conversely, could be given more advanced operative responsibilities with confidence. This policy was both safe and sensible because both the old and the new operating theatres had been designed as twin suites so that senior surgeons were always immediately to hand to supervise the work of trainees working in the other theatre.

Training of junior surgical staff was on a personal one-to-one basis therefore, and courses to prepare for the Primary FRCS and the final FRCS examinations were arranged for several years in the late 1960s and early 1970s. These were open to any staff in the Newport Hospitals as well as staff from other hospitals in the area and they were free. The syllabus of the courses was based on lectures in general surgery and orthopaedics but was especially valuable to candidates because practical sessions to examine patients with a viva voce examination by the consultants was arranged in the Out-Patient Department during evenings. This followed the pattern used in London, especially at St. Bartholemew's and The London Hospitals. The success rate of trainees at examinations for the various Royal Surgical Colleges was very high, so much so that at one stage in the early 1970s, there were no trainees requiring coaching.

On-call duties

Surgical on-call duties meant that each consultant and his team were on duty one day each week and once every four weekends. Every Thursday, the Senior Registrar assumed the role of Consultant covering a surgical registrar which was excellent training for future consultancy responsibilities and was a unique feature in Wales. While on call, the duty senior registrar/registrar lived on the hospital premises to be immediately available for emergencies. House surgeons were provided with living quarters in the Doctors' Residence as did other junior staff in general medicine and there were few, if any, married house officers.

A particular feature of life as a consultant surgeon in Newport from the 1960s onwards was the professional support and easy communication between individuals. It is well known historically that the surgeons in Newport in the 1950s did not communicate with each other professionally or socially. From about 1968, it became the custom for the Newport surgeons to meet in each other's homes every six weeks to discuss departmental matters and these meetings soon became formalised as the General Surgeons' Committee. There was a Chairman, a Secretary who took minutes and matters were based upon a formal Agenda. Discussion took place about developments, policy towards management and other decisions, planning and agreement about cover for absence, assessment of juniors as well as the usual plans for social matters. These meetings became extremely important after 1974 when the influence of the Senior Medical & Dental Staff Committee was demoted by formation of the 'Cogwheel' design of Divisions of clinical specialties (ref. p.98). The general surgeons thereafter spoke for General Surgery (including Urology) with one voice as their views had been determined and clarified during their meetings. This proved to be important to protect the interests of general surgery and urology in the coming years in which management became a dominant factor in hospital policy. These regular meetings were the basis of the coherence and friendliness of the surgeons as a group which was well known among Welsh colleagues to be a feature of Newport.

Surgical sub-specialisation

Since the 1970s, general surgery in Newport as an individual specialty gradually fragmented into several subspecialties some of which have retained an overlap with general surgery especially for emergency cover. This has been the pattern throughout the country with developments of units concerned mainly with vascular surgery, breast disease, upper and lower gastro-intestinal conditions. Also, in common with other hospitals, urology was set up in 1974 in St. Woolos Hospital as a separate surgical specialty but in which interested general surgeons retained their place and influence.

In 1976, Mr. J.M. Price-Thomas was appointed as a further general surgeon from Oxford where he had worked as Senior Registrar with Mr. Joe Smith, a distinguished British urologist. Upon Mr. Roberts' retirement in 1979, Mr. Michael Butler was appointed as his successor but with a specific vascular interest. Sadly, Mr. Butler died in 1982 from metastatic malignant melanoma eight years after removal of a doubtful lesion while a Senior Registrar in Southampton. He was succeeded by Mr. K. Shute in 1982 as general surgeon with a special interest in vascular surgery who had been a senior registrar in Nottingham and had acted as locum for Mr. Butler during his illness. Mr. Shute laid the foundations of the Vascular Surgical Unit which was to come with the arrival of Mr. A. Shandall in 1992 and Mr. Ian Williams in 1998.

Further surgical sub-specialisation within the Department of General Surgery occurred in 1986 with the appointment of Mr. K.D. Vellacott to develop endoscopy and colo-rectal surgery. He had received training as a senior registrar in Bristol and previously had been with Professor J.D. Hardcastle in Nottingham where he had taken part in a large screening study for colon cancer to which he continued to contribute from Newport. This aspect of surgical work increased with the appointment of Mr. B. Stephenson in 1995 who had received part of his senior training in Newport to be followed by training in colo-rectal surgery at St. Mark's Hospital, London. Since his arrival in Newport, Mr. Stephenson has also developed a specialist interest in hernia repair for which he has received national as well as international renown. In fact, in 2001, he organised a most successful international Masterclass about management of hernia with closed circuit television transmission from the operating theatre to the Postgraduate Institute at The Friars.

In 1995, Mr. Wyn Lewis was appointed to establish a surgical service for diseases of the upper gastro-intestinal tract, especially cancer of stomach and oesophagus and in the relatively short time of his career in Newport has received much acclaim nationally and internationally for contributions to surgical treatment of cancer of the stomach.

From the 1960s, The Royal Gwent has always been recognised for up-to-date management of breast cancer largely due to the influence of Mr. L.P. Thomas and in 1995 sub-specialisation for breast disease arrived when Mr. C. Gateley was appointed to set up a Unit for diseases of the breast. He was joined in this Unit by Mr. P. Holland in 2000 who also has in interest in endocrine surgery.

While these moves into surgical-subspecialisation within general surgery in Newport have been going on, development of laparoscopic techniques have become common-place in the surgical unit in The Royal Gwent Hospital and, especially for gall bladder surgery, have largely replaced earlier open surgical techniques.

Accounts of the developments in these subspecialties follow this overall review of general surgery in Newport.

The modern Operating Theatre (2004) with some staff. Back row, left to right Anthony Bird, John MacAllister, Lee Miskin, Gareth Pocock. Front row Jan Clist, Vicky Hodson, Mandy Fry, Lesley Watson, Gayle Dracott, Karen Young, Helen Williams, Clare Walters, Derek Edwards and Annie Holloway.

(photograph Andrew Ponsford)

Vascular Surgery
Ahmed Shandall MCh FRCS

Before 1979

Vascular surgery was introduced to Wales by Mr. L.P. Thomas who was the first Welsh surgeon to carry out transabdominal aortic aneurysm grafts. He did these operations while Senior Lecturer with Professor Lambert Rogers at Cardiff Royal Infirmary shortly before taking up his post as Consultant Surgeon at The Royal Gwent Hospital. Previously, he had become involved with vascular surgery while working in the United States of America at Boston. After 1961, he did a number of cases at The Royal Gwent of ruptured abdominal aortic aneurysms, as well as arterial endarterectomy, embolectomies, femoro-popliteal grafts and sympathectomies. He also introduced, and carried out, aorto-femoral angiograms to the hospital (see Radiology section).

Mr. Derek Richards also had a previous interest in vascular surgical problems in the 1960s and carried out lumbar sympathectomies for peripheral vascular insufficiency. When he died in 1967, Mr. Peeling took over his vascular commitment and also carried out some lumbar and cervical sympathectomies, embolectomies and even vena caval plications for recurrent pulmonary emboli which had a transient vogue in those days.

In fact, all the general surgeons were called upon when an embolectomy was indicated as an emergency.

After 1979

However, vascular surgery acquired a sub-specialist flavour with the appointment of Mr. Butler in 1979 and after Mr. Butler's death, was developed further during the next ten years by Mr. Ken Shute.

In fact, Mr. Shute was the only consultant surgeon at The Royal Gwent Hospital with a dedicated interest in vascular surgery and at that time, about eighty major vascular cases were treated each year. These ranged from transperitoneal abdominal repair of aortic aneurysms, femoro-popliteal bypass, axillo/ileo/femero-femoral bypass. A moderate number of iliac and femoral angioplasties were also carried out.

In 1992, Mr. A. Shandall was appointed to be a second vascular surgeon. He introduced carotid endarterectomy to Newport firstly under general anaesthesia then in 1996 under regional anaesthesia. In the United Kingdom, the first eversion carotid endarterectomy under regional anaesthesia was carried out at The Royal Gwent.

A Vascular Laboratory was set up in 1994 and there are now three accredited Vascular Technologists. They carry out a full range of non-invasive vascular investigations (over 5,000 each year). Consequently, there is now no need for venograms, carotid angiograms and diagnostic angiograms, all of which are associated with some morbidity and have been replaced by non-interventional methods.

Some members of the Vascular Team. Left to right Tracey Brown, Jane Trumper, Chris Davies, Marion Dwyer, Lynne McRae, David McLain, Ahmed Shandall and Pete Kempshall.

(photograph Brian Peeling)

Order ID: 203-1837015-2707525

Thank you for buying from Oxfam Shop F2717 on Amazon Marketplace.

<table>
<tr><td>
Delivery address:
William T. Graham
23 Withenfield Road,
Northern Moor,
Manchester
England
M23 9BT
United Kingdom
</td>
<td>

Order Date: 3 Sep 2012
Shipping Service: Standard
Buyer Name: W.T.Graham
Seller Name: Oxfam Shop F2717
</td></tr>
</table>

Quantity	Product Details
1	**The Royal Gwent and St. Woolos Hospitals: A Century of Service in Newport [Hardc...** **Merchant SKU:** 6I-JYSU-EP6N **ASIN:** 1874538085 **Listing ID:** 0930I3Y4VW7 **Order-Item ID:** 43594674722067 **Condition:** Used - Very Good **Comments:** V. good condition. Signed by author together with inscription. Dust jacket with only slight indentation. Map intact at back of book. (10.364)

Thanks for buying on Amazon Marketplace. To provide feedback for the seller please visit www.amazon.co.uk/feedback. To contact the seller, please visit Amazon.co.uk and click on "Your Account" at the top of any page. In Your Account, go to the "Orders" section and click on the link "Leave seller feedback". Select the order or click on the "View Order" button. Click on the "seller profile" under the appropriate product. On the lower right side of the page under "Seller Help", click on "Contact this seller".

We would welcome feedback on our service when you have the time. Thanks.   *LL pp. Oxfam Cirencester*

Recent developments

Many vascular techniques have been introduced to The Royal Gwent including distal bypass to tibial arteries, thoracoscopic sympathectomy for hyperhidrosis and cell salvage. Also all aortic surgery is now carried out retroperitoneally including operations for pararenal and suprarenal aneurysms which were not previously undertaken in this way.

Endovascular repair of aneurysms was started in 1998 and The Royal Gwent was the first hospital in Wales to be accepted into the National trial (E.V.A.R. - Endovascular Aneurysm Repair).

With time, the demand for vascular surgery has increased and in 1998 Mr. Ian Williams was appointed as a full-time vascular specialist.

At the present time, over three hundred major vascular cases receive surgical treatment at The Royal Gwent Hospital each year.

Mr. Shandall and Mr. Williams do not take part in the general surgical emergency cover rota. They run a vascular surgical rota which is now linked in with the vascular surgeons in Cardiff as The South East Wales Vascular Service.

Mr. D. McLain was appointed to the Vascular Service in 2003 and Mr. Ian Williams now divides his work between The Royal Gwent Hospital and The University Hospital of Wales, Cardiff.

Surgical Gastroenterology and Endoscopy Services
Keith Vellacott DM FRCS

As with many developments in hospital medicine, endoscopy services came into being in The Royal Gwent Hospital in a haphazard way that depended upon the interests and skills of individual consultants. Gastroscopy was started on the surgical side in the mid-1970s by Mr. Gwilym Griffith and developed in 1975 by Dr. Brian Calcraft for investigation of medical patients referred with upper gastroenterological problems. This was the usual pattern of progress with endoscopy in many hospitals in the country as surgical and medical experience continued separately. For some time, Dr. Calcraft continued as the sole exponent of gastroscopy among the physicians, and some of the general surgeons took up this investigation in addition to Mr. Griffith.

While the surgeons were able to use the environment and facilities of the new operating theatres to carry out examinations, Dr. Calcraft had to make do at first with a 'cubbyhole' in the Gynaecological & Obstetric Building in 'B Block' before moving into a side room attached to the Coronary Care Unit which at that time was sited in the first floor of the Administration Block of the Old Hospital. Eventually, after the E.N.T. surgeons had moved into the new operating theatres in 1977, Dr. Calcraft set up a medical endoscopy unit in the old operating theatres that they had vacated in the East Wing of the hospital.

When Mr. Keith Vellacott was appointed as Consultant Surgeon in 1986, one of his major tasks was to expand and develop endoscopy and, in particular, colonoscopy and E.R.C.P. (endoscopic retrograde cholangiopancreatography). Up to that time, E.R.C.P. had not been undertaken at the Royal Gwent but had been referred to The University Hospital of Wales. When the equipment for colonoscopy and E.R.C.P. was purchased, it was evident that there was no room in the Department of Radiology for the procedure to be carried out there. Consequently, Keith Vellacott developed an effective system for undertaking E.R.C.P.s using mobile image intensifiers in the operating theatres. The examinations were recorded by video for a later opinion of a consultant radiologist.

Day Surgery and Endoscopy Units

It became evident that parallel but independent development of endoscopic skills in both surgical and medical departments was an illogical way to proceed, and Mr. Vellacott proposed that a single site be sought for all endoscopy in the hospital to be brought together, preferably close to the main operating theatres. Mr. Vellacott, together with Mrs. Ita Armstead who was Theatre Manager at that time, identified a large floor area immediately adjacent to the main theatres that had been used as changing rooms for female staff. It was proposed to convert this into a new Endoscopy Unit and Dr. Calcraft agreed to join the project. Eventually, the scheme was funded (for location see Pull-out Plan 2 - Site 10).

Two theatres were designed as endoscopy rooms but it was felt appropriate to install theatre-type ventilation while these were under construction so that they could be used as full operating theatres if necessary. At the same time as the work was going ahead, there was a national drive to increase facilities for day surgery so it was decided that, because of the position of the unit close to the main theatres, that the unit should function as a combined Day Surgery and Endoscopy Unit. The waiting area was funded by pharmaceutical companies and fund raising efforts which led to creation of a more friendly, relaxed atmosphere than the standard waiting area associated with the National Health Service. This Unit opened in 1990.

With the drive to increase day surgery, it was soon apparent that this combined unit was too small to cope with the demand. Consequently, despite the initial intention that the unit should be developed for endoscopy, it was considered that its function should be purely as a day surgical centre.

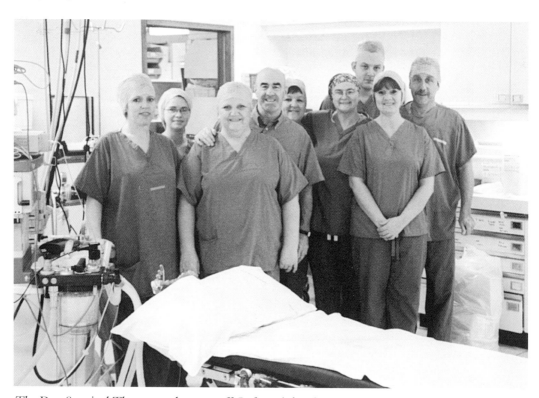

The Day Surgical Theatre and some staff. Left to right Fiona Grew, Ceri Screen, Cath Wharton, Bob Manship, Tracy Thomas, Helen Payne, Lee Miskell, Karen Purchase and Martin Penny.

(photograph Brian Peeling)

Consequently, a new unit solely for endoscopy was built adjoining the day surgical unit. This new Endoscopy Unit consists of two Examination Rooms which had to be built within existing structures and supporting walls with a waiting and trolley area. It was opened in 1994 but it is sad to record that Dr. Calcraft did not see the final outcome of this work for he died at the age of 53 from colon cancer. The department was named 'The Calcraft Endoscopy Suite' in memory of Dr. Calcraft, a very popular physician of considerable skills who had done so much for the hospital and who was respected so widely by his colleagues, staff and patients (p.111).

With the development of a dedicated unit, specific endoscopy nurses were appointed from the outset. This resulted in improved care of endoscopes, which cost in the region of £25,000 each. It was also possible to start an on-call rota whereby nurses and consultants would come in to the hospital to carry out emergency endoscopies when required - usually for gastro-intestinal bleeding.

The original fibre-optic instruments have now largely been replaced by videoscopes which give better quality images and provide excellent opportunities for training doctors and nurses. Two Nurse Practitioners now appointed to the Royal Gwent carry out flexible sigmoidoscopy to reduce delays in the investigation of patients with lower gastro-intestinal symptoms.

Research and Academic Activity

In addition, the facilities allowed both medical and surgically orientated research programmes to be developed in collaboration and the unit has taken part in several national studies for screening to detect colorectal cancer and polyps.

Upper Gastro-intestinal Surgical Subspecialisation
Wyn Lewis MD FRCS

Before 1995

During the past forty years, the role of surgical management for upper gastrointestinal disease has diminished dramatically. In the 1950s and 1960s, general surgical trainees would expect to meet perforated peptic and gastric ulcers frequently as emergencies, and persistent upper gastrointestinal bleeding from these would usually require emergency gastrectomy, an operation which experienced senior registrars regarded as part of the bread and butter of their training. In fact, until the introduction of vagotomy and pyloroplasty to treat duodenal ulcers in the early 1960s, partial gastrectomy was considered by many general surgeons as the optimal choice for this condition. This was the picture in Newport in the 1960s which later moved on to vagotomy and pyloroplasty.

All has changed since then partially due to real change of the natural history of peptic ulcers, to the success of medical therapies for this problem but especially from the development of fibre-optic technology which has provided a vehicle for diagnosis of disease and treatment of bleeding by laser therapy. This is now carried out by medical as well as surgical operators in Newport as elsewhere. The exception has been gastric cancer (cancer of the stomach).

Gastric Cancer

Gastric cancer is now the second commonest cancer worldwide, accounting for eleven thousand deaths per year in the United Kingdom alone. In Britain and much of the West, surgery for these cancers has, by tradition, been performed by general surgeons as has occurred in Newport. The operation of choice has usually been complete removal of the stomach. Despite sporadic reports to the contrary, the prognosis for patients diagnosed with gastric cancer remains poor. Furthermore, the procedure itself carries a significant level of morbidity and also mortality.

Although surgery remains the prime therapeutic modality, opinion about the best type of surgical resection for patients with gastric cancer remains divided, and the literature is polarized. Impressive outcomes after a specialised operation (D2 gastrectomy) have been published in large retrospective series from Japan, but these have not been reproduced in randomized comparative studies from Europe. In Britain, and Wales in particular, patients with gastric cancer tend to be older, more overweight, and less fit than in Japan. Furthermore, such patients often have diverse and complex clinical needs, best addressed by site specific multi disciplinary teams (M.D.T.).

From 1995

At the Royal Gwent Hospital, general surgical subspecialisation to treat gastric cancer has developed from 1995 onwards. This followed an executive decision by the Directorate of General Surgery to develop cancer (oncological) services specifically targeted at gastric and oesophageal cancer by which all surgical management of these malignancies was to be provided by one surgeon with a special interest. This development was in keeping with National Cancer guidelines that emerged shortly thereafter.

In March 1995 Mr. Wyn Lewis was appointed as Consultant Surgeon with a special interest in oesophagogastric cancer. He had spent five years working and training in this subspecialty under Professor David Johnston at the University Department of Surgery at the General Infirmary at Leeds.

Mr. Lewis set out from 1995 to investigate whether a modified D2 gastrectomy (preserving pancreas and spleen where possible), allied to a specialist multi disciplinary team approach, might improve outcomes after treatment for gastric cancer when compared with the traditional D1 gastrectomy performed by general surgeons working outside this framework.

The results showed that operative mortality after the D2 operation was lower (8.3% vs. 12%), had fewer complications (28% vs. 36%) and cumulative survival at five years was higher when compared with D1 operations (56% vs 11%). This was statistically highly significant (p<0.00001).

Furthermore, cumulative survival of MDT-enhanced oesophagectomy (removal of oesophagus for cancer) was higher when allied to immediate (neoadjuvant) chemoradiotherapy, than outcomes after surgery alone (51% vs 11%).

The findings from these studies have received considerable national and international recognition such as The Welsh Surgical Society Medal (1999), invitations for presentations at the International Gastric Congresses in Rome (1999), New York (2001) and Rome (2003) and an invitation to speak at The Association of Surgeons of Great Britain and Ireland in 2003. Recently, the Newport group under Mr. Lewis has been given a prestigious award by the Japanese journal 'Gastric Cancer' for one of the top three publications about gastric cancer in the world literature of 2003.

(Editor - Mr. Lewis acknowledges the invaluable help of three clinical research fellows (Messrs. Paul Edwards PhD MRCS, Jonathan Barry MRCS, and Guy Blackshaw MRCS). This clinical research is a most important and valuable contribution to treatment of gastric cancer and the fact that it has attracted so much professional interest is an indication of its merit. There have been 12 publications and 64 Abstracts in principal Scientific Journals, and 40 presentations to UK and International learned bodies).

Breast Disorders
Lewis P Thomas MCh FRCS & Christopher Gateley MCh FRCS

Traditionally, surgical treatment of breast disorders, especially breast cancer, was the concern of general surgeons. There was no surgical subspecialisation for breast cancer in Newport until 1995.

Before 1994

In the 1960s and before, the general surgeons at The Royal Gwent and St. Woolos Hospitals relied on clinical skill and knowledge to interpret the findings of examination of the breast by palpation and mastectomy was the sole management of primary breast cancer with some backup from radiotherapy.

Treatment of recurrent disease or metastatic spread was restricted to removal of the ovaries (oophorectomy) as a first line of attack. Removal of the adrenal glands (adrenalectomy), a major operation usually carried out through the abdomen, was the treatment for further relapse of these cancers. Adrenalectomy often gave considerable relief from pain arising from bony metastatic deposits by repressing growth of tumour tissue but required hormone replacement that sometimes could prove to be difficult to keep stable. These were procedures that all the general surgeons in Newport carried out when necessary and this treatment preceded the development of Tamoxifen which became the treatment of choice for advanced disease in the 1970s.

In the latter years of the 1960s, the general surgeons collaborated with breast cancer clinical trials set up by Professor A.P.M. Forrest at Cardiff Royal Infirmary and in the late 1960s and 1970s they provided breast tissue to help with pioneering studies about breast cancer receptors being carried out by Professor Keith Griffiths and his staff at The Tenovus Institute for Cancer Research at The Heath in Cardiff.

The arrival of mammography in the 1970s at The Royal Gwent together with the development of targeted biopsy and techniques to improve the precision of tumour localisation in the breast, as well as other diagnostic tests, did away with the relatively unsophisticated ways of earlier times and led directly to more interest in early detection of breast cancer.

From 1994

Therefore, the concept of a specialist Breast Unit for detection of early breast cancer and treatment of breast disease at The Royal Gwent slowly took root and in 1994 Louise Davidson was appointed as Specialist Breast Care Nurse to the hospital. This was the birth of the present Breast Unit.

In 1995, Mr. Christopher Gateley was appointed as a general surgeon with a subspecialist interest in breast disease. He developed a multi-disciplinary approach to diagnosis and management, especially for breast cancer. A Rapid Access Breast Clinic was set up in 1999 in collaboration with the Departments of Radiology and Histopathology. This development enables all necessary diagnostic procedures to be carried out during a single visit by patients, including percutaneous needle biopsy often undertaken under ultrasound guidance by a consultant radiologist. Results are reviewed within three days by a Multidisciplinary Team for review with patients and their relatives. The outcome of this process has led to correct pre-operative diagnosis of breast cancer in 96% of patients.

All patients with breast cancer can now be seen by a cancer specialist (oncologist) at a Joint Breast and Oncology Clinic held at The Royal Gwent with Dr. Chris Gaffney from Velindre Hospital, Cardiff.

The Breast Unit also has a team to provide assessment of women with breast abnormalities detected by screening through Breast Test Wales.

The success of the work of the Breast Unit at The Royal Gwent Hospital was made possible by expansion of staff by appointment of other consultants with a special interest in breast disorders. These have been two consultant radiologists, Drs. Anne Wake and Nest Evans and a second histopathologist, Dr. Majid Rashid to join Dr. Emyr Owen. A second consultant surgeon, Mr. Philip Holland was appointed in 2000.

By the year 2001, the Breast Team received over 2500 referrals annually and treated over 200 women with breast cancer each year.

Some members of the Breast Team receiving the Chairman's Certificate of Appreciation. Left to right Dr. Nest Evans, Denis Jessopp (Chairman N.H.S. Trust), Louise Davidson, Sarah Hacker, Mr. Phil Holland, Mr. Chris Gateley, Sheila Thomas, Margaret Matthews and Martin Turner
(photograph Nigel Pearce, Medical Illustration R.G.H.)

Urological Surgical Services
Richard Gower FRCS & Winsor Bowsher MChir FRCS FEBU

Apart from a Department of Urology at The Cardiff Royal Infirmary, there had been no other specialist urological unit in Wales until April 1974 when a urological department was set up in Newport.

Before 1974

Before 1974, all general surgeons had carried out urological consultations and treatments as part of general surgical practice. Mostly these had been related to urinary retention for which open prostatectomy was the standard operation although Mr. Roberts and Mr. Sturdy offered transurethral resection to some men with smaller prostate glands. Cancers of the prostate invariably presented with advanced disease in older men and in common with almost every hospital in the U.K., these were treated either with large doses of hormones (stilboestrol) or by castration. These men were usually referred back to their doctors for further care and rarely seen again in a surgical clinic on a routine basis. Urinary

150

stones were common in South Wales but, apart from removal of small stones blocking ureters, there was no tradition for other surgical treatment. Bladder cancers were also common; small tumours were treated by endoscopic diathermy and large cancers referred to Velindre Hospital for radiotherapy. Cystectomy (removal of the bladder for cancer) was a rare event.

The initiative for a specialist urological service in Newport came from The Welsh Hospital Board in 1973 in response to pressure from The British Association of Urological Surgeons that District Hospitals in the United Kingdom should move in this direction. The Newport general surgeons recognised that up to 1973, one third of their work had been urological in type and it was agreed that after the appointment of Mr. G.H. Griffith in 1972 as a fifth general surgeon, surgical services could be re-arranged satisfactorily in Newport to set up a specialist service in urology. To enable this to come about, The Welsh Hospital Board was advised that Mr. W.B. Peeling should be re-designated from general surgery to become a full-time urologist without a residual commitment for general surgery.

It was decided that the new urological department would be set up at St. Woolos Hospital with effect from 1st April 1974; which, by sheer coincidence, coincided with the start of the new Gwent Health Authority.

It was agreed that at St. Woolos there should be 32 beds designated for general surgery (Mr. H.G. Roberts) and 30 beds for urology (Mr. W.B. Peeling). Mr. G.H. Griffith, who had worked at St. Woolos following his appointment in 1972, moved to The Royal Gwent and took over the beds and general surgical sessions previously undertaken by Mr. Peeling at The Royal Gwent and Pontypool & District Hospitals.

From 1974

Consequently, Messrs L.P. Thomas and G.H. Griffith relinquished accepting urological referrals and emergencies (which on their Intake days were admitted to St. Woolos) whereas Mr. Roberts and Mr. Sturdy continued their established urological commitments.

In 1981, all general surgical work at St. Woolos Hospital was transferred to the Royal Gwent Hospital thus centralising general surgery at that site and all urological work at St. Woolos Hospital. To achieve this, Mr. Sturdy and Mr. Price-Thomas (who had opted to take over Mr. Roberts' interest in urology) moved some sessions from The Royal Gwent to St. Woolos Hospital.

A second urologist, Mr R.L. Gower FRCS, was appointed in 1985. He had been trained at St. Thomas' Hospital, London and had particular experience in treatment of urinary incontinence and management of urinary stones especially by lithotripsy.

In 1991, Mr. Peeling was appointed Honorary Professor in Surgery/Urology of The University of Wales College of Medicine.

However, the long-term plan of The Gwent Health Authority had been to move The Department of Urology to The Royal Gwent in order to centralise all surgical services under one roof. This occurred in 1992. The accommodation consisted of two wards (40 beds), eight Day Surgery beds in a side ward and three operating theatres designated for urology all in the undercroft of 'D' Block. Administrative offices and a library, Out-Patient department and an investigative unit (prostatic ultrasound and urodynamics) had been converted from the previous paediatric wards which had been moved elsewhere from the floor above the Fracture and Orthopaedic Unit (for location see Pull-out Plan 2 - Site 9). It is of interest that the urologists were given a free hand by management to plan the arrangement of this new unit. The final layout proved to be of general interest because urologists and planners from a number of hospitals in England and Wales that were considering new or updated urological services visited Newport to obtain ideas and advice.

Thus, the environment for urological surgery was transformed from its home in 'B' Block at St. Woolos Hospital built in the mid-nineteenth century to a state of the art modern theatre complex with all modern services including air-conditioning. Nevertheless, the move was a time of sadness for staff who had many happy memories of the old wards and especially the theatre despite its apparent primitive appearance which usually caused astonishment among visiting American surgeons - *'do you really do surgery here?'*.

A third urological surgeon, Mr. W.G. Bowsher MChir FRCS FEBU, was appointed in 1992 from The London Hospital and St. Vincent's Hospital, Melbourne where he had received specialist experience with prostatic cancer and in particular the operation of radical prostatectomy.

In 1995 Professor Peeling retired and was succeeded in 1996 by Mr. C.P. Bates MChir FRCS FEBU who had received his urological training in London (The Royal Marsden, Hammersmith and St. Mary's Hospitals).

A fourth urologist, Mr. Adam Carter BSc MS FRCS FRCS(Urol), has been appointed to and took up his post in December 2003. He received his training at Southmead Hospital, Bristol.

Mr. Suresh Pandelai FRCS was appointed to a Staff Grade post in 2000.

By 2003, various re-arrangements of ward accommodation had occurred so that the Urology Department consisted of thirty-one In-Patients beds in 'D' Block and a new Day-Case unit of 10 beds that had been opened adjacent to the Operating Theatre Suite in the undercroft of 'D' Block.

In 2002, the Urological Theatre Unit received a Chartermark Award.

Some of the Urology Theatre staff and Chartermark Award. Back row, left to right Registrar Mr. Murali Mohan, S.H.O. Dr. Simon Weaver, S.H.O. Dr. Ian Cambridge, C/N Raf Joomun, Senior Radiographer Andrew Ponsford. Middle row S/N Rose Armour, S/N Caroline Bates, S/N Sarah Gallagher, Sister Jan Meredith, S/N Julie Coslett, S/N Julie Williams. Seated Consultant Urologist Mr. Richard Gower and Sister Bridie O'Connor.

(photograph Andrew Ponsford)

Development of Urological Services

The Urological Department was, therefore, a *de novo* development in 1974 and the following account outlines the various stages of development of urological services that took place aiming for standards of service comparable with the best urological units in the UK.

The first task was to equip the department with a recently developed generation of endoscopic instruments using state of the art solid rod-lens telescopes that gave immensely improved, wide angle and clear vision over the old tools. In 1974, these had only recently become available on a commercial basis*.

> *It is not widely known that solid-rod lens technology was invented and developed in the United Kingdom. This was due to the genius of Professor Harry Hopkins of Reading University in the early 1950s but it is remarkable that his discovery was of no interest to British instrument makers at that time. By contrast, it was eagerly taken up by Karl Storz, a small time instrument maker in Germany, and the success and popularity of these new telescopes worldwide rapidly made Storz a very big-time producer of high quality endoscopic equipment for all medical specialties. It is sad to note that Professor Hopkins received no acknowledgement nationally or elsewhere for his work which had revolutionised endoscopic medical and surgical care throughout the entire world. In his later years, he was a very good friend and frequent visitor to The Department of Urology at The Royal Gwent. - Editor

It was a credit to the newly created Gwent Health Authority that funds were quickly provided to replace the old tools with a comprehensive range of Storz instruments (£50,000 spent over four years). The equipment at St. Woolos became a showpiece for other District Hospitals in Wales most of whom followed suit and purchased Storz endoscopes. There was, however, no marketing benefit from the suppliers for this!

2) Prostatic and Bladder Surgery. With an up-to-date urological armamentarium, from 1976 it was possible to undertake endoscopic prostatic and bladder surgery with confidence, effectiveness and safety and to move away from the traditional open prostatic and bladder operations with the discomfort and increased hazards that went with them.

Safety and comfort for patients was further increased by the introduction of spinal analgesia by Dr. G.D. Thomas, consultant anaesthetist, from 1976 onwards, an alternative to general anaesthetics. This was a therapeutic milestone that immediately made prostatic and bladder surgery a reasonable risk for patients with even the most perilous medical states. In fact, in Wales, for several years this was a routine procedure only at St. Woolos and in Cardiff. Patients rapidly showed approval of these new developments and it became the custom to offer them a Sony 'Walkman' to listen to music during the operation. One old gentleman was effusively delighted with this and commented afterwards *'it was a lovely operation, doctor and I really enjoyed it. But did I have to listen to Shirley Bassey all the time?'*

3) Treatment of Stones. In Gwent management of kidney stones, especially large 'staghorn' stones, posed considerable problems to surgeons and hazards to patients.

Several new procedures were set up to provide a comprehensive range of management for urinary stones to provide a service comparable with leading centres. These were introduced into routine practice at St. Woolos Hospital as they became available as follows:

i) Kidney Cooling: in 1977, funds were made available to purchase equipment to remove large kidney stones by using kidney cooling techniques developed at St. Bartholemew's Hospital in London. This method offered increased effectiveness and safety but the main downside was a long scar in the flank. In Wales, this operation was available only in Newport.

ii) Percutaneous nephrolithotomy (P.C.N.): this technique was introduced from 1982 onwards to avoid large flank incisions of open surgery. It was the forerunner to 'key-hole surgery' that is in vogue in most surgical specialties nowadays. Kidney stones were removed by special instruments passed into the kidney through a small puncture wound in the flank and the stones could be reduced to small fragments by ultrasound shock-wave or laser energy so that the debris could be extracted by suction. Most patients were home and back at work within one week and therefore, escaped the large scar in the flank associated with open surgery. This was much appreciated by the ladies.

The incentive to develop P.C.N. followed demands in 1981 from a delegation of ladies from Cwmbran who had undergone open operations at St. Woolos to remove kidney stones and had witnessed a TV programme showing P.C.N.. They arrived with a cheque for £10,000 to purchase the necessary equipment. The consultant urologist therefore had no option but to visit colleagues in London to learn the how to do the operation!

Therefore, P.C.N. was set up jointly with Dr. J.R. Harding, consultant radiologist. Thus, 'keyhole surgery' came to Newport in 1982 and, for kidneys, was a first in Wales. It was continued by Mr. R.L. Gower from 1985 but is now a rare operation due to the development of lithotripsy.

iii) Lithotripsy: Lithotripsy is a non-surgical technique developed in the 1980s to reduce kidney stones to dust by shock waves applied from outside the body. The stone dust should be passed out in urine afterwards. This was essentially an Out-Patient procedure that could replace open operation or 'keyhole surgery' as options for treatment.

A ten-year campaign to acquire a lithotripter for Newport started in 1985. This was ultimately successful following public fund-raising by a local Estate Agent, Mr. Bill Sage, of £300,000. The machine was installed in the Urological Operating Theatre Suite in The Royal Gwent Hospital in 1996 and the Unit was to have been opened by Lord Tonypandy, the much revered Welshman George Thomas, who had been Speaker of The House of Commons. Unfortunately, he was unable to do this due to illness from which he

The Storz Lithotripter and the original team. Left to right: Andrew Ponsford (Senior Radiographer), Louise MacMillan, Kath O'Donnell and Tracey Harris (Staff Nurses), Deb Turner (secretary) and Bridget Long (Patient Scheduler).

(photograph Andrew Ponsford)

died shortly afterwards. The Lithotripter Unit was opened on his behalf by Professor Peeling on 31st May 1996. It has been operated since then by a full-time ultrasound technician, Mr. Andrew Ponsford, with Mr. Richard Gower as consultant-in-charge.

The lithotripter at The Royal Gwent is the only 'Stone Buster' in Wales and receives many referrals from South Wales and elsewhere. Its arrival in Newport was, therefore, the final of a sequence of events that took stone surgery in Newport from operations through big holes, to operations through little holes, to operations with no holes!

4) Cancer Services. It is only since the late 1960s that management of urological cancers, especially prostate cancer, has been regarded with much interest probably because many of these cancers occurred in older men, and the fact that most cancers were advanced on presentation often made treatment unrewarding. This was a general attitude throughout the country.

In Newport, a particular interest in prostatic cancer has developed since 1970. Earlier work was concerned with advanced prostate cancer but with time, attention focused on detection and treatment of early, potentially curable cancers, just as early detection of breast cancers, for instance, is now of top priority.

Advanced Prostate Cancer. From 1970 to 1995, Brian Peeling and Professor Keith Griffiths of The Tenovus Institute for Cancer Research in Cardiff collaborated to study prostate cancer. Many studies by the Newport/Tenovus Group have resulted in over fifty publications in scientific and clinical journals and books. One important study was to direct a multi-centre UK trial from Newport to show that a new British drug 'Zoladex' (goserelin) could replace castration as standard treatment for advanced prostate cancer. Patients have given this medical therapy their vote of confidence.

Early Prostate Cancer: Until the early 1990s, most prostate cancers in Britain were detected when they had become advanced and were incurable. A high priority for the work of the Newport/Tenovus Group was, therefore, towards detection and treatment of early cancers that might offer curability. The programme for this was set up in three phases:

i)   detection of early cancers by ultrasound
ii) screening for early cancers in the community
iii) treatment of early cancer by surgery (radical prostatectomy)

Detection of prostate cancer by Transrectal Ultrasound. In 1979, a grant of £5,000 was made by The Tenovus organisation to the urological department to purchase equipment for scanning the prostate by ultrasound to detect early cancers. The late Dr. Glaslyn J. Griffiths MD FRCR, consultant radiologist at The Royal Gwent, and Mr. Peeling set up a collaborative study in 1979 with Professor K.T. Evans, Professor of Radiodiagnosis at the University of Wales Hospital to investigate the feasibility of this concept. The project was the first in the United Kingdom to scan the prostate and the third in Europe to work in this important field (the others being in Antwerp and in Copenhagen). The Gwent Health Authority supported the work with a grant to employ a Research Registrar (Mr. P.J. Brooman FRCS) to carry out the scanning which was done in Cardiff with Professor Evans' Senior Instructor (Mr. E.E. Roberts). Over a period of four years, over 10,000 men were scanned (including Professor Evans, and Messrs Peeling, Griffiths, Brooman and Roberts!). The findings created considerable interest in this country and abroad but some Americans wondered how the images of the prostate had been 'faked' because they had had no success with their earlier attempts. (It has to be stressed, however, that once they found out how to proceed, they moved like lightning).

Following on with this early work, the Department of Urology received a Capital Development Grant from The Welsh Office to set up a Prostatic Ultrasound Unit at

St. Woolos Hospital. This began its activities in 1984 and was the first Unit in the United Kingdom dedicated to imaging of the prostate by ultrasound as a clinical service.

Dr. Griffiths was the pioneer in the U.K. with an early technique that he developed for ultrasound guided prostatic biopsy and the first brachytherapy treatment in the U.K. (insertion of radio-iodine needles into early prostate cancers), also under ultrasound guidance, was designed at St. Woolos by Dr. Colin Keen, visiting consultant radiotherapist from Velindre Hospital.

Since those early days, the prostate ultrasound unit has developed but, sadly, Dr. Griffiths suffered a severe incapacitating illness in 1992 from which he died in 2000. His work was taken over by Dr. Richard Clements who has continued in charge of the Prostatic Ultrasound Unit which moved with the Urology Department to the Royal Gwent Hospital in 1992. Its work as a clinical service department has also had associated research activities from which many publications have come and many invitations have been received from Universities and professional bodies to deliver lectures and presentations. Dr. Clements is a member of several national advisory groups concerning screening and early detection of this disease.

Dr. Glaslyn J. Griffiths MD FRCR (1940-2000).
An internationally recognised pioneer of prostatic
imaging by ultrasound
(photograph courtesy of Mrs. Jill Griffiths)

Detection by Screening. In 1991, Professor Peeling and Professor Keith Griffiths designed a protocol to screen men in Gwent for early prostate cancer. It was, and still is, the only full-scale screening study to detect early prostate cancer to have been undertaken in the U.K.. Funding came from educational grants of £200,000 from pharmaceutical sources. There was no commercial element to the study and no financial support from the N.H.S..

Between March 1993 and March 1994 over 2,000 men were screened with no morbidity or adverse psychological problems. Follow-up has been over ten years and is the longest longitudinal study in time of screening for prostate cancer that has been done (10 years follow-up). Ninety-five early cancers were detected (4.7%) and over eighty per cent of these were potentially curable judged by clinical criteria.

Treatment by Surgery (Radical Prostatectomy). A cornerstone of the treatment of early prostate cancers is radical prostatectomy to remove the prostate. It has been a routine procedure in the United States since 1905 and in Europe and other countries for twenty or more years, but has only entered British urological practice within the past ten years.

The first radical prostatectomy in Newport (and, in Wales) was carried out at St. Woolos Hospital in 1991 and this operation became a routine procedure subsequently at The Royal Gwent Hospital with the arrival of Mr. Winsor Bowsher, firstly in association with the Screening Study. In fact, Mr. Bowsher was the first urologist in Wales to set up a routine service for radical prostatectomy and this operation is now a standard procedure in Welsh Urological Units for clinically proven early prostate cancer. It has received the seal of approval by Newport patients and their wives who have formed a group called 'Progress' that meets regularly in the Department of Urology. It was set up by Mr. Bowsher with patients and its Patron is Mr. Paul Murphy MP for Torfaen, now H.M. Secretary of State for Northern Ireland.

Winsor Bowsher (1957-2004). His unexpected death from myocardial infarction in May 2004 occurred while this book was in preparation. He was a dedicated, talented young surgeon with much to offer to urology and in his short professional lifetime made many research and clinical contributions especially to surgery for early prostate cancer - Editor.

Other Developments

Urodynamics: A urodynamic service to investigate various forms of urinary incontinence was first established at St. Woolos Hospital by Mr. R.L. Gower and then moved to The Royal Gwent. The Unit has been supervised by nurses, in particular Ceri Badham and Coral Seymour, and provides an All-Gwent service for specialised tests. One member of the urodynamic team, Ms. Karen Logan, has progressed to become a Consultant Nurse Specialist in Gwent.

Treatment of Male Impotence: Mr. R.L. Gower was one of the first urologists in Wales to offer a service for impotent men. Clinics were mostly carried out during evening hours.

Overview: Since 1974, urological services in Newport have improved and developed to offer standards in line with the high standards of other surgical services in The Royal Gwent Hospital.

Thoracic Surgery
information provided by Mr. Tom Rosser FRCS and others - Editor

There are few people who are associated with The Royal Gwent and St. Woolos Hospitals at the present time who realise that until 1979 there was a consultant thoracic surgeon visiting St. Woolos Hospital twice weekly.

Mr. T.H.L. Rosser ('Tom' to all his friends and staff) was a consultant at Sully Hospital, Penarth and Glan Ely Hospital, Cardiff until 1971 when he moved to The University Hospital of Wales, Cardiff, as part of the cardiac surgical team set up at that time and at Llandough Hospital where he headed the Thoracic Surgical Unit.

His first association with hospitals in Monmouthshire began in 1953 when he saw patients with thoracic disorders at Mount Pleasant Hospital, Chepstow. Work there was difficult for the facilities were primitive and he was made to feel unwelcome by some of the senior staff at the hospital.

In 1956, he began a thoracic surgical service at St. Woolos Hospital with one operating session weekly when major cases such as pneumonectomy, lobectomy, and hiatal hernia repairs were undertaken as a routine. He even carried out a small number of mitral valvulotomies in the heart successfully. In fact, on one occasion he was asked by a gynaecological colleague to do this operation on a lady who was in urgent need of a hysterectomy but whose cardiac status was severely compromised. So uneventful and easy was the mitral surgery that the consultant gynaecologist decided to follow on straight away with the hysterectomy. The patient made a spectacular recovery from both procedures. One wonders whether nowadays such an operation would have been followed by an enquiry sparked off by audit!

Clearly, major surgery at that level required three qualities. The first was an expert surgeon which Mr. Rosser was. The second was an expert anaesthetist and throughout most of his time at St. Woolos anaesthetics for his patients were given by Dr. Alan Phillips using up-to-date techniques of the time. And thirdly, recovery was dependent on excellent nursing which came from Sister Myris Smart who supervised McMahon Ward which had been divided into two-bed cubicles where it was routine for thoracic patients to have 'special' nursing. In fact, this ward was shared with general surgical patients under the care of Mr. Hywel Roberts whose seriously ill patients, perhaps needing ventilation, would be nursed individually if necessary. As has been mentioned elsewhere in this book, McMahon Ward often functioned as an Intensive Care Ward and was the first of its kind in Newport. This was due to the foresight and planning of Hywel Roberts.

Mr. Rosser also developed a close working liaison with Dr. Grahame Jones and Dr. Dipple from 1956 with joint clinics at The Royal Gwent and bronchoscopy sessions at St. Woolos Hospital. When Dr. Gerald Anderson was appointed in 1968 and took over much of the thoracic medicine from the Royal Gwent, these bronchoscopy sessions continued until Mr. Rosser's retirement in 1979. These examinations were undertaken with rigid bronchoscopes which needed special skills from anaesthetists to provide simultaneously a route for the instrument to pass, an airway for the patient to breathe and a live patient at the end of it all. From 1971 until Mr. Rosser's retirement, this was expertly carried out each week by Dr. Audrey Peeling who had learned this balancing act at The London Hospital as a registrar some years previously.

Open thoracic surgery ceased at St. Woolos in 1971 when the specialist units at the University Hospital and Llandough Hospital opened. Patients from Newport were therefore, transferred to Mr. Rosser in Cardiff. In the years leading up to Mr. Rosser's retirement in 1979, bronchoscopy with fibre-optic instruments under local anaesthesia arrived in Newport at St. Woolos with the appointment of Dr. Ian Petheram and is now standard practice.

Obstetric & Gynaecological Surgery
Robert Golding FRCOG, Mary Smith MB BCh & Jo Wiener FRCOG

Before 1948, practically all obstetrics was in the hands of general practitioners and mid-wives and hospital delivery was in the minority. Mr. R. Glyn Morgan was Honorary Consultant Gynaecologist at The Royal Gwent Hospital and the main obstetric unit in Newport was at Woolaston House with Mr. S. Beswick as Specialist in charge. There were only two obstetric beds at The Royal Gwent: these were in a side ward off Ward 6. In the 1950s, there was an Obstetric Unit at County Hospital, Griffithstown and there were busy G.P.-serviced units at Cefn Ila Maternity Home in Usk and Lydia Beynon Maternity Home in Newport.

In 1947, Dr. Mary Smith joined Mr. Beswick as a junior associate at Woolaston House Hospital and remained in Newport throughout her long and distinguished career in Newport until her retirement as Associate Specialist in 1987. In everything but name, her status in the hospital and community was that of a consultant and she became a pillar of the O & G Department.

Mr. Glyn Morgan retired in 1955 and was followed by Mr. J.M. Bowen. In the 1950s and early 1960s, Mr. Bowen's work took him to clinics and some operating sessions far and wide in Monmouthshire. He visited hospitals at Aberbeeg, Blaina, Blaenavon, Tredegar, The Victoria Cottage Hospital in Abergavenny, Pontypool & District Hospital, County Hospital and Monmouth Hospitals as well as overseeing The Royal Gwent, Lydia Beynon and Cefn Ila Homes. He especially enjoyed visiting Aberbeeg Hospital and the Victoria Cottage Hospital where 'the food was so good'. At the beginning of his appointment, his car had to go in reverse up some steep hills such as at Aberbeeg because of the gravity feed to the carburettor! On top of all this travelling, he was the master-mind behind the far reaching developments in gynaecology and obstetrics at The Royal Gwent in the mid-1960s leading into the following decade based upon the new building for these specialties arising from the Scheme 1 re-development of the Royal Gwent Hospital.

Mr. Arthur Williams was appointed as the second gynaecological consultant to The Royal Gwent Hospital in the early 1960s. He had trained in Oxford after a short career in engineering and carried out the first vaginal hysterectomy in Monmouthshire. He also developed a simple and safe original vaginoplasty ('The Newport Vagina') to correct post-radium problems after treatments for cancer.

In 1964, Dr. Nora Keevil retired from Lydia Beynon Maternity Home where she had been a senior resident doctor. Mr. Israel Rocker ('Rockie') came to Newport as an additional consultant at that time from Cardiff where he had been Senior Registrar. Previously he had worked at Bromley and Cambridge. In Cardiff, he established Infertility Clinics in the 1960s and carried this interest over to Newport. Mr. Rocker also instigated research in Newport into patient administered analgesics in labour and was in the team that produced the 'Stroud Report' in 1989 that stimulated debate and major improvements in obstetric and neonatal services in South Wales.

In 1966, Mr. Pat Gasson was appointed from Bristol to replace Arthur Williams who had returned to Oxford in that year.

In 1971, Pat Gasson moved to Australia and was succeeded by Mr. Gwyn Daniel from his previous post as Senior Lecturer at Cardiff Royal Infirmary. He was one of the first surgeons in Wales to take prophylactic measures against post-operative deep venous thrombosis in his patients by administering intravenous Dextran 70 during surgery. The next new appointment was in 1976 when Mr. Robert Golding followed Mr. Stan Beswick who had retired after a long and distinguished career spanning the days of Woolaston House Hospital before 1948 and the eventual transition of Obstetrics into its new home in The Royal Gwent in 1966.

Jack Bowen retired in 1980, his successor was Mr. Martin Stone who had been Senior Registrar at St. George's Hospital, London.

Israel Rocker retired in 1991 and his place was taken by Mrs. Jo Wiener and Mr. Asoka Weerakoddy. Jo Wiener has been the prime mover in several important developments. These have included 1) a Labour Ward Protocol which was a huge task that has been vital for clinical practice and medico-legal protection for all staff 2) establishment of the early pregnancy Assessment Unit 3) development of the Joint Medical Obstetric Antenatal Clinic which began as a Joint Diabetic Antenatal Clinic (p.113) with Dr. Owain Gibby 4) a training programme in ultrasound (unique in Wales) for junior staff. She also gives second opinions in ultrasound for obstetric and radiological colleagues and is now a Committee Member and Examiner of the Joint Diploma of the Royal Colleges of Obstetrics & Gyanaecology and Radiology.

Gwyn Daniel retired in 2000 and has been followed by Mrs. Rohini Gonsalves who has a special interest in colposcopy. During Gwyn Daniel's time as consultant he took a particular interest in the welfare of junior staff, especially those new to this country. This important commitment has been continued by Asoka Weerakoddy who has also developed courses for junior staff for the DRCOG and MRCOG examinations. These are highly regarded and much sought after.

Robert Golding retired in 2002; his successor is Miss Ann Wright whose special interest is obstetrics and which also includes the Joint Antenatal Clinic mentioned above *(leading up to his retirement, Robert Golding was appointed Medical Director but he now spends much time directing his yacht - Editor)*.

More recent appointments have been Robert Howells who has a subspecialty training in oncology and works part-time between The Royal Gwent and University College Hospitals, and Mrs. Leena Gokhale (appointed as an additional consultant in 2003).

In 1986, Mr. Sri Sanikop was appointed as Staff Grade specialist and proceeded later to Associate Specialists status. In 1998, Mrs. Jehan Khatib was appointed as a Staff Grade specialist.

'A Golden Age of Obstetrics'

In the 1960s, there was a 'Golden Age of Obstetrics' because of huge investments in obstetrics following the publication of the Perinatal Mortality Report by Professor Neville Butler of Bristol and the recognition of the significance of the Confidential Enquiries into Maternal Deaths by the Royal College of Obstetricians and Gynaecologists. The Royal Gwent Hospital benefited from these reports by obtaining funding to build an Obstetric & Paediatric Department which was the first scheme to be planned for the re-development of the Royal Gwent Hospital. When this opened in 1966, obstetric beds from St. Woolos Hospital were transferred into the new building. There was also an active Obstetric Unit at County Hospital, Griffithstown which provided a local service to people living in the Pontypool area.

The Abortion Act

In 1967, the Abortion Act came into being. Its introduction into clinical practice created an atmosphere which, to some, was the end of gynaecology as an attractive clinical profession. In fact, Mr. Gasson resigned in 1971 and moved to Australia because he was over-faced by the difficulties of working within the Abortion Act. While it was possible to obtain pregnancy terminations within the National Health Service in South Gwent at The Royal Gwent and County Hospitals, the only outlet for those who preferred to receive treatment on a private basis was the single private N.H.S. bed at Chepstow & District Hospital. Termination of pregnancy was not permitted at St. Joseph's Private Nursing Home in Newport and there were no other private beds for surgical treatments in the south of the County as it was the policy of the Newport & East Monmouthshire H.M.C. to oppose development of private beds within the National Health Service hospitals under its control.

Closure of Lydia Beynon Maternity Hospital

A major event for obstetric care in Newport was closure of the Lydia Beynon Maternity Hospital in 1979 (p.73). This hospital had operated as a General Practitioner Unit. Its work was moved to 'B' Block in Scheme 1 of The Royal Gwent Hospital as a G.P. Unit called the 'Coldra Unit' and was run principally by Dr. Bernard Palmer and Dr. Peter Jones to be followed a few years later by Dr. John Dodoo. Its name was taken presumably because Lydia Beynon Hospital had originally been called 'Coldra House'.

Special Services

At first, there were no sub-specialisations at a service level within the department although Mr. Rocker took up some new innovations as they came along. He carried out research into Cornual Tube anatomy and also in foetal assessment in early pregnancy. This work culminated in worldwide recognition in particular when he became one of the first to use clinical foetoscopy successfully. Foetoscopy was a 'key-hole' technique to examine the foetus while still in utero to search for developmental abnormalities, especially spina bifida, and he received invitations to contribute to national and international conferences on this topic in The United States and China. In fact, the first intra-uterine photograph of a foetus was made by Mr. Rocker in association with Mr. Nigel Pearce, Head of the Medical Illustration Department at the Royal Gwent Hospital. Further interest in this technique waned when biochemical tests for spina bifida were developed.

Colposcopy increased significantly and this service was established and run for over twenty years by Dr. Margaret Davies as an Associate Specialist in Cytology. Mr. Martin Stone raised money through his Rotary Club for a laser to be available for the Colposcopy Clinic. This was an important addition towards early detection and diagnosis of cervical cancer especially as Dr. Davies' other professional hat was her role as cytologist in the Department of Pathology.

An epidural service for obstetrics was set up with Dr. John Butler, consultant anaesthetist, in the late 1970s and the first caesarian section under epidural was carried out by Mr. Golding and Dr. Hywel Jones, consultant anaesthetist.

Ultrasound scanning for obstetrics made huge strides in the late 1970s and early 1980s largely due to Dr. A. Jones, consultant radiologist, and Mrs. Wiener. Later, when Dr. Jones moved to Cardiff, this work was taken over by Dr. Fiona Brook.

Obstetrics was the first speciality to be audited in the N.H.S., with the first National reports on Maternal Deaths in the 1950s and Perinatal Deaths in the 1960s. The departments at Nevill Hall and the Gwent led in population studies on perinatal deaths, effectiveness of screening, and recording of congenital abnormalities, the work being led and co-ordinated by Dr. M. Matharu, who produced annual reports from the early 80s. Mrs. Wiener (in addition to everything else she did!) initiated auditing the work of the department years before it became mandatory.

Outside the county, Mr. Gwyn Daniel upgraded an Antenatal and Gynaecological Clinic in the Brecon War Memorial Hospital with an operating session there. He did this for twenty-five years and this was much appreciated and praised by the local general practitioners.

Closure of Obstetrics at County Hospital

The Obstetric Unit at County Hospital, Griffithstown closed in 1989. This change in the pattern of obstetrics was driven by a decision by the Gwent Health Authority to centralise services at the Royal Gwent Hospital so that up-to-date technology would be available to all women undergoing delivery. However, there was some difference of opinion about the wisdom of this move especially among the midwives but also among the consultants. From the general public and the Trade Unions there was vociferous opposition which led to demonstrations outside the headquarters of the Gwent Health Authority which extended even to within the Board Room of the Authority during one of its meetings.

Nevertheless, the change took place and obstetric care was transferred to The Royal Gwent. The refurbished Labour Ward was opened by Mr. Rocker in 1991.

Over the next ten years progress was made towards sub-specialisation with the development of an Early Pregnancy Assessment Unit, Combined Medical and Obstetric Clinic run by Dr. Owain Gibby (consultant physician) and a Combined Vulval Clinic established by Dr. Cynthia Matthews (consultant dermatologist) and Mr. Robert Golding. As bladder problems are common gynaecological referrals, a close working relationship was created with Mr. Richard Gower (consultant urologist) to provide urodynamic facilities to assess bladder function and continence: this enables patients to be managed more appropriately than previously.

Chartermark Award

The Midwifery Unit received a much merited honour in 2002 with a Chartermark Award.

Members of the Midwifery Unit with their Chartermark Award (2002). Left to right: Enid Bowen, Susan Alderson, Linda Giles, Glenys Roberts, Maggie Davies, Gill Moss and Jenny Barrell.

(photograph Nigel Pearce, Medical Illustration R.G.H.)

Merger with Caerphilly Hospital

In May 1995, a major event occurred when the department was joined with the Obstetric and Gynaecological Department of Caerphilly Hospital. This was not an easy marriage as the agenda of the two groups of consultants did not always coincide. This merger was a pre-cursor of the eventual emergence of the Gwent Healthcare N.H.S. Trust in 1999 when the Glan Hafren, Nevill Hall, Mental Health and Community Trusts in Gwent amalgamated with addition of the hospitals in Caerphilly. One consultant described the whole process as it affected Obstetric and Gynaecological services as 'a difficult conception, a frustrating pregnancy and a painful delivery but to the parents a beautiful baby'. However, it appears that the potential of re-configuration of these services is beginning to come through as in 2002 the three O & G surgeons at Caerphilly have become an integral part of the routine and emergency service at The Royal Gwent

Hospital. These are recent replacement appointments and are Mrs. Makiya Ashraf, Mrs. Ros Goddard and Mr. Gareth Edwards.

Overview - The Changing Face of Obstetrics and Gynaecology (Gwyn Daniel FRCOG, DCH)

Obstetrics and Gynaecology has been moulded probably more than any other specialty in medical practice by the changes of social pattern that have affected this country since the Second World War.

In the 1950s and 1960s, gross pathology and life threatening emergencies abounded. Stillbirths were common, post-partum haemorrhage before the days of ergometrine killed women even in the 1960s. Hyperemesis was common (what happened to it and why?). Criminal abortion and deaths from incomplete abortion was a major problem and the Flying Squad was a feature of clinical life for obstetric and anaesthetic registrars even into the 1970s although this made a big difference to maternal mortality.

However, the Abortion Act, the arrival of the contraceptive pill, intrauterine devices as well as Women's Lib could be considered to have improved the overall health of women. Nevertheless, they might also have laid the seeds for present day problems of teenage pregnancies, an epidemic of chlamydia infection with ensuing infertility and even hepatitis and HIV - all of which can also affect children.

On the positive side, improved nutrition and iron supplements saw off anaemia but increased obesity and incipient diabetes brought on their own problems. Babies born at 24 weeks now have an evens chance of survival but there is now an increasing expectation that each baby should be perfect when born.

The rate of Caesarian Section has increased from 5% to 24% between the years 1970 and 2000 but this operation is now safer because of regional anaesthesia.

By 1980, the horrors of rhesus incompatibility had virtually gone thanks to post-delivery screening and prophylaxis. Later, screening for neural tube defects came in (of which Israel Rocker made his important contribution) and by 1990 the whole population was offered a chance to be screened for chromosomal and structural abnormalities. Counselling for 'positives' had to be provided and even more difficult was counselling those with 'negative' screening. Termination of pregnancy was unfortunately the only way forward for many cases but in some women foreknowledge of a potentially correctable abnormality allowed arrangements to be made in advance at the best paediatric surgical units. Screening for hepatitis B came in the mid-1990s (with appropriate immunisation of the newborn) and now HIV is screened improving the child's chance of escaping infection.

Options for treatment have improved with access to Intensive Care facilities (which were established in the 1970s as a result of Dr. Martin Sage's efforts).

In gynaecology severe prolapses and advanced carcinoma of the cervix have gone from being common to rare. Pulmonary embolism is now given due respect and 'prevented'. One can give some hope to women with advanced carcinoma of the ovary now, and chorion carcinoma has gone from incurable to 98% curable. There are now many alternatives to hysterectomy. Minimal access surgery and day surgery now make major contributions. 'Threatened miscarriages' has gone from days (weeks even) in hospital to nearly outpatients care.

Unfortunately, attitudes by some members of the public towards medical, midwifery and nursing staff have changed in recent years. Previously there was great respect for the work of professional staff but now it is not uncommon to have offensive disrespect and even physical abuse which has needed 'switch card' locks for wards and and employment of security staff. Litigation problems have accelerated almost to epidemic proportions which causes professional staff to adopt a defensive attitude to their practice. *(These remarks apply across the board for most specialties in the hospital and illustrate a situation that is now a fact of life - Editor)*

Ear, Nose & Throat Surgery
Marcus Brown FRCS

Before 1948

The first E.N.T. Department in Wales was established in 1891 at Cardiff Royal Infirmary by Dr. Patterson Brown, a physician with an E.N.T. interest, but little is known or recorded of the origin of the department to treat disorders of the ear, nose and throat at The Royal Gwent Hospital.

However, in 1937 the Chairman of The Newport Health Committee writing upon the health of Newport, noted that 'machinery is in operation for the ascertainment, education and general welfare of persons affected - deaf and dumb' which was possibly the beginnings of an embryonic Community Health Service. In the same year, the Newport Encyclopaedia (1937), which was compiled to celebrate the Coronation year and the Royal visit of His Majesty King George VI, lists under 'Honorary Staff' at The Royal Gwent Hospital J.A. Lee Esquire MB CM FRCS (Ed) as Consulting Surgeon to the Ear, Nose and Throat Department and D.B. Sutton Esquire MB BS (London) FRCS (Ed) DLO as Surgeon to the Ear Nose and Throat Department. The prefix 'Consulting' would have conferred seniority over his junior colleague. Nevertheless, it is evident that an active E.N.T. Department was in place at the time of handover of the hospital to The National Health Service in 1948 because both Mr. Sutton and Mr. J.L.D. Williams appear in the photograph of Honorary Staff in 1947 that features in *'The History of The Royal Gwent Hospital'*.

After 1948

In the post-war era, Mr. J.L.D. Williams MD BSc FRCS dominated E.N.T. practice being an all-round accomplished surgeon. His surgery with the scalpel was matched by his skill with the artist's brush. Several of his paintings adorn the walls of The Royal Gwent Hospital (and St. Joseph's Hospital in Malpas) and are a testimony to his artistic talents. He also obtained the degree of MD (Manchester) while a consultant which was no mean achievement. A Mr. Peter Thorpe MB FRCS worked as a colleague with J.L.D. Williams. He went to Australia where he was killed in a road accident in 1958. Mr. Gilbert Leitch joined J.L.D. Williams in 1960. In those days, the E.N.T. Department was scattered around Monmouthshire with clinics and operating sessions held throughout the county which is a far remove from present centralisation of services.

A major advance for management of deaf children was the first multi-disciplinary sensorineural clinic established by Gilbert Leitch at the Clytha Clinic in the centre of Newport. However, clinical demands continued to increase with an ever-increasing burden of E.N.T. practice in the county, so that Mr. Viswanathan FRCS (Ed.) was appointed as a third E.N.T. surgeon in 1963.

Specialisation in E.N.T.

The work pattern of the E.N.T. consultants was of a general nature but, as with other specialities, the era of specialisation in E.N.T. surgery began in 1974 with the appointment of Mr. I.T.G. Evans FRCS who had trained as a Fellow in Otology with Dr. Ted McGee in Detroit specialising in tympano-mastoid surgery. In 1978, he was joined by Mr. M.J.K.M. Brown FRCS (Ed.) FRCS who had been Fellow and Chief Resident in Head and Neck Surgery with Professor Douglas Bryce at Toronto General Hospital working particularly with head and neck cancers. Successive appointments have maintained and increased specialist interests in the department with Mr. M.I. Clayton's appointment in

1988 (otology and paediatric otolaryngology), Mr. J.M. Preece's appointment in 1996 (nasal and endoscopic sinus surgery) and Mr. D.R. Ingrams' appointment in 2000 (head and neck surgery, and thyroid) and most recently, in 2002, Mr. Ali Raza (Otology and Vestibular Disorders).

Accommodation of the E.N.T. Department

In the post-war era until 1979, the E.N.T. beds were shared with the general surgeons but with the departure of the general surgeons from wards in the Old Hospital to new accommodation in 'C Block', 40 beds became available to the E.N.T. Department in the old hospital (20 female beds in A3 East and 20 for men in A3 West). The Senior Sister for these wards was Ms. Mair Jones who supervised these wards from 1967 until her retirement in 1994. Sadly she died in December 1998. There were also eighteen paediatric beds with the majority in Ward 9. These were the halcyon days of bed availability.

Two Operating Theatres had become dedicated for E.N.T. surgery in 1967 when general surgery moved into the new theatre accommodation in the Scheme 1 development. As has been mentioned previously in this history, the facilities in these theatres were totally unsuitable for modern surgery, for there was no recovery ward and there was only natural ventilation so that on hot summer days the windows were opened wide to the outside air. The writer recalls carrying out a laryngectomy with neck dissection in the presence of sparrows flying overhead!

When the front of the old hospital was demolished in 1992, the E.N.T. Department moved to a purpose-built E.N.T. Ward of forty beds and a Treatment Room in the new 'D' Block (Ward D5 West). More recently, E.N.T. accommodation has moved to a different level in 'C' Block (C7 East) which has been purpose-built as a diagnostic and treatment unit and includes a progressive care Unit for patients with head and neck cancers. However, pressure for beds to care for medical patients has reduced the number of beds to twenty-eight and these are now shared with the Maxillo-facial and Plastic surgeons. Theatre accommodation moved to the main operating theatre complex and is fully equipped for microsurgery, endoscopic surgery and laser surgery. The paediatric beds are within the Paediatric Department on two floors according to age.

Audiology

Facilities for audiology remained basic until the appointment of Gavin Davies MSc in 1975 as the first Scientific Officer to the Department. As Principal Audiological Scientist, he has established the Hearing and Balance Unit with a staff of two Principal Audiological Scientists and twelve Medical Technical Officers which gives an audiological service based in The Royal Gwent Hospital to the whole of Gwent and The Rhymney Valley. Full cochlear and vestibular evaluation and investigations are available.

E.N.T. in 2003

The geographical distribution of the E.N.T. Department has The Royal Gwent Hospital as the core unit where all In-Patient and Day Case surgical procedures are undertaken. The Main Out-Patient Department is now housed in a new block ('E Block') built on the site of the Nurses' Home and was opened in the year 2000. The Hearing and Balance Unit is also located here. There are fully equipped consulting and treatment rooms, each with a microscope and flexible endoscopic equipment. Peripheral clinics are carried out at Nevill Hall Hospital (Abergavenny), County Hospital (Griffithstown) and Ystrad Mynach Hospital. The present catchment area for patient care is 600,000 people. Specialised clinics are multi-disciplinary based such as head and neck cancer clinics, neck lump clinics, voice clinics, paediatric assessment clinics and vestibular clinics.

The current four consultants are supported by three Specialist Registrars and four Senior House Officers.

Overview of Changes in Practice

The last fifty years in Newport have seen the emphasis in E.N.T. service move away from mastoid infection and laryngectomy to sophisticated reconstruction of the middle ear, digital hearing aids, cochlear implants and coping with the challenge of head and neck cancer with improved surgical reconstruction, voice restoration, radiotherapy and chemotherapy.

Ophthalmic Surgery
David Hughes FRCS

Sources for this brief history are current and retired colleagues, the surgical logbooks and files kept by Medical Staffing. Especial thanks go to Mr. Lewis P. Thomas ('LP') for his recollections and to Mr. Nigel Walshaw. The story prior to 1968 is patchy and relies on anecdote, but after this there are the surgical log books which were and still are kept up-to-date by nursing staff in theatres. They provide a fascinating insight to changing practice over the years.

Before 1968

It is difficult to ascertain much about eye care in Gwent prior to the 1970s. Mr. R. Coulter, honorary consultant to the Newport and Monmouthshire Hospital, was appointed in 1901. Gareth Jones in his book on Nevill Hall has copied lists of activity in Blaina Hospital where Mr. Coulter carried out 375 consultations in 1918 and 390 in 1919. A Mr. Iles saw 232 ophthalmic patients in 1936 at Ebbw Vale Hospital and 339 in 1939, he was probably a visiting surgeon but it is not certain that he was linked to Newport. Mr. F.W. Robertson ('Robbie the eye') was appointed sometime in the 1930s. He lived at 196 Stow Hill which is now the 'Longfield' private consulting rooms. He is remembered as a gregarious, generous Irishman who grew orchids, liked fishing and owned a racehorse even decorating his consulting rooms with his race colours. He evidently refracted in local opticians' shops, which apparently landed him in some trouble with the Inland Revenue. He travelled to provide an ophthalmic service in many of the hospitals in Monmouthshire. After retirement he moved to 29 Stow Park Circle, Newport.

In 1945, patients were seen in the Eye Department, which comprised a room in the Out-Patient block of the Royal Gwent Hospital.

Mr. George Hoare arrived after being demobilised in 1945. He lived at 'Holmeswood' near the Civic Centre where he also had a private practice. Later he moved his rooms to 'Longfield' and went to live near the Sugar Loaf mountain in Abergavenny. He was considered by colleagues to be a good surgeon. His N.H.S. practice was divided between the Royal Gwent and Caerphilly Miners Hospital where he had an operating session and beds. Clinics at Caerphilly ended in 1972 when the University Hospital of Wales opened and new patient referral patterns were established at Cardiff. After 1969, all the Newport consultants would almost certainly have had clinics in Nevill Hall Hospital.

It is uncertain when Mr. Vaughan Jones was appointed. He had been a doctor in the Royal Navy and lived in Cyncoed in Cardiff.

Mr. Ken Barber was appointed in 1962 and retired in 1978. He lived in Fields Park Road, Newport where he also had private rooms. During the war he had served in the Eighth Army in North Africa and it may have been through this that he developed his passion as a ham radio enthusiast. He was a chain smoker even smoking in clinics between patients. He was liked by all, but unfortunately his habit was probably the cause of his final illness.

After 1968 - Move to St. Woolos Hospital

Prior to 1967, eye surgery at the Royal Gwent Hospital had been carried out in one of the two operating theatres built at the east end of the hospital in 1916 sharing theatre time with general surgery, E.N.T. and other disciplines in what appears to have been two hour slots. When the new building for maternity services was completed on the Royal Gwent Hospital site (the 'New Hospital' in the Scheme 1 Re-development programme), the Eye Department moved to refurbished accommodation at St. Woolos Hospital in 1968 (located in Block 'F' see Pull-out Site Plan 1). This included a full Orthoptic Department with 3 consulting rooms, an operating theatre, 2 wards and an Out-Patient clinic. In 1971 there were three consultants, a Medical Assistant (Mr. G.M. Lalla), a Registrar and two Senior House Officers.

View of the Ophthamic Department at St. Woolos Hospital. The Out-Patient department and Operating Theatre was on the ground floor and the Wards were on the first and second floors.

In 1973 patients recovered from general anaesthetics in the corridor under infra red lights, and although this may sound strange, the department functioned very well. In 1974 North and South Monmouthshire Districts of the Welsh Hospital Board were amalgamated into the Gwent Area Health Authority. One of the first duties of the new Authority was to develop a Health Service Plan. Part of Scheme 6 of the 1976 plan for rebuilding The Royal Gwent was to move Ophthalmology back to the Royal Gwent site. This, in fact, took a further 25 years to accomplish.

Late in the 1970s, a blistering report following an inspection by the Royal College of Surgeons led by Mr. Cross provided the impetus for modernisation of ophthalmic services. At its peak the department had 32 beds on two wards in St. Woolos Hospital (Kingfisher and Nightingale) and 6 paediatric beds in a specially refurbished Christopher Robin ward opened by the Welsh International footballer Emlyn Hughes. A temporary Portakabin operating theatre was installed which lasted longer than intended.

Mr. Nigel Walshaw, trained in Manchester and replaced Mr. Vaughan Jones in 1973. He had sessions outside Newport in the new Nevill Hall Hospital in Abergavenny. Eye clinics had been transferred there from Blaina hospital on the 24th March 1969. Mr. Walshaw was appointed on a whole time contract, which was very onerous but not untypical of the time. It comprised two and a half operating sessions and seven and a half clinics a week with a Saturday morning ward round. Unfortunately after almost 30 years service to the hospital, he was forced to retire because of ill health, but during his time the department underwent huge changes and expansion. He now lives in Christchurch, Dorset and finds that retirement has enhanced his sailing skills.

When Mr. Hoare retired in 1976, Mr. Alec Karseras was a member of the committee to appoint his successor. Mr. Karseras represented The University of Wales for at that time he was Senior Lecturer in Ophthalmology in Cardiff. Unfortunately, the successful applicant when offered the post, declined the appointment apparently for financial reasons. The post was re-advertised and once again Mr. Karseras was nominated for the panel as University representative. In the meantime, he had decided to apply for the post himself! Obviously, another University member sat on the committee and Mr. Karseras was appointed. He retired in 2000. Previously, Mr. Hoare had carried out refractions at the War Memorial Hospital in Brecon and Mr. Karseras developed this session into an Out-Patient ophthalmology clinic where, in later years, he performed day case surgery for cataract. He lives in Whitchurch and was appointed OBE for his work with handicapped children in Cardiff.

Mr. Holt Wilson joined the staff early in 1978 as a replacement for Mr. Barber. He had been working in Kuwait. His post was largely split between Nevill Hall Hospital and the Royal Gwent. He played a leading role in developing ophthalmic services in the north of the county. He lives on a smallholding near Raglan which has been the source of many turkeys that have adorned many medical Christmas tables in and around Newport. He retired in 1999 to take up voluntary work in Ethiopia.

The appointment in mid-1978, of Mr. Yunis Khan, was the first expansion of consultant numbers in the Ophthalmic Department for many years. He had been trained in Sheffield and Birmingham and replaced Mr. Lalla, who had worked in the department as Senior Hospital Medical Officer since the 1970s and had moved on to a consultant post in Merthyr.

The number of consultants did not change for a further 20 years until David Hughes was appointed from a consultant post in East Anglia in 1997. This marked the beginning of a period of great change for the department. Not only were plans for the long awaited new building for ophthalmology well underway, but three consultants were coming up to retirement. They were replaced by Mr. Chris Blyth in 1998 who also has sessions at the University Hospital of Wales, in 2000 by Sue Webber and Mr. Des O'Duffy and in 2001 by Mr. Andrew Feyi Waboso.

Orthoptics in Gwent

The history of Orthoptics in the county is of interest. There was no hospital-based service in the early 1960s. Children with squint were treated in community clinics - those from Monmouthshire in Stanley Road, Goldtops where facilities were crude and the consulting room was divided from the waiting room by a curtain. Children from Newport Borough were seen at the Clytha Road clinic where there were cubicles for refraction. Mr. Hoare and Mr. Vaughan Jones attended these clinics on alternate weeks. Adults with squint were seen at the Royal Gwent Hospital by Mr. Robertson in small refracting cubicles. In July 1960, Mrs. Jenny Savage, who was Head Orthoptist, pioneered the first outreach clinic travelling to Tredegar each Friday by local bus with 72 stops! This process resulted in a network of community clinics and a pre-school screening programme which at its height, comprised 12 community clinics. The community orthoptic service and these clinics were transferred from the Community Paediatric Directorate to the Ophthalmology Directorate with the demise of the pre-school screening programme in 1999.

Training of Junior Doctors

The Senior House officer complement of the Ophthalmic Department increased to four in the early 1990s. By 2000, a staff grade surgeon and an associate specialist had been appointed. An unfortunate report from the training committee of the Royal College of Ophthalmologists led to the withdrawal of recognition for training registrars for a period in 1996/97. The required changes were made to the departmental timetable to improve supervision and training status was re-instated in 1997.

From 2000 - Move to The Royal Gwent Hospital

In 2000, the long-planned new building (Block 'E') was completed on the site of the old Nurses' Home previously called 'Colditz'. This was part of a refurbishment project that included a new Out-Patient clinic for E.N.T. and a new Ophthalmology department. The Ophthalmic accommodation is now housed in the upper 2 floors of 'E' Block. The facilities are a huge improvement over those at St. Woolos Hospital and consist of a day case ward, two operating theatres, nine consulting rooms and pharmacy, two treatment rooms, a minor operations theatre and an assessment suite. There is also an orthoptic department together with space for clerical staff. The ward now has eight beds and children are housed in the paediatric ward if required.

Some members of the Opthalmic Department in their new home in 'E' Block. Back row, left to right Julie Jenkins, David Hughes, Yunis Khan, Des O'Duffy, Anita Prajad, Scilla Greenland, Andrew Feyi-Waboso, Chris Blyth, Gill Williams, Pam Sage, ? Anuradha and Brigette Gadd. Seated Janice Lloyd, Jane Lessimore, Linda Passey, Elaine Lynch, Suzanne Webber, Diane Ausebrook and Mary Witchard. Kneeling Younis Masih, Regina Lepelanza, Mary Overland, Sarah Preece, Pip Mason and Helen Payne.

(photograph Andrew Ponsford)

Over the last 30 years for which there are records, there have been huge changes in ophthalmic practice. The changes in the configuration of the ophthalmic service in Newport reflect national trends. Some developments have relied on the generosity of individuals who have donated to the endowment fund enabling the purchase of equipment now considered essential, for example the first phacoemulsification machine and the digital fundus camera. The following table demonstrates some of these changes.

1960s	Move to St. Woolos Introduction of cryoextraction for intracapsular cataract removal (1968) Use of Cryoprobe for glaucoma and Diabetic retinopathy First modern retinal detachment operation (1968)
1970s	First modern glaucoma operation (trabeculectomy 1971) Modern operating microscope replaced Keeler microscope Mr. Walshaw's first operation (Cataract extraction 6/11/73) Xenon arc photocoagulator introduced for diabetic retinopathy Mr. Karseras' first operation (4 muscle squint 17/11/76) First recorded intraocular implant (Mr. Karseras, Federov implant 8/2/78)
1980s	Intraocular lens implants established Retinal photography introduced by Nigel Walshaw and Nigel Pierce Introduction of extracapsular cataract extraction by Mr. Khan
1990s	Introduction of medical audit Planning for new build on Royal Gwent site (Block 'E') First phacoemulsification operation (30/9/91) Establishment of day case cataract surgery Subspecialty clinics introduced Appointment of 2 new consultants Phacoemulsification established for cataracts with foldable lenses Assimilation of community orthoptics Development of a nurse practitioner led assessment team Daycase surgery introduced at Nevill Hall Hospital Digital retinal photography introduced Regular medical student attachments

Orthopaedic Surgery
Keith Tayton FRCS

In the early part of the 19th Century trauma services were largely managed by G.P. surgeons and if the case was complex then it was usually referred to a general surgeon with an interest in the subject. However, with no blood transfusion service available until the 1940s and only basic knowledge of blood biochemistry, the chances of surviving any injury involving multiple trauma must have been little different from the battlefields of the Somme.

During the latter part of the First World War, Sir Robert Jones was put in overall charge of the British War casualties on the Western Front and in this task he was ably assisted by a number of relatively junior officers, all of whom were destined to become very famous orthopaedic surgeons in their own right.

Shortly after the First World War ended the Government charged Sir Robert Jones with the task of organising orthopaedic services for the whole of the British Isles. He did this by dividing the country up into large areas, each of which had a single large orthopaedic centre directed, usually but not exclusively, by one of his original junior army colleagues.

The southern half of Wales, (from Aberystwyth across to Monmouth), was run from the Prince of Wales Hospital which was situated in The Walk (near Albany Road) in Cardiff and which had been originally opened by Edward Prince of Wales during the First World War, for the treatment of battle casualties who had sustained injuries to their limbs. The first and later senior orthopaedic surgeon directing the service for this extremely large parish was A.O. Parker. Whether he was able to provide a significant service for Monmouthshire in these early days is not known, but he certainly provided a service for the management of complicated congenitally dislocated hips in babies and later one for Perthe's disease.

Orthopaedics in Newport before 1948

The first orthopaedic surgeon associated with the Royal Gwent Hospital was Arthur Rocyn Jones, FRCS, but little is known about him as his main practice was at the Royal National Orthopaedic Hospital in London. Apparently he was affectionately known as Uncle Arthur and would visit Newport on an occasional basis in order to give an opinion, presumably to help out the local G.P. surgeons and general surgeons on site, with their more difficult cases.

Many years ago Mr. Keith Tayton met the senior surgeon from Oswestry Mr. Roland Hughes, who had been Arthur Rocyn Jones' House Surgeon in 1941/42 at the R.N.O.H.. On enquiring what the old man was like, he replied with a smile that 'his lists consisted of an orgy of sub-malleolar operating!' In other words, Arthur Rocyn Jones carried out a very large number of foot operations but little else.

Mr. Tayton also had one patient, now very old, who was born in Newport with complicated congenital abnormalities. She was referred from Newport to Oswestry for Sir Robert Jones' opinion on what should be done, despite the fact that Arthur Rocyn Jones was around: it is thus likely that he was not available to treat long-term problems locally.

Of course it must not be forgotten that specialised orthopaedics in those days was largely concerned with the management of poliomyelitis, rickets, tuberculosis of bone, osteomyelitis and complicated fractures, all of which needed long term treatment and which were treated mainly by G.P. surgeons and general surgeons. Elderly patients with hip fractures had not yet become the serious problem that they are today, and in any event they were largely treated on traction in the Poor Law Infirmaries (Wooloston House later St. Woolos Hospital being the one in Newport) and most would die from complications. With very few specialists available for second opinions, advice on complex orthopaedic problems was obtained via regular regional meetings. In the main however orthopaedics as we know it today did not exist.

In approximately 1935 Arthur Rocyn Jones' nephew Nathan Rocyn Jones became the first appointed orthopaedic specialist in Newport. The Rocyn Jones family had a moderate monopoly of the medical services in Gwent for Dr. Gwyn Rocyn Jones, who was Nathan's father, was the chief medical officer for Newport and East Monmouth Hospitals around that time.

Nathan Rocyn Jones was employed exclusively in South Wales but had sessions also in Cardiff and as far west as Haverfordwest. For certain, he carried out operating lists in the Prince of Wales Hospital in Cardiff and in the Royal Gwent Hospital and in the County Hospital, Panteg, Griffithstown. He carried out the orthopaedic service for

Monmouthshire, no doubt assisted to some extent by the general surgeons of the Royal Gwent Hospital, but otherwise single-handed until approximately 1953.

However, it should be remembered that the regional nature of orthopaedic referrals meant that although super-specialists were not common, access to them was possible. Via this system Dilwyn Evans in Cardiff provided a South Wales service for club feet and A.O. Parker provided the service for the management of Perthe's disease in Crossways - an old stately home in Cowbridge where the children were kept in bed for up to 3 years while being treated.

In 1938, it seems that some forward thinking governors at the Royal Gwent Hospital and in the town decided that a fracture and orthopaedic unit should be constructed at the hospital in order to anticipate the forthcoming hostilities from Germany. As a result the present F.O.U. block at the Royal Gwent Hospital was built and opened in 1943 for the treatment of fractures.

This unit was a three-floored building, with just over 50 trauma beds on the first floor. On the ground floor was a combined Out-Patient and operating theatre suite. Staff Nurse Glenys Boddy who worked in this trauma theatre in its latter days recalls that fracture clinics took place on a daily basis in the Out-Patients area of the suite. On Mondays, Wednesdays and Fridays the operating theatre also functioned and 'fracture cases' were brought past patients sitting in Out-Patients to the theatre where they received their operations before being taken back through the Out-Patients to the ward.

Normally, the theatre would cease operating early in the evening but would be available for treatment of major injuries after this time, when it would be staffed by Nurses from casualty. Similarly, in the evenings after 8.00 p.m. 'walking wounded fracture cases' would be treated in the trauma theatre by casualty staff.

This theatre remained the main orthopaedic and trauma theatre until the early 1970s when it was superseded by the present one in the new hospital. The old theatre was subsequently turned into an Out-Patients clinic, which it remains to this day.

Orthopaedics in Newport after 1948

After the Second World War the Prince of Wales Orthopaedic Hospital in Cardiff was moved from The Walk to a temporary war hospital, which had been constructed at Rhydlafar just north of the city. Nathan Rocyn Jones moved his elective orthopaedic practice to this new site along with his other South Wales colleagues. The buildings were all temporary war-time constructions and apparently on the orders of Aneurin Bevan himself they were dismantled and the brick-built huts which lasted until quite recently were put up on the old concrete foundations. These were finally demolished when the Prince of Wales Hospital closed and was replaced by a housing development in 1997.

i) 1953 to 1983

With the advent of the N.H.S. the orthopaedic service in Gwent began to expand. In 1953 T.C. Howard Davies, FRCS, was appointed to the Newport and East Monmouth Hospital Management Group, as the second specialist orthopaedic surgeon. He was a charming, enthusiastic and friendly man, and for his day was a very well trained and skilful surgeon who was given a solid grounding to his art in Montgomery's 8th Army during the Second World War. He was appointed as a general orthopaedic surgeon for the whole of the county of Monmouthshire and on the day of his appointment he found he was on the staff of eleven separate hospitals - these were the Royal Gwent Hospital, St. Woolos Hospital, Chepstow Cottage Hospital, St. Lawrence Hospital, County Hospital, Griffithstown, Tredegar Hospital, Blaina Hospital, Ebbw Vale Hospital, Nevill Hall Hospital, Abergavenny, Monmouth Hospital, and the Prince of Wales Hospital in

Rhydlafar, Cardiff. In the early days he used to travel to all of these hospitals looking at the various patients, which the G.P. surgeons and the G.P.s of those days, often would have been managing without extra assistance.

Sometimes the management of various problems was a little unusual and Howard Davies later recalled of his visits to Ebbw Vale Hospital, (which is now a rehabilitation unit), where he used to carry out pin and plate operations on fractured necks of femurs. If there were no radiographers available, the chief porter used to take the X-Rays for him and obtained very rapid pictures by over exposing the patient with X-Rays and then under-developing the films!

At some stage during the early 1950s St. Lawrence Hospital, Chepstow, which had been set up as a regional plastic surgery unit, opened up two wards for elective orthopaedic surgery, (numbering about 50 beds in all) and about half a ward for paediatric orthopaedic surgery. From that time on, the elective orthopaedic surgery of Gwent was split between St. Lawrence Hospital in Chepstow, and the Prince of Wales Hospital, Rhydlafar, in Cardiff.

Orthopaedics was now changing dramatically, tuberculosis, rickets and poliomyelitis having largely gone. (The last epidemic of polio in Gwent occurred about 1958 and was managed by Howard Davies admitting most of the patients to Tredegar Hospital for isolation - there were 25 or so cases). The population was healthier and the patients began to get older. Nevertheless, during this period arthritic problems were still largely managed conservatively, with physiotherapy, walking aids and anti-inflammatory drugs. Operations for arthritis were carried out, but not in the vast numbers that we see today and in the case of hips and knees consisted of arthrodesis, osteotomy and pseudarthrosis procedures.

Howard Davies' principal sub-speciality was spinal surgery, and in particular, scoliosis surgery in children, which he carried out for South Wales almost single-handedly for about 30 years in Cardiff. During this time he fused around 1200 adolescent spines by the classic post Second World War technique of jacking out the spine straight in a Risser type plaster jacket using turn buckles and then fusing the spine through a window cut in the jacket and keeping the child in bed for the next 6-7 months while the fusion took place. This process required almost a whole ward in Rhydlafa to be dedicated to the spinal children and a school was set up which inevitably had to take them up to O Level G.C.E. standard. The exams were taken in Rhydlafa during the 50s, 60s and 70s.

Nathan Rocyn Jones retired in approximately 1966 and he was replaced by Hilton Harrop-Griffiths, FRCS, a Mancunian with Welsh connections who had already been appointed as a Consultant in Hull but wished to come back to Wales to be near his wife's family. Hilton Harrop-Griffiths was a quiet man with a very dry sense of humour who was famous for saying very little to his patients. However, he was a very accomplished surgeon and was renowned for operating through very small incisions.

During the 1950s John Charnley in Manchester developed what was probably the greatest medical breakthrough of the Twentieth Century, in that, he solved the problem of reliably replacing joints and obtaining fixation of the plastic and metals to bone. The first total hip replacement in South Wales was carried out in approximately 1971 in the Prince of Wales Hospital, Rhydlafar, Cardiff, by Howard Davies from Newport. He used to recount that the operation was not without its problems and that the depth of the acetabulum was far greater than the plastic cup which he had available to put in. With typical ingenuity he took the head of the femur, which he had just excised from the patient and packed it into the base of the acetabulum as a bone graft before cementing the plastic cup on top of it. This is now a well recognised technique for revision surgery, but in 1971 had to be thought of on the spot without any advice from other experienced surgeons to ask whether it could be done or whether it would work. A first from a Newport surgeon.

Mr. Howard Davies, Sr. Margaret Parkin and Mr. Raj Dutta.

(photograph courtesy of Margaret Parkin)

Approximately 1971, a third surgeon was appointed to the Royal Gwent Hospital, Raj K. Dutta, FRCS, a Burmese Surgeon who had come to the UK in the late 1950s and trained in London, Birmingham and latterly Cardiff. His appointment marked the next leap forward in orthopaedics, in that he introduced modern fracture fixation techniques in the form of plates, screws and intra-medullary nails, against it must be said considerable conservative opposition from the resident surgeons. Like Hilton Harrop-Griffiths and Howard Davies, Raj Dutta also had sessions at the Prince of Wales Hospital in Cardiff and at St. Lawrence Hospital in Chepstow, and carried out an operating list a week in each. Although Hilton Harrop-Griffiths having inherited Rocyn Jones' sessions at Cardiff still ran an Out-Patient clinic there and Howard Davies ran a scoliosis clinic in Rhydlafar Hospital, Raj Dutta's Out-Patient sessions were limited to R.G.H. in Newport with one clinic and one operating list also in Nevill Hall Hospital, Abergavenny. However, the Abergavenny commitment became difficult to keep up, so that Peris Edwards, FRCS, was appointed there as a single-handed specialist surgeon, and Raj Dutta gradually dropped his commitment in that hospital.

Raj Dutta was the first of the modern trained orthopaedic surgeons and brought a technical expertise to total joint replacement, which his colleagues had had to learn by trial and error. In his later years he studied the techniques of arthroscopy of the knee joint and attended many courses in order to acquire a reasonably high skill at this particular technique.

By the early 1980s the body of the new Royal Gwent Hospital which had been under construction for some years and which Howard Davies had been promised would be his to occupy in the late 1950s was nearing completion. Unfortunately, Howard Davies only just worked long enough to move into the new building before he retired on 1st January 1983, having previously supervised the closure of the orthopaedic unit in St. Lawrence Hospital, Chepstow, which then reverted to a whole time plastic surgery unit.

ii) Subspecialisation of Orthopaedics in Newport

Howard Davies was replaced by Keith Tayton, FRCS, a Royal Free Hospital trained surgeon who had completed his training in Cardiff and had been senior lecturer/

consultant in the Professorial Unit there for the previous 4 years. He was the first orthopaedic surgeon appointed exclusively to South Gwent, without commitments in Cardiff.

On appointment on 1st January 1983 he was charged with the task of bringing the orthopaedic services of South Gwent right up-to-date, and this he undertook with enthusiasm and considerable assistance from the management, the nursing staff and his orthopaedic colleagues.

The traditional style operating theatres in the 'new part' (Scheme 1) of the Royal Gwent Hospital were soon drastically altered to provide vertical down flow air systems to ensure maximum sterility during total joint replacements. The rehabilitation wards in Panteg Hospital, which for many years had simply been overflow wards for the Royal Gwent Hospital, were turned into post-operative ortho-geriatric rehabilitation wards and an orthopaedic clinic was set up in Chepstow.

Keith Tayton started and ran the paediatric orthopaedic service for over 20 years developing specialist children's clinics and operating lists at the Royal Gwent Hospital in order to provide a good local service for club feet, congenital dislocation of the hips, leg length discrepancies, etc. He began the regular teaching for registrars and S.H.O.s and with this approach a determined effort was made to attract high quality juniors on a regular basis.

The Out-Patient clinic in Pontypool and District Hospital was gradually run down over the next few years and when that hospital finally closed it was transferred to the County Hospital, Griffithstown, where orthopaedic operating lists persisted into the late 1980s.

Keith Tayton pressed hard for an increase in the complement of orthopaedic surgeons and in 1985 Witek Mintowt-Czyz, FRCS, another London trained Surgeon was appointed. His training included a spell in the army and latterly in Cardiff. Witek Mintowt-Czyz brought specialised techniques in arthroscopy with him and to this day provides a service of major knee surgery via the arthroscope and especially the reconstruction of major knee ligament complexes. This was yet another example of the use of keyhole surgery resulting from fibre optic technology replacing open surgery. His appointment greatly enhanced the teaching available to the junior surgical staff.

In 1988 Hilton Harrop-Griffiths retired with his wife to a small sheep farm which he had inherited in West Wales where he lives out his retirement into the early 21st Century.

Hilton Harrop-Griffiths was replaced by D. Gregory Jones, FRCS MRCP, a Cardiff trained surgeon who had spent some time in the Royal Navy before completing his training in Cardiff. He brought spinal surgery as a speciality to Newport, and in particular the techniques of excising vertebral bodies and replacing them with bone grafts in order to clear secondary carcinomas. He organised the spinal service and linked it with pain clinics which had the convenient effect of removing back and neck problems from other orthopaedic clinics but with the foreseeable effect that G.P.s could unload all of their problem cases onto the hospital service.

With the waiting lists swamping the National Health Service's ability to cope with patients rapidly, now becoming apparent, further increases in consultant staff were sought and granted. In 1990 Robert Savage FRCS, yet another London surgeon who completed his training in Cardiff was appointed as an orthopaedic consultant specialising in hand surgery, a service which complemented the one previously being provided by the plastic surgeons, but which was destined to move with them to Swansea in a year or two.

Further consultant appointments followed with Andrew Grant, FRCS, a Cardiff trained orthopaedic surgeon specialising in back surgery and who brought much needed extra assistance to the service being provided by Greg Jones. Soon after in 1996 Phillip Alderman, FRCS, who trained in Bristol initially and then in Cardiff, and who specialised in total joint replacement, particularly their revision, was appointed and his service was soon complemented by Paul Roberts, FRCS, a Birmingham trained surgeon who also specialised in this type of surgery. In 1998 the need for a specialist foot surgeon was identified and Kartik Hariharan, FRCS, a surgeon trained in Madras, and latterly in Cardiff, was head hunted from his post in the Prince Charles Hospital Merthyr Tydfil and recruited to the Gwent. His appointment brought the solving of problems in adult feet up to modern standards and added formal links with the diabetic department for the management of diabetic feet.

Also, in the late 1990s Dr. Simon Hannaford-Youngs, MRCP, trained in London and later in Bedford was appointed as a consultant orthopaedic physician to complement and later replace the service provided by Dr. John Merrick, MBBS, a local G.P., who had been providing a back and neck manipulation service since the early 1970s.

Finally, in 2001 Rohit Kulkarni, FRCS, a surgeon initially trained in Manipal, South West India and latterly in Cardiff, was appointed as an orthopaedic surgeon specialising in shoulder and elbow surgery.

As can be seen from the resumé above, the orthopaedic and trauma services from Newport have progressively and dramatically been up-dated from very humble beginnings at the turn of the twentieth century when it was largely provided by G.P. surgeons to the inter-war period when the first specialist orthopaedic surgeon was appointed to provide a consultancy service for problem cases which the local G.P.s and local general surgeons could not handle. From the early 1960s the service has gradually improved with the appointment of each consultant up to the present day when it has really come of age covering a full range of sub-specialties within the overall umbrella of traumatic and orthopaedic surgery.

Academic Opportunities and Staff Training

Academic opportunities began to open up seriously in the 1980s particularly with the new training systems for Registrars and S.H.O.s Publications in reputable journals began to appear from the Royal Gwent Hospital on a yearly basis and Keith Tayton was invited to give a lecture to the Royal Society of Medicine in 1998 on 'Isoelastic hip replacements'.

The number of junior doctors increased from two Registrars and three S.H.O.s in the 1970s to eight SpR's, one Fellow, three Staff Grades and nine S.H.O.s by 2003 and the number of nursing supportive administrative staff has similarly increased.

Overview of Orthopaedics Services in 2003

The present orthopaedic teams in Newport are able to offer a service equal to the best in the United Kingdom, the only procedures unavailable locally being the management of bone tumours, which are treated nationally in Birmingham, London and Edinburgh, scoliosis surgery which is treated regionally in our local centre in Cardiff and high risk paediatric procedures where a paediatric intensive care service is required, and this again is available in Cardiff and Bristol.

Unfortunately, as the population grows in size, and ages considerably, the load on the trauma and orthopaedic service increases drastically year by year and it is quite clear that the present elective service which has expanded so dramatically over the last 30 years is likely to contract equally dramatically, as the available beds become filled progressively with psycho-social geriatric problems suffering moderate to major fractures. Unless this problem is faced firmly by our political masters then, with the exception of children it is likely that the provision of elective orthopaedics will move exclusively into the private sector and the National Health Service will be providing a trauma service only when the next chapter of the history of the Royal Gwent Hospital is written. In another 40 years time it would be interesting to see if the editor of those days has to reflect rather ruefully on the accuracy of these predictions which could be sorted out now by imaginative and far-sighted politicians, but alas will be totally insoluble by then.

Oral & Maxillofacial Surgery
Max Gregory BChD FDSRCS
and John Llewelyn BDS MBChB FDSRCS FRCS

Although there were two Dental Surgeons, Messrs Desmond J. Dalton and Partridge Jackson, listed as members of the Honorary Staff of The Royal Gwent Hospital before 1948, there is no information or records of the work of the Dental Department for some time after 1948. Presumably, these gentlemen worked as general dental practitioners to the hospital after 1948 in addition their own dental practices in the town. There is no information about Mr. Jackson but some retired consultants remember Mr. Dalton in the hospital in the late 1960s which is, presumably, about the time that he retired from the hospital.

Mr J.R.V.B. (John) Gibson was appointed in the 1950s as a Consultant Dental Surgeon to the Plastic Unit which was based at Gloucester. This unit subsequently split to form the plastic surgery units based at St. Lawrence Hospital, Chepstow and Frenchay Hospital Bristol. Mr. Gibson was based at St. Lawrence Hospital with sessions in The Royal Gwent Hospital, Newport and emerging Dental Hospital in Cardiff. His commitment at The Royal Gwent was for two sessions, one theatre and one clinic session. In the early days, Mr. Gibson provided the only Oral surgery Service in South Wales. He retired in 1985 and will be remembered by all who knew him as a true gentleman, always courteous and never too busy to enquire with interest about the hospital especially from younger members of staff.

In 1976, Mr. Alan Quayle was appointed as the first Consultant Oral Surgeon to the South Gwent District. It had been intended by management that Mr. Quayle would develop a specialty unit of Oral Surgery but no support came for him and he worked from one room in the Out-Patients Department which was shared with the paediatricians (see p.131). He resigned after two years and moved to Manchester as Senior Lecturer. However, he felt so strongly about the absence of administrative support and lack of clinical facilities that he had experienced while in Newport that he wrote a critical report to the Royal College of Surgeons. Their response to management was sufficiently robust that a suite of three rooms in the 'New Hospital' (later to be re-assigned as 'B' Block) were designated for Oral Surgery.

Mr. Max Gregory was appointed in 1978 to follow Mr. Quayle in the development of the service in Gwent. He had qualified in Dental Surgery at The University of Leeds in 1967 and had trained for four years as Senior Registrar in Oral and Maxillofacial Surgery at St. Lawrence Hospital and The University Hospital of Wales. On appointment, his work plan as a consultant was modified to include clinical sessions at St. Lawrence Hospital with a teaching link established with the Dental Hospital in Cardiff.

The work of the department quickly expanded. Two theatre lists were inherited at The Royal Gwent Hospital, there was one theatre session at St. Lawrence Hospital and a weekly day case list at Nevill Hall Hospital, Abergavenny in addition to clinic sessions. The appropriate secretarial and (eventually) nurse infrastructure slowly came about and two Senior House Officers were created to support the consultant.

The need for a specialist Orthodontic Service was quickly evident and in March 1980, Mr. Simon Wigglesworth was appointed as the first consultant in this specialty in Gwent. He graduated from Newcastle University in 1972 and subsequently joined the staff of The Eastman Dental Hospital for postgraduate orthodontic training. When appointed in Gwent, he set up consultant orthodontic clinics at The Royal Gwent, Nevill Hall and St. Lawrence Hospitals. It was not long before joint clinics for orthodontic and surgical treatment of appropriate problems were established. Today, the department is very active with five orthodontic Specialist Registrars on rotation with The Dental Hospital, Cardiff.

In 1995, the regional plastic surgery unit at St. Lawrence Hospital was transferred to Morriston Hospital, Swansea and the hospital was closed. Therefore, the work of the Maxillofacial Department previously carried out at St. Lawrence Hospital had to be transferred to The Royal Gwent Hospital. To cope with this very considerable workload, an enlarged department was built alongside the ground floor of 'B' Block and this unit was opened in July 1995. It consists of two dedicated Day Case Theatres with a Recovery Ward and an Admission Ward, a separate Oral and Maxillofacial clinic and consultation suite, and three Orthodontic Rooms (for location see Pull-out Plan 2 - Site 'Oral').

The increased workload required an additional consultant and it was decided to appoint someone with a specialist interest in oro-facial cancer. Mr. John Llewellyn was appointed and took up his post in January 1995. He had graduated in Dental Surgery from The University of Wales in 1975 with a further qualification in Medicine from The Royal Free Hospital in 1986. Mr. Llewellyn is an Examiner for the new Collegiate examinations in this specialty.

Overview. This specialty has gone a long way since the early days of the hospital in the N.H.S. especially since the late 1970s. In Newport, there is now a department that provides a full range of Maxillofacial and Oral Surgery for Gwent. The consultants are supported by an Associate Specialist, Mr. Sirikumara and a Staff Grade Specialist Surgeon, Mr. M. Murphy. There are currently six Senior House Officers and one Specialist Registrar on rotation with Cardiff. The Orthodontic Department continues to grow to meet increasing clinical demand and is now a major training centre for Orthodontic Specialist Registrars.

Chapter 9: Other Specialties

Accident & Emergency Services
Bill Morgan FRCS, Francis Richardson FRCS, A.R. Vaghela FRCS & Mrs. Caryl Jones [1]

[1] Mrs. Caryl Jones is the daughter of Mr. Vernon Jones

In the original hospital of 1901, a Casualty Unit was established, adjacent to the Operating Theatre at the east end of the building on the ground floor (ref. p.11). Presumably, these two units worked together when necessary. In 1916, the Casualty Unit was greatly improved and extended as part of a new three floor block attached to the east end the hospital. As this new development included two operating theatres on the top floor, the original theatre on the ground floor became dedicated as a Casualty Theatre. (ref. p.26/2) This arrangement continued for the next forty-five years.

There is no record of medical cover for the casualty service at The Royal Gwent Hospital in those days but Mr. Lewis Thomas, who was Resident Surgical Officer at that time, recalls that the establishment to cover casualty calls was the following:

Resident Surgical Officer	1
Resident Medical Officer	1
Resident Orthopaedic Officer	1
Resident House Officers	4 (surgical 2: medical 2)

Junior House Officer (at night) aided by house surgeons
House surgeons gave the anaesthetics

Mr. R. Vernon Jones became Surgeon-in-Charge in about 1952. He had trained in Cardiff and had qualified about 1940 and obtained a position at The Royal Gwent Hospital along with several other student colleagues who later became consultants at the hospital - such as Messrs J.M. Bowen, R.D. Richards and Dr. Chris Griffiths who became a well respected general practitioner in Newport. He married a Royal Gwent nurse in 1941, was called up into the Royal Navy and served on a ship in the Mediterranean. He was due to sail back from Naples but was confined to shore because he had contracted either measles or chicken pox. His ship was torpedoed with hardly any survivors.

On return to The Royal Gwent, Vernon Jones became Registrar to Mr. Bowker with ambitions to specialise in neurosurgery. He decided to specialise as a Casualty Surgeon at The Royal Gwent. His initial grade was as Senior Hospital Medical Officer (S.H.M.O.) but it was not long before he was re-designated as Consultant-in-Charge.

It was Vernon Jones who masterminded a purpose-built and up-to-date Casualty Unit which opened in 1962. This department was located adjacent to the site of the old casualty unit and was a pre-fabricated single-floor building (ref. p.26/A). The unit included a resuscitation suite with direct access from the ambulance park, a plaster room, a fracture unit, several examination rooms, waiting areas for relatives and offices for consultant and secretary.

In the early 1970s, a Short-Stay Unit was added for twenty-four-hour observation of patients with head injuries, abdominal pain and renal colic and other problems for observation which created much needed relief to In-Patient wards that could rapidly become overloaded by emergencies. This was located in the area between the eastern block of the hospital and the central block containing the Board Room (ref. p.26/B). It was under the administrative care of Mr. Jones but staff from the clinical firm responsible for admission were expected to clear the bed the following morning either by admission to an In-Patient bed or by discharge home for Out-Patient follow-up if indicated.

Vernon Jones developed a Major Incident Team that was called upon to attend several major incidents including a coach crash on the new Severn Bridge carrying Tesco employees on a night out. However, its activities could be difficult to coordinate and control as occurred on another occasion, this time as a Sunday morning Major Incident Exercise, a practice incident that occurred in the Severn Tunnel. The various teams from the hospital, the emergency services, the police and elsewhere were deployed at Bronze to Silver and to Gold levels at the exit from the Severn Tunnel awaiting 'casualties' from within the tunnel. The first snag occurred when it was discovered that the driver of the engine for the rescue coaches was not registered to drive on the main line so a suitably qualified driver had to be rushed from Cardiff to take his place. The second snag was the delay of several hours before the train carrying the 'casualties' emerged from the tunnel: this had been to allow a delayed Secretary of State to descend down a service shaft to reach the incident area for an inspection. However, the 'casualties', with one exception, were remarkably cheerful after their prolonged period under the River Severn and it was rumoured that the bar in the Buffet Car had mysteriously failed to close. The exception was a most belligerent lady who exasperated the Triage Surgeon with her demands and complaints of delay. However, she became very thoughtful when he informed her that unfortunately the nearest hospital for her treatment was Aberdeen. Then there was the unconscious man whose eyes suddenly opened, said in a clear whisper 'head injury', and then relapsed back into his official coma. Most people on parade for this, including the Chief of Police, viewed the occasion as a muted success as most had missed their Sunday lunch *(Editor's recollections of the event)*.

Vernon Jones retired in 1980 after long and loyal service to The Royal Gwent Hospital and was a highly respected colleague and friend to medical staff and to his nurses.

Vernon Jones' retirement party. Back row, left to right: Vernon Jones, Pauline Whiting N.A., Thora Davies, Barbara Harris S.E.N., Joan Bonsay (Domestic), Hilda Matthews N.A.. Front row: Winnie Payne, Hazel Taylor, Daisy Ford and Gill Piper.

(photograph courtesy of Mrs. Caryl Jones)

He was succeeded by Mr. W.J. ('Bill') Morgan who converted to a part-time contract in 1995 and retired in 2002. A second consultant, Mr. G. McCarthy was appointed in 1995 and was joined by Mr. F.J. Richardson in 1996. A fourth consultant, Mr. G. Quinn was appointed in 1999 but in 2002 both Mr. McCarthy and Mr. Quinn returned to their native Ireland so that the current consultant establishment in the Accident Unit is - Messrs. F.J. Richardson, S. Jones, A.R. Vaghela with Dr. S. Jones and Miss A. Palmer who have been Associate Specialists since 1996.

The Casualty Unit that Vernon Jones had developed ended its days when the new Accident & Emergency Department in Scheme 6 of the hospital's re-development opened in 1990.

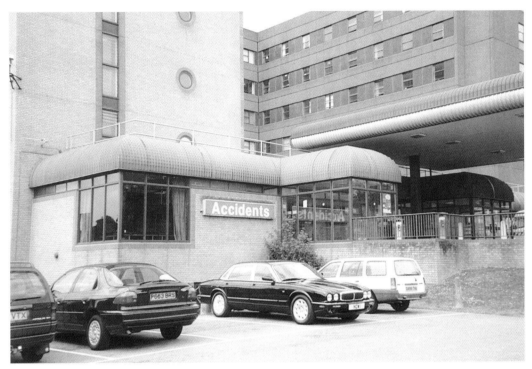

The entrance to the new Accident & Emergency Unit in 'D' Block (1990).
(photograph courtesy of Cliff Knight)

Vernon Jones' daughter, Mrs. Caryl Jones, recalls his great pleasure at the arrival of this 'state of the art department' together with a short-stay unit but his one complaint had always been that, as a Casualty Surgeon, he had never been able to follow his patients through their hospital stay for they arrived in Casualty, were 'put together' and then went 'upstairs'. It has never been established what he meant by 'upstairs'.

Accident & Emergency Medicine as a Speciality

Before 1980, the Accident Unit had no specialist staff and its staffing structure was similar to other units in District Hospitals of the U.K.. The total staffing was one consultant and eight Senior House Officers. The work of the unit was therefore, carried out by non-specialist trained junior doctors. However, in 1982, the Accident Unit at The Royal Gwent Hospital was recognised for Senior Registrar training in this specialty and was the first District Hospital in The United Kingdom to achieve this status. In 1997, this post converted into a Specialist Registrar Training appointment to be in accordance with similar changes that had taken place in other specialties. This grade had been introduced in 1975 in this country specifically to train doctors in Accident and Emergency care. Also, a new Staff Grade level was introduced in the mid-1980s to give experienced day-to-day care in Accident Units. It was not until 1994 that Staff Grade appointments started in Newport. The grade of Associated Specialist in the Accident Unit was started in Newport in 1993.

Accident & Emergency Unit in 2004

The Staffing complement of the Unit in 2004 is therefore:

Consultants	3	Nursing Staff (W.T.E.)	76
Associate Specialist	1	Sisters H. grad.	2
Staff Grades	4	I Grade	1
Specialist Registrars (SpR)	5	G Grade	4
Clinical Fellows	3	Senior Clinical Nurse Manager	1
Senior House Officers	10	Departmental Manager	1

Students from the University of Wales College of Medicine join the A. & E. department on a regular basis as part of their medical training.

There is also a dedicated Radiology service with two X-Ray rooms in the department and a 24 hour service.

In common with other departments in the hospital , its workload has doubled in ten years from 40,000 casualties in 1991 to about 80,000 currently. Of these, about 25% have been children. Therefore, creation of a Children's Assessment Unit attached to the A. & E. Department has been a visionary development which includes a Play Area and cubicles for examination and treatment (ref. p.132).

In the Resuscitation Area, there are three Trolley Bays. Most thrombolysis (clot-busting drug treatment) is started here. In the general part of the Unit there are twelve Trolley Bays, a Plaster Room, Treatment rooms and an Operating Theatre.

There is a Short-Stay Unit consisting of nine beds with clinical control by the A. & E. staff: these beds are provided for patients admitted with problems such as drug overdosage and head injuries.

Anaesthetics & Pain Relief
Gwyn Thomas FRCA

There is no doubt that the arrival of the National Health Service in 1948 produced the biggest change in the practice and organisation of general anaesthesia in the United Kingdom since its inception one hundred years previously. For the first time, anaesthesia was recognised as a specialty in its own right to be staffed by appropriately trained and accredited practitioners. The training period would be supplemented by suitable examinations after which a practitioner could be suitable to apply for one of the new consultant posts that were being created. Anaesthetists who were already working full-time in anaesthesia at accredited hospitals with a good record of competence and skill were accepted as consultants in the new regime. In Newport, during the next fifty-five years, these changes have continued so that the shape and scope of anaesthetics as a specialty in its hospitals has kept pace with trends throughout the country and offer a modern comprehensive service as the twenty-first century begins.

After 1948

In 1948, at the time of transition to the National Health Service, there were eight anaesthetists who were honorary members of Staff of The Royal Gwent Hospital and two of these, Dr. Harvey Nicholl and Dr. K.A. Thom had previously been appointed as

Consultant Anaesthetists. Theirs was, therefore, the important task of initiating an anaesthetic service under the new system. Of the remaining anaesthetists, Dr. Lister Wilson increasingly specialised and eventually was appointed as a consultant, while two of the part-time general practitioners, Dr. P.W. Martin and Dr. S. Rosehill, continued their anaesthetic sessions at St. Woolos Hospital until the mid 1970s.

In 1955, the first Consultant Anaesthetist to be appointed to Newport with a teaching hospital training was Dr. D. Glyn Davies who had qualified and trained at Guy's Hospital, London. He was closely followed by J.W. ('Johnny') Thomas who had previously seen service with the R.A.M.C. in the Eastern Mediterranean and trained at Cardiff Royal Infirmary. Dr. Thomas retired in 1985 and is well remembered for his infectious good humour. In 1959, Dr. Alan H. Phillips was appointed from the Cardiff training programme; a major part of his work initially was to anaesthetise patients undergoing thoracic surgery at St. Woolos Hospital under the care of Mr. Tom Rosser and he subsequently became involved in many initiatives including setting up the intensive care unit in the mid sixties.

Dr. Audrey Peeling was appointed in 1971. She had received her initial training in anaesthesia at The London Hospital but for family reasons had withdrawn temporarily from formal training until 1970 when she was appointed senior registrar at The Royal Gwent Hospital. Dr. Lister Wilson retired in the late 1970s: at the time of retirement he still maintained a few patients in his general practice which went back to the pre-N.H.S. days.

After a lengthy period of serious illness, Dr. Glyn Davies resigned as a consultant anaesthetist in 1971, and was replaced by Dr. David O. Jones in 1972. He had re-trained in anaesthesia from general practice having worked in Aberfan at the time of the waste tip disaster and was senior registrar at Swansea and Cardiff prior to his appointment in Newport.

Since those years, the Anaesthetic Department in Newport has expanded considerably in its expertise but particularly with regard to Critical Care, Pain Relief in its various aspects and in its well-recognised reputation for post-graduate education.

Intensive Care Cover at The Royal Gwent:

The 1960s saw rapid progress in surgery and anaesthetics and as more complex operations became available for conditions previously thought to be untreatable, many more poor risk patients were being presented to anaesthetists.

It became appreciated that to ensure good survival rates, post-operative care on general wards was inadequate. To overcome this, it was considered a matter of urgency to set up an Intensive Care Unit and the foundation for this was laid by Mr. L.P. Thomas, Mr. Vernon Jones and Dr. A.H. Phillips. A high nurse-patient ratio was considered the basic necessity together with up-to-date equipment for respiratory and cardio-vascular monitoring and support within a dedicated unit for seriously ill patients. As time went on, the Anaesthetic Department assumed an increasingly central role although for some time the primary responsibility for care of these patients rested with the consultant surgeons who had carried out the surgery. Consequently, although surgeons initially retained overall control of their patients, in time anaesthetists became responsible for this ward.

It is interesting to record that the special needs of post-operative thoracic cases at St. Woolos Hospital had prompted re-design of McMahon Ward in that hospital in the early 1960s, under the initiative of Mr. Hywel G. Roberts, to convert the unit into six two-bedded cubicles. Here patients could receive 'special' nursing on a one-to-one basis if necessary with ventilation if required to ensure respiratory adequacy. Ventilation was supervised by the anaesthetist who would be available on-call, and while this arrangement fell short of modern standards of intensive care, it was a visionary situation that served the hospital well until an Intensive Care Unit was established at The Royal Gwent Hospital.

Since its early days, the Intensive Care Unit at The Royal Gwent Hospital has become an extremely busy department involving specialist consultants, registrars and nurses under the direction of a Consultant Anaesthetist, presently Dr. S.W. Dumont. However, its capacity has always been inadequate despite many pleas for more accommodation to be created to cope with an increasing demand from clinicians for its services.

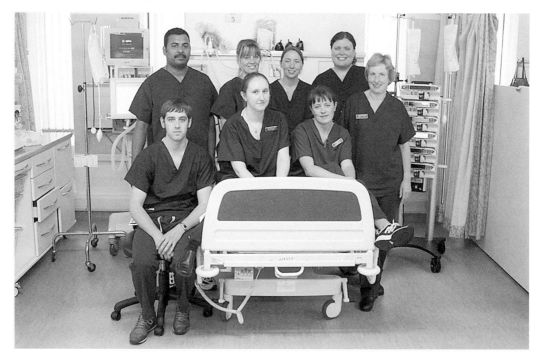

Intensive Care Unit (2004) and some members of staff. Back row, left to right Bino Mathew, Tracey May, Una Cronin, Emma Eccleston. Front row Paul Taylor, Caroline Patton, Alison Kirton and Jane Reynolds.

(photograph Andrew Ponsford)

Regional Anaesthesia:

In the mid-1970s, there was a return of interest in regional anaesthesia. Intrathecal and epidural anaesthesia was originally seen as a way of avoiding some of the unwanted side effects of general anaesthesia especially in poor risk patients. As their use increased, it became apparent that these techniques had other benefits and in the Urological Department at St. Woolos, for instance, regional anaesthesia became the method of choice for many procedures.

At the same time, the benefits of epidural analgesia for relief of pain in childbirth was becoming appreciated as was its use, together with intrathecal anaesthesia for interventional procedures such as caesarian section. In Newport, this developed over the years until a fully staffed anaesthetic obstetric service was established that gives a first class service at the hospital.

Regional Anaesthesia and local analgesia are now used routinely in all surgical specialties and all trainee anaesthetists are fully trained in their use.

It is true to say that these techniques have revolutionised many of the technical aspects of surgery and obstetrics in Newport and, for patients, have reduced the fear of operations of which, to many, a general anaesthetic was the most feared.

Pain Relief Services:

As a spin-off from the interest and expertise gained in regional anaesthetic techniques, anaesthetists became increasingly involved in pain relief outside the confines of operating theatres. At St. Woolos Hospital, Dr. Gwyn Thomas had increasing numbers of patients referred for alleviation of persistent pain, many from advanced spinal cancer, so that a clinic was set up in 1979 originally based in McMahon Ward Recovery Unit (re-named 'The Hywel Roberts Ward' in 1981 in honour of Hywel Roberts after his retirement). As often happens when a new facility is offered, demand for this clinic rapidly increased so that in 1984 a new purpose-designed Newport Pain Relief Clinic was created within a new Medical Day Case Unit at St. Woolos Hospital to cope with the increased work load. In 1989, soon after his appointment, Dr. John Gough joined Gwyn Thomas in running this clinic and both were supported in their work by Dr. W. Raj, Associate Specialist Anaesthetist. Eventually, the Medical Day Case Unit moved to more substantial quarters at The Royal Gwent Hospital in 1995 and finally in 1997 to its present accommodation.

The demand for improved relief of post-operative pain followed that for chronic pain relief. This led to development of a team to initiate and maintain safe analgesia in the post operative period and high dependency units. This type of analgesia involves mainly indwelling epidural catheterisation or self-administering and therefore self-controlled intravenous apparatus that delivers pain relieving drugs. This requires a high degree of professional skill and painstaking monitoring to keep acute pain control safe for the patient. Much credit for this service goes to a number of anaesthetists and especially to Drs. Chris Callander and Allison Williams.

Administrative Changes:

A number of radical administrative changes were made in the 1970s. It has been noted in an earlier section of this book that after the 'Cogwheel' recommendations had been introduced, clinical specialties split off from the main clinical body represented by The Senior Medical & Dental Consultants Committee and became Divisions - each with a Chairman and Secretary. Consequently, the Division of Anaesthesia was formed. With time, the number of Consultant Anaesthetists in Newport has increased from two in the 1950s to thirty-four in 2004. This has been necessary to keep up with the proliferation of surgical specialties and subspecialties recorded in the previous chapter as well as the number of sessions now undertaken outside operating theatres. These fullfil the needs of intensive therapy, obstetric anaesthesia, acute and chronic pain relief.

Associated with the changes of structure of the department, there has been an ever increasing but obligatory educational requirement of anaesthetists in training which created a need for the Department to work from a dedicated, central base for the Division of Anaesthesia. Thus, in February 1997, the Division of Anaesthesia moved into a custom-made suite of rooms in 'C' Block of the hospital. In addition to rooms for consultant and other staff and accommodation for secretarial and supportive staff, there are seminar rooms for teaching and conferences.

In recent years, post-graduate teaching, often in cooperation with Bridgend Hospital, has been open to trainees from other hospitals and regions and has achieved considerable standing. These courses have been very successful and the initiative behind them has come largely from Dr. Hywel Jones whose commitment to education has widened recently with his appointment as Sub-Dean of Medicine of The University of Wales College of Medicine at The Royal Gwent Hospital. He is also Assistant Medical Director of The Gwent Healthcare N.H.S. Trust.

Members of Anaesthetic Division in the department's Conference Centre. Those pictured are Matt Turner, Matt Dallison, Steve Dumont, Ian Greenway, Jo Jones, John Gough, June Nicholls, Iljaz Hodzovic, Tan Mian, Iwan Morris, Ken Craddock, Hugh O'Dwyer, Dave Howells, Hywel Jones, Jill Curtis, Raouf Michael, John Butler, Pat Hallary, Chris Callander, Dave Thomas, Tracey Haynes, Victor Francis, Harjeet Singh, K. Zakrzewski, Derek Dye, Emma Knight, Keshra Barker, Farouk Kermani, Akilan Velayuvan, Pauline Donne, Vimla Victor, Shoba Dugari, Christine Everett, Paul Nichols, Sonia Warton, Alison Cavling, Lisa Bassett and John Barnes. The following Senior Anaesthetists were not able to be present Drs. G.F. Clark, J. Griffiths, L. Harding, D. Hughes, T. Stoilova, J. Janes, D.I. Jones, S. Krishnan, S. Lloyd-Jones, M. Sage, S. Watson, R. Walpole, K. Woods, W.A. Raj and P. Prasad.

(photograph Andrew Ponsford)

Overview (1948 to 2003):

From a starting point in 1948 of two Consultant Anaesthetists and several part-time general practitioners, the Anaesthetic Directorate is now the biggest in The Royal Gwent Hospital with a total staff of 62 of whom 24 are consultants.

Doubtless, the two consultants who started the process off so many years ago would be well content, if not extremely surprised, at the progress made in the intervening fifty years with the scope and complexity of anaesthesiology and the size of the department.

Pathology Services
Michael Penney MD FRCPath

It is unlikely that anyone would deny that Pathology Services provided by the laboratories of the hospital are an essential element to clinical management of most patients. Laboratory tests are often the first step in clinical investigations to confirm or refute an initial diagnosis or to provide assessment of fitness to undergo treatment such as surgery. Increasingly laboratory tests are used to evaluate progress of patients in response to treatment and in many cases these tests can now provide a definitive diagnosis. And yet the Pathology Department is rarely seen by most patients and is mostly seldom visited by clinicians and other professionals for the work carried out there is highly specialised.

As with other medical skills, laboratory services have grown exponentially from small simple beginnings to the large, highly scientific, specialised and automated departments of today. For instance, in the late 1950s and 1960s, clinical laboratories in Newport (as elsewhere) had a restricted repertoire of tests limited to simple procedures such as measurement of haemoglobin, blood sugar and blood urea which were carried out in test tubes. Examination of tissue biopsies and blood films was done by simple staining techniques and microscopy. More sophisticated tests would require working up special procedures for the occasion which could only be carried out by specific agreement between the clinical consultant and the consultant pathologist. In those days the majority of clinicians relied on clinical knowledge allied to detailed, careful physical examination and observation of patients. There was great pride and satisfaction in the reliance on clinical skills and acumen.

In the 1960s, enormous advances began in biochemistry, cell biology, immunology and microbiology. Since then, many methologies and technologies have been introduced to assist clinical diagnosis. In Newport, laboratory expertise has kept up with the best since the 1960s and much credit for this must go to Dr. G.S. Andrews, consultant in charge of laboratory services during these formative years. His vision and administrative skills laid the foundation for the future expansion of the laboratories in the hospitals of Newport and the south of the county.

In the early 1960s, the main unit of the Pathology Department was sited at The Royal Gwent Hospital with satellite laboratories at St. Woolos Hospital, County Hospital in Griffithstown, Pontypool Hospital, St. Lawrence Hospital in Chepstow and Llanfrechfa Grange Hospital. All these units carried out some basic tests to provide a quick return of results to the parent institution. Microbiology services were provided independently from the main Pathology Department and came from the Public Health Laboratory Service (P.H.L.S.) based in its own building at the Clytha Square entrance to the Royal Gwent site (ref. Pull-out Plan 2 - Site 1). These services moved to the Main Pathology Department in 1977.

Cervical cytology:

It was at this time that an exfoliative cervical cytology service commenced, initially based at St. Woolos Hospital with Dr. Margaret Davies (Associate Specialist) in charge. This unit was one of the first comprehensive services of this kind to be established in the United Kingdom.

Expansion of Chemical Pathology and Haematology

As the scope and extent of new technology increased and more sophisticated tests became available, the role of the central laboratory at The Royal Gwent Hospital became dominant. To accommodate the need to expand services, the chemical pathology and part of the haematology units were relocated in prefabricated huts on the roof of part of the Out-Patient building in the old hospital.

Radioimmunoassay

Another satellite facility was opened in Allt-yr-yn Hospital in 1969 to provide working space to accommodate the rapidly emerging technique of radioimmunoassay. This new technology was pioneered as a service in Wales firstly at St. Woolos Hospital and then at Allt-yr-yn Hospital providing some of the first assays in Wales for thyroxine, growth hormone and testosterone.

Centralisation of Services

As space became increasingly cramped, in 1974 the major parts of chemical pathology, haematology and histopathology were transferred to the newly commissioned building located to the north of 'C' Block as part of the Scheme 5 redevelopment of the Royal Gwent Hospital. This is the present site of the Pathology Department. Medical microbiology services, previously managed by the P.H.L.S. (Public Health Laboratory Service), moved to the new laboratory and came under hospital management. Cytology services moved from St. Woolos Hospital to take up space vacated by P.H.L.S., the remaining accommodation on the ground floor being occupied by the Department of Genito-urinary Medicine.

Rationalisation (ie. closure) of the smaller laboratory sites continued throughout the 1980s but it was not until 1995 that the laboratory at Allt-yr-yn Hospital closed and was incorporated into the main laboratory building at The Royal Gwent Hospital.

Overview of Pathology Services

The Pathology Department of The Royal Gwent Hospital has striven over many years to keep its services as modern and reactive as possible to the needs of the clinical services. The repertoire of tests available has expanded enormously and particular innovations in recent years have included introduction of pre-natal screening for Down's Syndrome and the development of liquid based cytology for screening of cervical cancer - both first in Wales. As the available laboratory space has contracted during the past thirty years as services have been centralised, the workload and demand has increased several fold. This has required substantial investment in modern high capacity automated laboratory equipment, robotics and advance computer technology. Future developments in the 21st century will require additional space and further specialist technical, scientific and medical input.

Currently, the consultant staff of the Pathology Department are Drs. Emyr Owen, Abdul-Majid Rashid, Ian Thompson and Elise Wessels (histopathology), Drs. Colin Hewlett and Elizabeth Moffatt (haematology), Dr. Elizabeth Kubiak (microbiology) and Dr. Michael Penney (chemical pathology). Recently retired pathologists are Drs. G.S. Andrews, Robin Gray, Howard Jones, John Glencross and Windsor Fortt.

Radiological and Imaging Services
Richard Clements FRCR FRCS and Stan Jordan DCR (R.&T.)

In the 1960s and 1970s, imaging by X-Ray was often imprecise. Consequently, it was not unusual for a question mark to be left over a diagnosis so that physicians and surgeons frequently were forced to rely on clinical judgement and intuition arising from experience rather than make decisions based on hard evidence from investigations. Surgeons not infrequently needed to resort to internal exploration to establish a true diagnosis but physicians had no such luxury and might find out the truth in the post-mortem room.

This began to change in the latter part of the 1960s and early 1970s, when technological innovations mostly based upon computers, especially in the field of diagnostic ultrasound, resulted in ever-increasing precision of imaging upon which to base clinical diagnosis. Furthermore, accurate image guided needling of suspect tissue is now routine to obtain a pathological diagnosis without resort to exploratory surgery. Radiographic and other techniques have been developed for precise display of internal structure of organs from which the specialty of interventional radiology has been born and this, also, has replaced surgery in many fields.

In Newport, these aspects of clinical investigation by ultrasound, CT, MR imaging and nuclear imaging have kept pace with the best centres in the country even from the earliest days of the hospital.

Before 1948: An X-Ray Room was equipped at the new Newport & East Monmouthshire Hospital in 1905, and the Annual Report in 1908 identified the Medical Officer to the Electrical Department as Dr. F.W. Daniels. However, there was no other reference of radiological facilities at the hospital until 1921 when it appeared that a new X-Ray Department was established with equipment costing £2,000, and the appointment of an 'Honorary Radiologist'. This was Dr. T.I. Candy who wrote in the Annual Report of 1927 that 'an efficient X-Ray Department is one of the most important needs of a modern hospital, and in a populous industrial area it is a sine qua non. For this reason the large outlay involved in its equipment and maintenance, and in the additions necessary from time to time to keep abreast of all the latest developments, is money well spent'. That statement at the outset of radiology as a speciality at The Royal Gwent still applies today.

In 1927, equipment had been installed 'for diagnosis and treatment' and that year between five and six thousand 'photographs' had been taken 'for diagnosis' and there had been three hundred and fifty 'screen examinations without photographs'. In the X-Ray Treatment Section of the unit, there had been 873 treatments and it was reported that the new installation for deep X-Ray therapy 'was giving every satisfaction'. Of the Massage, Electrical and Ultra-Violet Ray Department, Dr. Candy wrote *the work performed in this department deserves more than a passing notice, not only on account of the volume of work dealt with in a year, but also because of the many excellent results that are obtained in the restoration of the injured and crippled, and in the alleviation of painful conditions for which no other form of treatment would be of service. As most of the cases of accident are referred to it (the department) for treatment, the figures given of the work done might be regarded as an index of the economic service which the Hospital renders to the community*. Prophetic ideas.

In 1929, a mobile X-Ray Unit was installed 'to enable photographs to be taken at the bedside with the minimum of disturbance and discomfort to the patient, and to the advantage of the surgeon, since the detrimental movement of bad cases of fracture to the X-Ray Department was no longer necessary'.

Dr. Candy died in 1931 from aplastic anaemia induced by self-treated radiotherapy for quinsy! *(information from Mr. L.P. Thomas quoting Dr. Candy's granddaughter. Apparently, radiotherapy to treat tonsillar infections was in vogue)*.

After 1948: Dr. Candy was followed as consultant by Dr. W.H. Hastings who advised the Directors in March 1948 to re-equip the department completely including a new deep X-Ray therapy unit.

However, by modern standards, at the start of the N.H.S. in 1948, the X-Ray facilities were limited. 'Main X-Ray' was a single diagnostic radiographic room by the Casualty Department with a single X-Ray machine, together with a portable machine kept in the adjacent corridor. There was also a separate set in the Fracture and Orthopaedic Clinic.

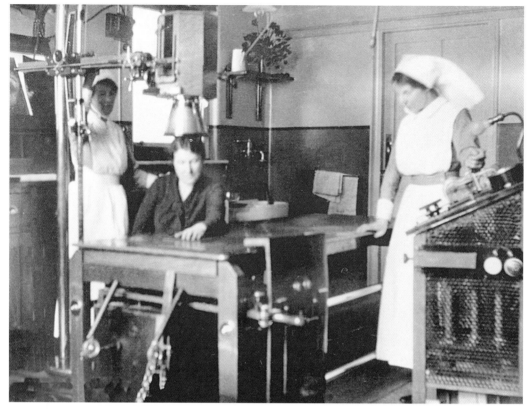

The Radiology Department 1934: note the simple machine, the operators being nurses without radiological protection and the control unit to the right.

(photograph courtesy of Messrs. J. Otley Rhodes Ltd., Newport)

There was still only one radiologist, Dr. Howitt Hastings. There was also a cobalt therapy unit in main X-Ray, where radiotherapy treatments were given by Dr. Glyn Evans- a radiotherapist from Cardiff - and by the departmental therapy radiographer Joan Burns. The cobalt source was kept in a cupboard behind the lift to upper wards and would be transported by a radiographer when it was required *(information from Mr. Stan Jordan)*. In fact, monitoring of staff for exposure to radiation was only set up in The Royal Gwent in the early 1960s.

The other radiology staff at that time consisted of one nursing sister (who also took X-Rays), one qualified radiographer and two clerks. There were four ex-servicemen 'student' radiographers attached to the department.

Dr. Hastings left in 1949 and was succeeded by Dr. T.J. (Jack) Thomas who stayed for about 5 years before emigrating to Canada. His successor as radiologist was Dr. Aneurin Williams and was later joined by Dr. Rex Owen as a Consultant Radiologist and subsequently by Dr. Harold Ansari, who had previously been a Registrar in the Department.

Throughout the subsequent fifty years, the radiological facilities in the Royal Gwent Hospital have been inadequate and inappropriate for the service demands. Various improvements have been undertaken but each time technological developments have overtaken the planning of the X-Ray department leaving X-Ray facilities that have struggled to cope with the demands of the service.

In the mid 1950s, a new 5 room 'main' department was commissioned adjacent to Jubilee Ward (Ward 6) of the main part of the hospital in the floor below the Doctors' Residence Quarters and the Medical Staff Dining Room and kitchen. One development at this time was an electrical tilting X-Ray table, which replaced a previous set, that could only be tilted by manual winding.

Fluoroscopy was upgraded at that time. With the first image intensifier, the radiologist had to wear a leather lead apron tied with rope, brown lead gloves and red goggles through which he would peer into its binocular periscope to see the X-Ray images in real time.

Film processing was by hand in a dark room and the films took about 10 minutes to dry. Surgeons were impatient for their films then, as now, hence the demand by surgeons for 'wet films' as they could see these a little earlier. The problem with these was that they were prone to misinterpretation in fracture work because of parallax effects between the two sides of the wet film, which could give a false impression of a fracture.

In the 1960s, lumbar angiography commenced - a hazardous procedure requiring the full staff of seven. This was first carried out by Mr. L.P. Thomas who introduced vascular surgery to The Royal Gwent Hospital. The procedure required a general anaesthetic and involved percutaneous insertion of a large needle into the aorta from the back to give the injection of contrast. The procedure was supervised by the radiologist, the superintendent radiographer operated the controls of the unit and 'timed' the exposures, and 3 radiographers pulled the films sequentially from under the patient to try and catch images of the contrast as it passed down the legs of the patient. Occasionally, other general surgeons carried out this procedure (R.D. Richards, W.B. Peeling) but, in time, the radiologist took over the injection routine and eventually the investigation was discontinued.

By the late 1960s the service had outgrown its accommodation and moved to a new location. Mr. Stan Jordan became superintendent in 1968 replacing Mr. Fred Oxford. The new department had the height of X-Ray technology of the time - a 'polytome' machine which could take X-Ray slices across the body. Main X-Ray has been on this site ever since and despite extensions across a corridor on the same level (Level 2) and upwards along the staff room corridor on level 3, the accommodation remains inadequate and inappropriate for the service demands of a modern radiology department in the year 2004.

In the mid 1970s, ultrasound scanning and a nuclear medicine gamma camera arrived. A CT scanner was installed in 1987 with MR in 1994.

There were considerable problems with installation of the huge magnet that is the core of the MR Scanner. It weighs nearly two tons and it was necessary to create a large hole in the side of the building for it to be winched in and put in place. There was therefore, considerable consternation when a final check revealed that it was 3cm out of place: this required services from a large hydraulic jack to line it up correctly. Unfortunately, the German engineers advising the process had gone home at that stage.

The workload of the department was 93,000 in 1982 and this had increased to 149,000 examinations by 2000. Increasing demand for In-Patient imaging has meant that many Out-Patient examinations and general practitioner services needed to be moved to St. Woolos Hospital in the mid 1990s. A second CT scanner was installed in 2002.

From this circa 1960s.

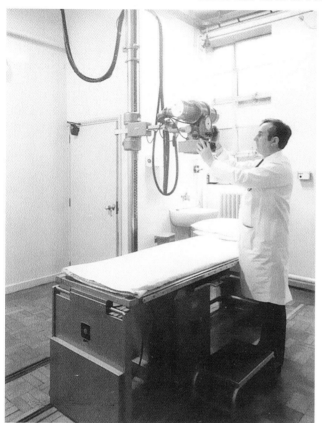

AE Dean Unit & Floating Table of the Royal Gwent Hospital and Mr. Stan Jordan (radiographer). This unit was a general-purpose machine typical of its time. Note: suspension of the X-Ray Unit from the ceiling.

(photograph courtesy of Mr. Stan Jordan)

To this in 2004.

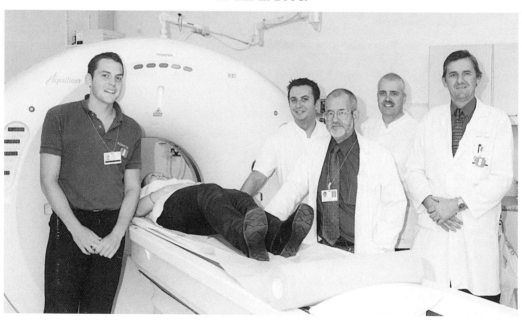

Multi-CT Scanner 2004. Left to right Callum Cheshire, Shaun Walsh, Graham Cheshire, Paul Widger and Andrew Edwards.

(photograph Nigel Pearce, Medical Illustration R.G.H.)

Computerisation of the department occurred in 1992 with the introduction of the Radis Radiology Administration System. The major change that is anticipated in the next few years is the conversion to a filmless digital department.

New radiologists also arrived in the 1970s - Dr. Glas Griffiths based in Newport and Drs. Rosemary Anderson and H.M. Davies based at Nevill Hall Hospital. Service demand has grown by at least 10% per year for the last 25 years and in 2003 there are 54 radiographers, 6 nurses, 21 clerical and secretarial staff and 9 porters with ancillary staff in the Royal Gwent Radiology Department. Twelve radiologists provide the service for the South Gwent Hospitals and Caerphilly. These are Drs. Fiona Brook, Richard Clements, Nest Evans, Richard Harding, Jennifer Haslam, David Jackson, Andrew Jones, Peter Stamper, Brian Sullivan, Gerald Thomas and Anne Wake. Dr. Barbara Williams recently retired.

Mr. Jordan retired in 1988 being replaced by Mrs. A. Cormack as District Superintendent Radiographer. Mrs. Cormack retired in 2000 and Mrs. Marilyn Williams became Radiology Directorate Manager with Mrs. K. Hatch as Superintendent of the Royal Gwent Hospital Department.

The Gwent School of Radiography opened in the late 1950s at the Royal Gwent and later transferred to Park Square, Newport. The Principal was Mr. D.W. McKears. The School closed in 1987, with transfer of radiographic training to Cardiff.

Nursing Services
Mrs. Hazel Taylor OBE JP RGN and Cliff Knight

Before 1948:

There is no mention in 'The History of The Royal Gwent Hospital' or other sources of the conditions or pattern of work of nurses in the Royal Gwent Hospital until 1927, when a report was made for the need of a Nurses' Hostel as a preliminary to completion of a Ward Unit over The Out-Patient Department. It was considered by the Directors that 'patients could not be accommodated unless there were wards and beds; if these were available they could not be used unless there were nurses to staff them; and it was of no use to advertise for nurses if they could not be housed. So, a Nurses' Hostel was a first necessity and the Directors moved.' !!

It seems that most nurses 'lived in', firstly over what is now the Out-Patients' Department (ref. p.26/5) and then in the Nurses' Hostel completed in 1933 (ref. p.26/6 and p.33). They would rise about 7am, have a communal breakfast of porridge, boiled egg and tea and then go onto the ward for the rest of the day. There was usually one day off each week which sometimes had to be given up for lectures. They were expected not only to carry out nursing duties but some cleaning of the ward as well. In 1925 the reward for this arduous work was the princely sum of £12 per annum which rose to £24 in 1928, and to help pay this meagre salary, nurses were sometimes delegated to attend local churches on 'Hospital Sunday' in their uniforms to take up the collection which was donated to the hospital.

Nurses at that time and later, were governed by strict discipline. It would be true to say that they were more part of the 'family' of the hospital than of their own families. They slept, worked and ate at the hospital, and although made to work hard and long hours, they were well looked after. They had regular nourishing meals in the communal staff dining hall with the Matron at the head of the tables and the rest of the staff seated in descending order of rank. The Matron and Sisters were seated first and the latest probationer nurse last. A nurse's life was to some degree governed by the hospital; they had to be back in the Hostel by a specified time at night and in certain cases if under the age of 21 they had to have permission to get married.

After 1948:

This pattern of life was still present after 1948 when, unlike now, the nursing and hospital environment was still a home to nurses. Most nurses were female and still strongly encouraged to remain single. Almost all were resident and there was a formidable 'Home Sister' who lived in the Nurses' Hostel who kept a firm but motherly eye on them. As in earlier days, the hours of work were long and all nurses were expected to work 'split' shifts consisting of a morning shift and a double-back to cover the afternoon and evening. Christmas at The Royal Gwent was very special and it was usual for nurses to spend all day on duty, taking meals on the wards and staying with patients and their families throughout the day. It was the tradition until the early-1970s for consultants to visit the wards at lunchtime, carve the turkey (usually wearing a chef's hat) and sometimes to dress up as Father Christmas to distribute gifts to patients. Consultants' children often joined in and served lunches to the patients. Not infrequently, consultants would admit very elderly or poor and lonely patients of theirs to make Christmas a special treat for them.

Courtesy was taught very early in a nurse's career at the hospital and respect and discipline was a central element to behaviour. It was customary to hold doors open for more senior nurses and consultants and to stand when they entered the room. In the dining room, it was still the custom that junior nurses would not sit until more senior nurses had been seated.

The ward environment was very strict and older nurses to this day would not dare to sit upon a patient's bed. Wards were run and ruled by Ward Sisters and patients were expected to conform to Sister's rules. There were rest hours in the afternoon and visiting was restricted to two visitors per bed, controlled by distribution of visiting cards. In the earlier days, no children were allowed to visit and no excess noise was permitted. Standards of cleanliness were high and the food was simple and plainly cooked.

Until the late 1960s and early 1970s, Sisters ate in their own dining rooms which were on the first floor centre of the Administrative Block of the old Hospital (this later became the site of the first Intensive Care Ward of the hospital in the late 1960s). Similarly, medical staff had their own dining room. Some Management Board members regarded this as elitist and incompatible with an egalitarian society. Those involved with balancing the financial books looked upon this arrangement as inefficient and unjustifiable on business grounds. In 1972, both dining rooms were closed for other uses as part of the Scheme 4 Redevelopment programme, and all staff, irrespective of grade or discipline, dined communally, and happily, in the Main Dining Room which had been opened in 1966.

Nurses' Accommodation

As mentioned earlier in this chapter, the nurses' quarters were originally situated above the Out-Patients Department in the main hospital. It was in 1920 that a suggestion had come from the Executive Committee of the Hospital Workingmen's Fund to build a purpose-built unit to accommodate nurses but it was not until ten years later that a contract was made and by 1933 a new building had been completed ready for occupation. The interim accommodation over the Out-Patients Department that had been used since 1927 was vacated and became a Children's Ward with another part used to house some of the domestic staff. As well as sleeping quarters, the new building contained a large recreation hall which was used for dances, concerts etc and could be partitioned off for use by the nurses for study rooms.

The building cost £62,000 to put up, and was constructed by Richard Jones (Builders) of Caerphilly. During the excavation work it was found that the site was near the old Stowe Quarry from which stone for the foundation of the building was provided. It was also discovered that the stone excavated from this quarry had been used to build the nearby 'Friars' and some of the more ancient buildings in Newport.

For many years the new Nurses' Home was used so much that in February 1948 the Directors bought two houses, 12 and 13 Park Square to accommodate night staff. As time went on and nurses tended to provide their own accommodation outside the hospital (and get married), less use was made of the building. Therefore, in 1986 it was decided to close the building as nurses' accommodation and alternative accommodation was provided by a pair of two-storey buildings constructed to the rear of the hospital on Friars Field (Block 9 & 10). Richmond House also was used for additional accommodation for nurses (p.29).

The appearance of the Nurses' Home was so solid, square and formidably dominating Belle Vue Lane that, although some people liked it, others thought it a monstrosity and in the 1950s dubbed it 'Colditz' after the celebrated, well-known castle in Eastern Germany. The long-term plan for this building was demolition to make way for a new Ophthalmology and Ear, Nose and Throat Unit which opened in 1997.

Nursing Training

There is no information about nurse-training in the earlier days of The Royal Gwent although it is known that a School of Nursing was established at the hospital in 1902 and it is clear that the Directors considered that system of training of nurses to be important. Later, the provisions of the Nurses Registration Act 1919 were incorporated by the hospital and a complete training school for nurses was set up. In fact, during the first Preliminary State Examination held in 1924, nurses from the hospital did exceedingly well.

The Matron of the hospital was usually present at their working meetings and it was at such a meeting in 1945 that Miss Frances Greene, the Matron at that time, announced that steps had been taken to establish a new Training School for Nurses. She said that trainee nurses would be better equipped if, rather than spending all their time on the wards, they had three months of tuition with one or two days on the wards each week. The rest of the time would be devoted to study rather than the old ways of 'learn as you go'.

So it was in 1945 that the *South Wales Argus* reported that a large house had been bought in Stow Park Avenue (No.29)[1] for £2,000 to accommodate a Nurses' Training School and at the same time made an appeal for £5,000 towards the project. This coincided with the end of the Second World War and the public was encouraged to give 'Thanksgiving Offerings'. These gifts together with a donation of £2,000 from the Newport Chamber of Commerce enabled the School to open debt-free which was a remarkable achievement in those troubled and hard times.

It was on November 27th 1946 that the first batch of ten students began their course at the Training School. The object of the course was threefold:

1) To enable the student nurse coming straight from home to obtain a grounding in nursing theory and practice
2) To give the student a chance to find out if she was suitable for nursing care and
3) To determine if the student was suitable, from the hospital's point of view, to embark on a nursing career

The course lasted three months - nine weeks in the School and four weeks in the hospital before being called upon to handle patients.

At the Preliminary Nurses Training School in 1945 it was suggested that males as well as females be encouraged to become nurses. This suggestion was realised in April 1954 when two nurses from St Cadoc's Hospital, Caerleon qualified as State Registered Nurses after training at the Royal Gwent Hospital. These were Stan Knight [2] and David Harris.

Training of nurses expanded and by the 1970s, a total of 600 nurses had been taken in during any three year period. The Royal Gwent was one of the first Welsh hospitals to offer general nurse training to male students and training has always been offered to nurses from other countries so that there is now a multi-cultural environment to nursing in Newport which is much valued.

In 1991, the School of Nursing was transferred to Cardiff where students were based at The University of Wales College of Nursing. This was a radical change for education for nurses. In the early days, nurses had learned how to look after patients by watching and working with experienced nurses as an apprenticeship supplemented by textbook learning to back-up essential hands-on learning. From 1991, nurses received more academic training and could no longer be used as a 'work force'. This gave opportunities for degrees in nursing which laid the foundation for the concept of 'Specialist Nursing' that could change the career and pathways of some nurses to make them specialists in a narrower clinical field. This would bring them more closely into decision making and responsibility previously expected of medical staff and in some cases, specialist nurses would work autonomously with their own caseload. Also, opportunities for involvement in clinical and other research programmes opened up.

So, nurses who 'learned the trade by trial and error' in the early twentieth century and were made to clean the wards in addition to their nursing duties were now being replaced by highly qualified staff supported by others who would carry out the more mundane duties of cleaning etc.

[1]   *This house is one of four built over the site of the motte and bailey built in 1071 referred to in Chapter 4 Editor.*
[2]   *Stan Knight (died 1998) was the brother of Cliff Knight, principal contributor to this book. He became Deputy Head Nurse at St. Cadoc's Hospital. - Editor*

Administrative and Organisational Changes

During the past thirty years, the profile and image of nursing has undergone a radical change. This commenced with the Salmon Report produced in 1971-72. It proposed a system of 'Unit Matrons' of the nursing hierarchy in hospitals, later changing titles to Nursing Officers. Wards were grouped into similar specialties which the Unit Matron supervised, being responsible for standards of care and management of the nursing team and all personnel issues. This system was introduced in 1971-72 in Newport (at both The Royal Gwent and St. Woolos Hospitals) after a period of 'trial'.

Consultant staff had accepted that a trial of these ideas should be carried out, but were extremely concerned when the Salmon recommendations were installed as a matter of fact by the authorities without further consultation because there was considerable scepticism that these changes would result in benefit in overall standards of care for patients. However, once these new Unit Matrons were appointed, the earlier anxiety faded and a close working relationship was established between the senior nurses appointed and the consultant staff.

The main immediate effect of the new system of nomenclature was the disappearance of the title 'Matron' but the title of ward sisters remained unchanged.

Clearly this development was a radical break with a long-standing tradition. The first Matron in Newport had been appointed 1867 at 'The Infirmary' on Stow Hill but there is no record of her name. The first recorded name of a Matron was that of Miss Irwin who was appointed in 1877. Five further Matrons followed in quick succession over the next 24 years until 1901 when Miss A.J. Ainsworth was the first Matron of the new hospital off Cardiff Road, soon to be followed in 1902 by Miss M. Evans. The first Matron of The Royal Gwent Hospital after the Charter Warrant in 1913 was Miss M. Arkey to be succeeded by Miss C. Staples (1915), Miss H.M. Vine (1917), Miss L. Foster-Feather (1920), Miss Margaret Husband (1926), Miss M.G. Wilkie (1931), Miss L.J. Ottley (1937), Miss Francis Greene (1944), Miss A.F. Hutchinson (1960). During the 1970s, titles and areas of responsibility changed and duties widened to cover 'District' and latterly 'Community' nursing. Amongst people responsible for the Royal Gwent Hospital were Miss Mary Coker, Miss Freda Honeybourne, Mrs. Vevers, Miss Janet Grant and Mrs. Hazel Taylor.

The longest-serving and perhaps the best-known of the Matrons who served at the Royal Gwent Hospital was Miss Frances Greene who had came from Ashby-de-la-Zouch in Leicestershire and had trained in Plymouth. When she came to the hospital in 1944 she only intended to stay two years, but liked the town and the hospital so much that she remained for sixteen. Her main achievement during her time as Matron was the setting up of the Nurses' Preliminary Training School, firstly at 29 Stow Park Avenue, which later moved to St. Lawrence Hospital in Chepstow, and then to the Friars at the Royal Gwent Hospital.

The last Matron at St. Woolos Hospital was Miss E.V. Davies SRN SCM.

In 1986/87 an attempt was made to recreate the matron role when two senior nurses were appointed as assistants to The Director of Nursing, Miss V. Martin. Mrs. Hazel Taylor was appointed 'Matron' at The Royal Gwent Hospital and Mrs. Val Evans was appointed as 'Matron' at St. Woolos Hospital. These titles were later dropped when N.H.S. Trusts began in 1993-94.

However, there is no doubt that changes of ward design which started in 1966 for the new buildings of the re-developed Royal Gwent had a significant impact on the organisation of working patterns for nurses and it is doubtful whether the ideas that worked so well for old-style Nightingale Wards could be applied today.

In the early years, there was little professional supporting staff for nurses and each nurse was expected to have a working knowledge of such things as dietetics and physiotherapy. In the present-day hospital, there are much larger numbers of support staff with a great emphasis on a team working together to give better care of patients.

The nursing teams at The Royal Gwent have always covered a wide range of clinical specialties, including nursing of sick babies and children. Midwifery has always been practised in the hospital and community midwifery and hospital midwifery have been merged recently and neonatal intensive care development.

Potential nurses today still enter the profession because they want to care for people and it is this devotion to caring that has continued throughout the years at the hospitals in Newport. It is an ethos that has continued through all the changes of the 20th century and it is this proud tradition that will carry forward into the future.

Obstetrics and Neonatal Nursing Services
from John Cawdery FRCP FRCPCH and Cliff Knight - Editor

Before 1948:

Before 1900, most women in Newport gave birth to their children at home. As there were no trained midwives at that time a neighbour would perform the necessary duties and there was certainly no pre or post-natal care. Consequently, it was not uncommon sometimes for the baby, and perhaps the mother to die.

In 1904, the wife of a ship repairer and prominent benefactor, Mrs. C.H. Bailey, CBE JP, decided that women expecting children needed better care, so she opened a Maternity Nurses Training Centre at 30/31 Herbert St. on the corner of Cardiff Road, approximately opposite the Royal Gwent Hospital. Nurses were trained to give advice to expectant mothers and to attend the birth in the home. Previously, the 'midwife' had usually been a neighbour. By 1908, the service had been so successful that adjoining premises were purchased so that the more difficult cases could be delivered on the premises.

In 1916, it was reported that in the 12 years the Nursing Home had been opened, 4,566 cases had been dealt with. There were no general maternity facilities at the Royal Gwent Hospital, although in 1904, the Directors decided to undertake the training of midwives at the hospital who would attend expectant mothers in their homes.

After 1948

In the following years, several maternity units were developed in the area, the consultant units being in St. Woolos Hospital, the County Hospital in Griffithstown and the Lydia Beynon Maternity Home by the Coldra (now part of the Celtic Manor Hotel.) However, with medical advances in obstetric and neonatal care, it became necessary to locate the main consultant unit in the Royal Gwent Hospital which was opened on June 8th, 1966 by H.M. The Queen Mother in 'B' block as part of the two-million pound development of the Royal Gwent Hospital. Since its opening, this unit has proved to be one of the foremost in Wales. Many mothers (and fathers) are grateful for the facilities provided at the maternity unit over the past 35 years, but the older generation still talk about being born at the Herbert St. Nursing Home.

Premature and sick neonatal care

Prior to the opening of the Royal Gwent Hospital unit, there were no proper facilities for nursing premature and sick newborn babies. Premature babies were nursed in the large nurseries in the post-natal wards. The main medical intervention in neonates at that time would have been exchange transfusion for rhesus haemolytic disease, the paediatricians carrying out between 30 and 40 exchanges each year. These were undertaken, not in the maternity unit, but in a sterilising room of one of the medical wards in St. Woolos Hospital, the steriliser being turned on full to create a warm moist atmosphere (or fug!).

When maternity services moved into the Royal Gwent Hospital in 1966/7, the Special Care baby work moved at the same time and after a short period of sharing in Christchurch ward, the Special Care Baby Unit (S.C.B.U.) moved in 1969 to its present position in 'B' Block. In September 1986, S.C.B.U. organised the first 405 course in Wales for the training of nurses and midwives in this very specialised area of neo-natal care and has continued to be actively involved in teaching until the present time. Since 1969, S.C.B.U. has been updated and refurbished on three occasions.

The Pharmacy or Dispensary
Eluned Price BPharm, FR PharmS and Godfrey Brangham MSc, MR PharmS

at The Royal Gwent Hospital

When the Royal Gwent Hospital was opened in 1901 a small dispensary supplying pharmaceuticals to wards, theatres and patients was situated in the Out-Patient building situated just inside the main gate to the hospital. Little is known of these early years except that the department was managed by a dispenser and pharmacy's relatively low rating was emphasised by a request to the hospital committee to have the roof of the department raised from a height of seven feet to eight feet and six inches.

In the 1930s, a new Dispensary was built next to a corridor near the Out-Patients Department. It remained in this area until the late 1970s. After a major expansion had taken place in the hospital in the late 1970s, a new dispensary (now called 'The Pharmacy Department') was built on the second floor of 'C' Block where it is located now.

The first pharmacist employed at the hospital was Mr R.E. Wagg in the late 1930s. However, a history of pharmacy at the Royal Gwent Hospital would not be complete without a reference to Mr. Harry Gibbor who spent more than three decades within its walls. He took up his position as Acting Chief Pharmacist in 1939 when the Royal Gwent Hospital was a voluntary hospital and was later appointed as Chief Pharmacist. His meagre staff during the Second World War consisted of one pharmacist, a senior dispenser, a junior dispenser and a dispensing assistant. Mr. Gibbor spent some time as a pharmacist with the Navy and during his absence his duties were taken over by Mr. John Hough. Fragments of letters during these years include remarks such as:

'...great savings can be made in making our own pessaries and suppositories'
'...we have rationed soft soap and also Imperial Drink as it contains sugar'
'...on the request of Matron I have given a series of lectures on Materia Medica'

Despite the small number of staff they exhibited some enterprise, by adapting a small section of the pharmacy stores to house an autoclave where they sterilised aqueous solutions such as intravenous products, irrigation fluids and eye-drops. This innovation sufficed for several years but with the inexorable rise in the throughput of patients and a need for a lengthier products list, it was eventually recognised that a more substantial unit was required.

By the early 1960s a greatly enlarged production unit had been built directly opposite the main dispensary. This incorporated autoclaves, a dry heat oven, a steamer, an intravenous fluid and ampoule filler, bottle washer and other state of the art machinery. The unit produced an extraordinary range of sterile pharmaceuticals, fully satisfying the demands of the hospital. In the 1970s, visits from the Medicines Inspectorate and new legislation concerning sterile products resulted in a decrease in the range of products from this unit, also the introduction of commercially produced intravenous fluids in easy-to-use packs phased out the demand for many of the locally produced sterile fluids.

During this period the pharmacy was also responsible for ordering and supplying surgical dressings, stoma products, sutures and medical sundries for wards, theatres and departments and as well as ordering and arranging repair of some surgical instruments.

In the late 1960s, with reorganisation of pharmaceutical services following the Noel Hall Report, Mr. Gibbor took extra responsibility for coordinating pharmaceutical services for South Gwent and in the early 1970s both he and his staff were actively engaged in planning a new department to meet the future needs of The Royal Gwent Hospital and those of smaller outlying hospitals in the district. Miss Eluned Price was appointed Chief Pharmacist at the Royal Gwent Hospital in 1974 when Mr. Gibbor moved to The Gwent Health Authority.

During the 1970s the range of services were developed in line with national guidelines and in anticipation of the planned move to new accommodation. A Ward Pharmacy service was set up whereby pharmacists visited wards to review prescriptions for In-Patients and to discuss pharmaceutical aspects of care of patients with other professional staff. The appointment of a Drug Information Pharmacist provided a source of information and advice on use of pharmaceutical products for professional and other staff (including general practitioners). Also, all products made in the Production Unit were subject to quality control tests which were carried out by a Quality Control Pharmacist in line with the requirements of the Medicines Inspectorate.

The Pharmacy became heavily involved with Education and Training. There was a close liaison with the Welsh School of Pharmacy and the Chief Pharmacist acted as Tutor in the Practice of Pharmacy for undergraduate students and postgraduate students completed their pre-registration training in the department. Student pharmacy technicians were also trained in the department.

In the late 1970s, a new Pharmacy department was opened in which there were greatly improved facilities which enabled new services to be developed. This included a new Aseptic Suite within the Production Unit to prepare parenteral nutrition products for premature babies, with an instant revision of the viability of low-weight infants. This unit also prepares sterile products for individual patients including the preparation of cytotoxic drugs.

In 1981, when Mr. Gibbor retired, Miss Price was appointed to the Area post and Dr. Richard Capstick was appointed as Chief Pharmacist at the Royal Gwent Hospital. He later moved to another Health Authority and Mr. Frank Mansell became Chief Pharmacist in 1983.

During the 1980s, Ward Pharmacy was developed into a clinical service with staff associated with clinical specialties such as Cardiology, Trauma and Orthopaedics and Wound Management. Pharmacists were trained for the Diploma of Clinical Pharmacy. Computerisation was also introduced which enabled the drug budgets of the hospital to be closely scrutinised by the Drugs and Therapeutics Group which has led to useful economic decisions and rationalisations in drug therapy.

During the past hundred years, the pharmacy service at the Royal Gwent Hospital has been very fortunate to have employed staff who have given many years of dedicated service to the hospital. These include Mr. John Hough who worked during and after the Second World War, Miss Pauline Bowen who became Deputy Chief Pharmacist and later moved to St. Woolos Hospital as head of department, Miss Peggy Davies Senior Technician at the department for many years who was not only a skilled technician in the dispensary but also was an expert in matters relating to sutures and surgical equipment. In recent years, Mr. Godfrey Brangham, Deputy Chief Pharmacist, has developed an expertise in Wound Management whose advice is available to clinicians and especially to surgeons and those concerned with trauma.

At one time, there was a plaque fixed to the wall of the dispensary which read:
'This plate was affixed to one of the earliest homes of the Institution, and was presented by Dr. H. Egerton Williams, The successor to Dr. R.F. Woolett, the first Secretary and Dispenser and afterwards Surgeon of the Institution'. This plaque links back to the earliest days of healthcare in Newport. It is a reminder of the enormous progress in drug therapy since those times when there was little scientific basis for drug treatment and treatment was often empirical. This compares with modern times when the work of the Pharmacy is based on scientific principles and quality control.

at St. Woolos Hospital

In the 1950s a small outhouse building was used as a dispensary which supplied pharmaceutical products, surgical dressings, sutures, stoma care products and surgical sundries to wards, theatres and all departments of the hospital. The Chief Pharmacist was Mr. E.V. Davies.

On his retirement in 1970, his place as Chief Pharmacist was taken by Miss Shirley Merritt who moved from St. Lawrence Hospital, Chepstow. In 1975 a new Pharmacy building was constructed. At that time, St. Woolos Hospital held the District Ophthalmic and Urology Departments as well as the Dermatological Unit, and was the centre for Chest Diseases. The new pharmacy provided a Ward Pharmacy service to In-Patients, dispensed

Out-Patient prescriptions and also a small aseptic unit was included where specialised eyedrops could be prepared. At a later date a cytotoxic cabinet was installed to prepare cytotoxic drugs for individual patients.

In due course, most of the specialties were transferred to the Royal Gwent Hospital so that the work load in the department at St. Woolos Hospital has become less and some staff have been transferred to the larger hospital. The department is still open and supplies the remaining needs of the hospital and also County Hospital, Griffithstown and St. Cadoc's Hospital, Caerleon. Chief Pharmacists since 1976 have been Frank Mansell, Pauline Bowen, Jean Matthews, John King and from 2000 has been Theresa Maclean.

Physiotherapy
Lucy Bryant MSCP SRP, Superintendent Physiotherapist

Historical Background

The first Society of Physiotherapy was founded in 1894 by four nurses who were trained in massage and 'medical rubbing'. The founders set up the Society of Trained Masseuses to protect their profession from falling into disrepute. Many newspaper articles were published at this time warning members of the public of unscrupulous people offering massage in conjunction with other services!

Examinations were devised and carried out regularly by the society to ensure that a high standard of practice was maintained, and rules of conduct were published to be circulated to other health professionals and organisations. By 1901, when the Newport & Monmouthshire Hospital was built, the membership of the society was 250 and it was given both legal and public status of a professional organisation, it became known as the Incorporated Society of Trained Masseuses.

During the early 20th century the profession continued to develop and expand the types of treatment modalities used to include remedial exercise and the use of electrotherapy. 1920 saw the Society granted a Royal Charter and became known as The Chartered Society of Massage and Medical Gymnastics with a membership of 5,000. The name again changed in 1942 to become the Chartered Society of Physiotherapy (C.S.P.) to be more representative of the service it provided and is still known as this today.

In 1960 the Council for Professions Supplementary to Medicine (C.P.S.M.) was established which became the regulatory body for eight different professional bodies, physiotherapy being one. This led to a compulsory requirement that all physiotherapists working within the N.H.S. should have state registration. The 1970s saw the profession gain increased independence and autonomy, eventually leading to a change in a Bye-Law, that allowed physiotherapists to treat patients without a prior medical referral. This enabled physiotherapists to assess and treat patients with the methods they deemed most appropriate. This change in practice had taken 83 years to achieve!

at The Royal Gwent Hospital

Against this historical background, the Physiotherapy profession in The Royal Gwent Hospital has developed and now following its centenary year, the hospital physiotherapists work in many different clinical areas. These include a physiotherapy Out-Patient Department and specialised Hand Unit, surgical wards, Adult Medicine, Intensive Care Unit (I.C.U.) and the High Dependency Unit (H.D.U.), Obstetrics and Gynaecology, Urology, Trauma and Orthopaedic wards as well as Paediatrics and the Accident and Emergency Department.

The Physiotherapy profession within the hospital is continuing to expand with increasing new opportunities, such as new posts developed for Extended Scope Practitioners and Clinical Specialists, enabling both patients and clinical staff to benefit from advanced skills.

Other new areas include Research posts and Lecturer Practitioner posts which are to be linked with the Department of Physiotherapy Education, Cardiff to provide support in training physiotherapists of the future.

In the clinical field, physiotherapists in Newport have an increasing educational and preventative role which can be seen through Back Care programmes, Cardiac Rehabilitation programmes and Health Promotion sessions based in the community to allow easy access for the public. The Health Promotion topics include Osteoarthritis, Rheumatoid Arthritis, Asthma and Osteoporosis.

The Physiotherapy Department within the Royal Gwent Hospital delivers a high standard of care to over 14,000 new patients per year and this is maintained through regular setting and monitoring of local and C.S.P.M. standards. The department keeps abreast of national service developments and N.I.C.E. (National Institute of Clinical Excellence) recommendations and adapts working practices if required to conform to them.

The future holds opportunities for the profession to expand further in many areas, including more posts incorporating advanced skills and with the anticipation of the development of Consultant posts. The expansion of the profession will ensure that the patients who are referred to the service benefit greatly by having easier access to clinicians working in many different environments, and also access to those who have advanced skills. Continual monitoring is carried out to ensure that the most recent advances in Physiotherapy are delivered within the Department.

Another major development for the future will be professional links with primary care and community services, by providing outreach clinics away from the hospital setting so that delivery of the service at the location most convenient and appropriate for the patient can occur. This process will be helped by forging links between Physiotherapy, Primary Care and Community Services.

All these advances envisioned for the future means that the profession is set to continue developing further and who knows where this will take us in the next 100 years!

Some members of the Department of Physiotherapy. Left to right Jeanette Parsons, Lucy Bryant, Clare Connor, Lyn Jennings, Rob Letchford, Rhian Jennings, Pauline Hawkings, Pauline Price, Louise Brooks, Roz Barker-Smith, Jackie Baker and Sharon Gardiner.

(photograph Andrew Ponsford)

Occupational Therapy
Mrs. Margaret North FROT, Head of Occupational Therapy

In 1982, Susan Baker (nee Woods) was the first Occupational Therapist to be appointed to the Royal Gwent Hospital. There was no department so she was based in the Physiotherapy Department. In 1983 a Head Occupational Therapist was appointed at St. Woolos Hospital also covering the Royal Gwent Hospital. In 1985, Mrs. Baker moved to St. Woolos Hospital and two additional Occupational Therapists were appointed (Lynne Robinson and Margaret North) to cover the medical wards in 'B' Block at St. Woolos as well as the wards of the Royal Gwent. However there was still no department and staff were working from room 501 in the Royal Gwent although staff were becoming very fit from the walk between the hospitals.

The Occupational Therapists were given a base for their department in 1986. This was the old medical library and the room at the front entrance of the 1901 hospital that used to belong to the porters. To assess activity and daily living (A.D.L.) a Portakabin was purchased and lifted into the front of the hospital by crane. This small unit contained a kitchen, a bathroom and a bedroom to test ability of handicapped patients to live independently but it was taken out two weeks later because of problems with access to drains. However, a second attempt to install this unit was successful in January 1987.

When 'A' Block of the old hospital was demolished the department moved to its present location in the old paediatric ward which is shared with the Dietetics Department and Cardiology (ref. Pull-out Plan 2 - Site 8).

In 2004 there are 17 members of staff covering medical, orthopaedic and surgical wards The demand for occupational therapy increases as hospital stays shorten. The O.T. Department is responsible for the safe discharge of patients from the wards and expanded its service into the new M.A.U. facility in September 2003.

Nutrition and Dietetics
Eirlys Cawdery SRD, Chief Dietitian

Diet - what one eats - has been of interest to people over the centuries and many beliefs and taboos abound regarding the virtues of certain foods. Unfounded claims are constantly made by the people who write in magazines or by products sold in Health Food shops.

Nutrition is the science of food and enables us to study the composition and to group various foods whilst dietetics is the application of this knowledge to health and disease. The first dietitian in the U.K. was a nursing sister who had developed a deep interest in her patients following the discovery of insulin in the 1920s. Several others followed suit in the 1930s, and in the late 60s in Newport, Dr. Dipple, at that time the physician with a special interest in diabetes, was the first consultant to request a post of dietitian to be established at the Royal Gwent Hospital. By the 1970s there were two dietitians in post, and they provided a service for In-Patients as well as Out-Patients. Furthermore, a dietitian was appointed in 1970 to provide nutritional education to the Gwent population under the umbrella of the Health Promotion Department at Caerleon.

In the early 1990s, a Diabetes Specialist Dietitian was appointed to provide a dedicated educational service to patients attending the Royal Gwent Hospital while a second post was established in 2001. These two dietitians are involved in some 60 clinics per month and are part of the multi-disciplinary diabetes team which is based in Richmond House. Many changes take place regarding the content of the diet recommended as research dictates, therefore patients need to be regularly updated during their visits to diabetic clinics.

Dietitians are involved in the treatment of many other conditions. Special diets played great importance before the days of kidney dialysis in the mid-1960s and transplants in the 1970s. The current Chief Dietitian recalls using the Giovannetti diet, named after an Italian doctor, which was extremely low in protein and used low protein spaghetti to boost calorie intake. However, very little spaghetti was consumed in the U.K. at that time, which is in marked contrast with the popularity of pasta nowadays.

Several research projects have been undertaken in Newport by a number of dietitians over the years, but the greatest challenge of all has been to encourage patients to take adequate nourishment following surgery and cancer treatments. Many lack appetite prior to admission to hospital and it is hoped that the 'hotel services' which came about in Newport in the 1990s will at last be seen as part of treatment and will meet the requirements of individual patients, following government promotion of 'Food as Treatment' using celebrity chefs. If this can occur, apart from the well-being of patients, the length of stay in hospital can be reduced.

Dietetic expertise has been evident for intensive care patients since the early 1990s and the tube feeding of patients has become a major part of our work for both adults and children.

A dedicated paediatric dietitian was appointed in the 1980s and this enabled diabetes and cystic fibrosis clinics for children and teenagers to flourish as the dietician was dedicated to work alongside the consultant paediatrician.

Several members of the dietetic department have developed an interest in Sports Nutrition. One member who is worthy of mention is Gill Regan, who joined the department in 1983 and has since built up expertise in paediatric dietetics second to none in the U.K. During her early days at the hospital, she regularly competed for Wales in the long jump, including two Commonwealth Games, namely Brisbane (1982) and Edinburgh (1986), and she still holds the Welsh long jump record. More recently, she became an Honorary Dietitian to the British Olympic Association and was the official dietitian to athletes competing in the Olympic Games held in Sydney in 2000. She took a leading role in establishing and organising activity weekends for children with diabetes. These were started in the late 1980s and have been a regular feature since then. They are always a lot of fun for the children but quite exhausting for the staff who give up their weekend to supervise them. It is an excellent opportunity to help educate the children and increase their confidence and independence.

Dietitians are frequently asked for advice from people who have been to an alternative medical practitioner to determine whether they have a food allergy. It has been noted in Chapter 3 that two 'Physicians to Allergy Department' were employed by the hospital in 1948. These posts have long disappeared but more people than ever reckon that they have got an allergy to a huge number of foods these days.

The dietetic department is recognised for the practical training of student dietitians. However, with only two small offices to house the department, the students are obliged to claim any unoccupied desk on the day as in 2004 the department has long outgrown itself. It is true to say that a staff of sixteen dietitians is still a very small number to meet ever increasing demands that are made on the department. It has become the battle of the bulge in more ways than one! The Good Life has not been all good as being overweight contributes to many medical conditions - a big challenge for this new century.

It is essential that the Dietetic Department is situated within the hospital site. Dietitians cover every ward and are often requested to see patients attending consultant clinics. The service is demand-led and many clinics for children and adults referred by consultants are held within the department. In the 1980s, the department was located in the

Members of the Nutrition & Dietetics Department at the retirement dinner for Mrs. Eirlys Cawdery. Back row, from left to right: Andrew Hayes, Bethan Mainwaring, Helen Shannon, Elaine Hibbert-Jones, Lorna Trick, Gill Regan, Rachel Knowles and Peter King. 2nd row from back Nicky Marment, Annabel Doolan, Eirlys Cawdery, Tabbasum Kabeer, Judith Davies, Jennifer Jones and Joanna Males. 3rd row Gill Huntington, Paula Murphy, Pamela Murch, Lisa-Marie Brown and Nia Rees Williams. Front row Jayne Lavin, Kim Chorley, Lucy Ford, Adriana Dias, Sheelagh Challenger, Anna Pain, Judith Kilroy, Helen Tooke, Carolyn Penn and Orla Hynes.

(photograph courtesy of Eirlys Cawdery)

old pathology department. It moved into the old post-graduate centre at the front of the hospital when this relocated to the Friars 1983. Before demolition of the old building in 1992, the dieticians moved to the present site in 'A' Block which became available following transfer of the children's ward to the newly built 'D' Block. During the 1990s, the Dietetics Department doubled up as the Major Incident centre for the hospital.

Due to the very broad workload the department has operated flexitime for staff thus enabling new mothers to return to work which has ensured that a full complement of experienced staff is always available. In turn, experienced staff oversee newer members of staff who join the rotational post-graduate scheme that is operated. Apart from covering out-reach hospitals, a dietetic service is also provided to all G.P. practices in the Newport area, along with Caldicot and Chepstow.

Reaching out to the community in this way has many benefits. Patients find it easier to attend their own surgery and this cuts down on the number of people coming to the hospital site. Good teamwork has enabled better care to be offered to patients with diabetes, as increasing numbers are now diagnosed and treated in the G.P.s surgeries. Diabetes has indeed been the bread and butter of the profession since its inception and dietitians are often requested to give talks to voluntary groups supporting diabetes and other medical conditions.

Education is taken very seriously by dietitians at the Royal Gwent Hospital, whether it is to the staff or the patients. However, it is a constant uphill struggle to reverse the effects of modern lifestyle and dietary habits which are vigorously promoted by the modern food industry. The department regularly takes diabetes and medical students but lacks the workforce and accommodation needed to carry out its present work load.

Speech and Language Therapy
Christine Smith MSc MRCSLT

Historical Background

The importance of speech as a means of communication and an interest in problems associated with it has been recognised since ancient times. In the Edwin Smith Surgical Papyrus by James Breasted (1930) references dating back as far as 3,000 to 2,500 B.C. are made to speech difficulties and swallowing - the two main areas associated with Speech and Language Therapists (S.L.T.s).

The history of S.L.T. as a profession however is more recent. Towards the end of the 19th century, interest of physicians was beginning to focus on certain aspects of speech and its disorders but it soon became clear that the medical profession did not consider that treatment of speech disorders to be within their remit and sought assistance from outside the medical profession. In Britain they looked to that group of people who already had a great deal of professional experience in dealing with speech and voice - singing and elocution teachers.

The first official provision for children with speech problems came in 1906 with Manchester Education Authority appointing remedial teachers for stammerers. The first hospital clinics were believed to have been set up in 1911 at St. Bartholomew's Hospital in London for people with 'a stammer and speech defects'. Two years later, clinics at St. Thomas' Hospital and Guy's Hospital soon followed and London County Council, in later years, funded four clinics for children with speech problems.

In these early days, therapists were employed within two main areas, health and education. However, a split developed into two professional bodies, the Association of Speech Therapists supporting those who worked in education and the British Society of Speech Therapy supporting those who worked in the health arena. For approximately 10 years these two organisations ran in parallel until, encouraged by Joan Van Thal who acted as a 'link' between the two associations, they merged in 1945 to form 'The College of Speech Therapists'. In 1995, this became The Royal College of Speech and Language Therapists.

S.L.T. and The Royal Gwent Hospital

Speech Therapy, therefore, has a long history. There is little documented information about an early association of S.L.T. with the Royal Gwent Hospital, most of which is anecdotal and based on the knowledge and memories of current staff. As recently as 1957, there were no S.L.T.s working with adult patients in the Cardiff or Newport areas, and there were few therapists working in Wales at all. A visiting therapist to The Royal Gwent at that time, Ruth Bennett, was one of the pioneers of the profession. She worked mainly with children with cleft lip and palate at St. Lawrence Hospital in Chepstow around the late 1950s through to the early 1970s.

It was not until 1989 that an S.L.T. service was provided at the Royal Gwent Hospital where sessions had only been only provided on an ad hoc basis. At St. Woolos Hospital, by contrast, an S.L.T. service to patients had been set up on a regular basis. In the early days before 1989, the main emphasis of the work had been focused on pre-operative counselling of patients scheduled for laryngectomy and also assessment of some stroke patients. For therapists working in The Royal Gwent at that time conditions were difficult. No rooms had been allocated for treatment and one therapist remembers sitting in the car park to write up her notes! Although conditions were not ideal, the S.L.T. department kept up with the cutting edge of medical developments. For instance, a current member of the team vividly remembers travelling to Charing Cross Hospital in London with one of the E.N.T. Consultants to see a demonstration of the first speaking valve for laryngectomy patients.

Elderly patients were usually transferred to other hospitals such as St. Woolos but younger patients were generally discharged home. Because accommodation was a problem, prior to 1989 the adult Out-Patient S.L.T. service was run on a predominantly domiciliary basis. It was through the dedication and perseverance of the S.L.T. staff working in the adult service in Gwent during the 1980s and with the support of Dr. Calcraft (who had a special interest in stroke patients) that a team to treat adults was set up to provide a service for The Royal Gwent Hospital. Initially, they were given temporary accommodation in the old Endoscopy Suite until the department moved to its current location in 'C' Block.

From those early beginnings the service has continued to develop with a service now being provided to children and babies as well as to adults.

Nowadays, there are three main service areas for assessment and treatment of communication and swallowing difficulties; (1) Adults, (2) Community and (3) Children Special Needs. The S.L.T. service in Newport aims to provide input to all the children's and adult wards as well as specialist clinics such as the Multidisciplinary feeding clinics, Videofluoroscopy and the newly developed E.N.T. Voice Clinic. As advances in medicine have been made, therapists have responded, and will continue to respond, flexibly to meet the changing demands that will arise.

References
Breasted J.H. (1930) The Edwin Smith Surgical Papyrus. University of Chicago Press: Chicago Illinois

Robertson S., Kersner M. Davies S. (1995) A History of the College 1945-1995. Royal College of Speech and Language Therapists: London

Acknowledgements
With thanks to members of the Gwent S.L.T. Department and to members of The Royal College of Speech and Language Therapists for their valuable contributions (C.L.S.).

Chapter 10: Education & Training

General Historical Review
Gwilym Griffith OBE FRCS and Brian Peeling CBE FRCS

Before the mid-1960s, formal postgraduate education for both doctors and general practitioners did not exist in Newport; consultant trainees occupied junior posts in hospitals and were reliant on a rather haphazard apprenticeship system to further their training.

In 1966, it became mandatory for all large hospitals to have some provision for postgraduate education and at The Royal Gwent Hospital, Mr. Israel Rocker who was a consultant gynaecologist, was appointed as the first Postgraduate Organiser. His task was to create a system of post-graduate education for junior staff in training.

An Administrative Assistant was appointed, Mrs. Olive Palmer, who was also responsible for maintaining and running a Medical Library. The facilities for this were very limited and consisted of a small room leading off the main corridor of the hospital with twenty-five medical textbooks but a reasonably good selection of journals. A particular problem for Mrs. Palmer was to keep track of the journals and trace them as they had a habit of migrating around the hospital. There was also an especially obnoxious occurrence of removal of pages from journals by persons unknown. This dishonest and anti-social habit apparently persists even to the present day in the hospital's library. The Library was funded by a meagre budget, some from the Hospital Management Committee which was directed towards purchase of journals but also from funds generated by donations from pharmaceutical organisations for books. Therefore, expansion of reading material for postgraduate studies was slow.

Post-graduate meetings, clinical meetings and lectures by visiting experts were held in The Board Room of the hospital which, when there was good attendance, became very cramped. Meetings were also liable to become very stuffy and hot for those were the days when smokers' rights were unassailable. However, in about 1968, The Senior Medical and Dental Consultant Committee (who also met in same Board Room) voted, with considerable internal dissent, to abolish smoking from their meetings: thus medical meetings also became smoke-free.

However, The Post-graduate Department at The Royal Gwent Hospital really came into being with its own identity when a pre-fabricated Lecture Theatre was built in 1968 at the front of hospital next to the main entrance costing £5,000 (ref. Pull-out Plan 2 - Site 13). An anonymous general practitioner donated £2,000 towards this and the remainder of the money came from The Welsh Hospital Board and the Newport and East Monmouthshire Management Committee. This important landmark in the history of the hospital was masterminded and completed by Mr. Rocker. The unit had accommodation for about seventy places, a projection room, a small office for Mrs. Palmer and a restricted lobby where limited exhibitions could be displayed. It was connected to the Library which was a single room off the main corridor immediately behind so that these became a self-contained unit for Post-graduate studies. However, a major drawback was the rumble and noise of lorries and other traffic travelling along Cardiff Road which was only about twenty yards away. Also, there was no air-conditioning so that the room could become stifling in hot weather and frigid in cold weather (until warmed up by body heat).

In 1973, Mr. Brian Peeling followed Mr. Rocker as Post-graduate Organiser but had to relinquish the post after a year to give time to set up a new Department of Urology at St. Woolos Hospital that had started in 1974.

The baton was taken over by Dr. Gerald Anderson in 1975. Post-graduate activities had increased in the years since its inception but it became apparent that the accommodation in the pre-fabricated building had become inadequate for future progress. Dr. Anderson negotiated re-siting the Postgraduate Department in the Public Health Authority building elsewhere on the hospital site but this came to nothing with the authorities. It was not until the late 1970s, when Mr. Gwilym Griffith had taken over as Postgraduate Organiser, that agreement was reached with the management of the day (Dr. Douglas Harrett, Chief Medical Officer of The Gwent Health Authority) to move the Postgraduate Department and Medical Library to 'The Friars' building. Mr. Griffith negotiated and approved plans for a new lecture theatre to be built alongside and connected to 'The Friars' but, due to difficulty in raising the necessary capital (£60,000), the new building was not opened until 1983. By that time, Mr. Griffith had been succeeded as Postgraduate Organiser by Dr. Ian Petheram who arranged for the official opening of the new centre to be carried out by Professor Raymond Hoffenberg, President of The Royal College of Physicians. The new centre consisted of an auditorium with a spacious stage and seating for up to one hundred and twenty people, a reasonably spacious Projection Room and a small Exhibition/ Catering area. The Library was housed at 'The Friars' together with a Seminar Room that could accommodate thirty to forty people. There were also two committee rooms and an office for the Administrator, Mrs. Sandra Workman, who had followed Mrs. Palmer after her retirement in 1986.

The Friars and Postgraduate Lecture Hall (2004).

(photograph Andrew Ponsford).

In 1990, postgraduate education came under the jurisdiction of the Postgraduate Dean at The University of Wales College of Medicine and facilities had to be increased year on year because of an increasing number of doctors under training at the Royal Gwent and St. Woolos Hospitals.

There had to be an increase in Library content and the first full-time Librarian, Mr. Graham Titley, was appointed in 1985. He remained in post until 1995 when Joanna Dundon (née Grey-Lloyd) was appointed as Library Services Manager. She now has an assistant Librarian who is Undergraduate Liaison Librarian for all the students who are on placement in Newport and a Library Assistant to help in the daily running of the Library service.

Dr. Anne Freeman took over as Postgraduate Organiser in 1994 and she presided over the much-needed expansion of support staff for Postgraduate Studies which increased rapidly in the 1990s. Sandra Workman supervises four full-time administrative staff. In 2000, Dr. Freeman handed over to Mr. Francis Richardson.

A review of future capacity of the hospital to accommodate and cope with increasing demands for both undergraduate and postgraduate studies for medical and other professional staff was carried out between 1996 and 1999 by Professor Peeling at the request of the Chairman of the Trust, Mr. Colin Hughes Davies and the Chief Executive, Mr. Martin Turner.

His report indicated clearly that great expansion of lecture room, seminar room and library facilities was urgently needed among other priorities such as an under-graduate centre and recommended closer links with the University of Wales College of Medicine (U.W.C.M.).

In the Autumn of 2000, Dr. Hywel M. Jones, Consultant Anaesthetist, was appointed Sub-Dean of U.W.C.M. to coordinate and administer undergraduate and postgraduate medical and dental education in Newport and in Gwent.

Some members of the postgraduate staff. Left to right Sandra Workman, Rosanna Carnevate, Barbara Hopcroft, Linda Coe, Brenda Gadd, Maureen Williams, Laurie Matthews, Joanna Dundon, Sarah Still, Caroline Newman, Dr. Anne Freeman and Dr. Richard Harding.

Also, in recognition of the increasingly demanding role of the Postgraduate Organiser the Sub-Dean of the Gwent Clinical School, Dr. Hywel Jones, the Medical Director of the Gwent Healthcare Trust, Dr. Stephen Hunter and Professor Tom Hayes, the Postgraduate Dean of U.W.C.M. agreed to fund an Assistant Postgraduate Organiser post to support Mr. Richardson. Dr. Al Shafi, consultancy microbiologist, was appointed in 2001. Recently, Dr. Al Shafi moved to a post in England and Dr. J.R. Harding, consultant radiologist, was appointed in June 2003 as his replacement.

Dr. Hywel Jones Sub-Dean in Medicine.

Undergraduate Training & The Gwent Clinical School
Hywel Jones FRCA: Sub-Dean of Medicine

It was in 1973 that undergraduate students from the Welsh National School of Medicine were formally attached to The Royal Gwent Hospital for part of their clinical training.

The secondment of medical students to units outside Cardiff had started earlier with clinical attachments firstly in General Surgery arranged by Mr. L.P. Thomas with Professor Forrest and later in General Medicine. Soon afterwards, this was extended to attachments in Paediatrics and Obstetrics and Gynaecology, with students being allocated to many District General Hospitals in Wales of which The Royal Gwent was a major contributor.

Clinical teaching is, therefore, not a recent development for the Royal Gwent, and the contribution that the hospital now makes to teaching in all five years of the undergraduate programme has significantly increased over recent years. The hospital's main involvement is in Year 3 education. The year 3 curriculum includes the Foundation Clinical Skills course. This is a crucial period in the curriculum because it lays the foundation for further clinical training, which is essential to the quality of medical practice in the future. Year 3 also includes the start of Clinical Systems training in Medicine 1, Medicine 2, Surgical Systems, Function Systems e.g. Orthopaedics and Rheumatology and General Practice rotations with practices in the locality.

There are, also, many student attachments from years 4 and 5 which include Child Health, Reproductive Medicine, Psychological Medicine, and Cardiovascular and Respiratory Medicine. Also included in year 4 is the Module of Sub Specialities (M.O.S.S.). This includes a series of 5-week attachments in E.N.T., Dermatology, Ophalmology, Haematology and Infectious Disease.

Advanced training in Medicine and Surgery continues with the Diagnostic Synthesis Module, which continues into Year 5 together with the Clinical Consolidation Module.

Many other specialties are involved with student education. These include Anaesthetics and Intensive Care Medicine, Radiology, and the sub specialties in Pathology. These departments along with others host Special Study Modules (S.S.M.) which now make up 20% of the curriculum. These are mainly self-directed modules, which include project work that contributes to the student's final assessment.

Continuing with the theme of assessment, the hospital also hosts the Year 3 Clinical Competence Exam in May each year, which is part of the Intermediate M.B. examination. Success in this exam is the gateway to progression to the Final Degree examinations after a further two years training. Many clinicians from the Royal Gwent are also involved with the Final M.B. examination held each summer.

These details of the undergraduate training programme in Newport highlights the breadth and depth of teaching activity not only within the hospital but throughout the Gwent Healthcare N.H.S. Trust.

The Gwent Clinical School

As a leading campus of the University of Wales College of Medicine (U.W.C.M.), the title of 'Gwent Clinical School' has been bestowed by the Senate of the University of Wales College of Medicine. This is in recognition of our major contribution to clinical teaching in Wales particularly in relation to the expansion of student numbers that has occurred.

It is intended that The Gwent Clinical School will undertake nearly 15% of all clinical teaching which is second only in Wales to the Cardiff hospitals.

The increase in medical student numbers across the U.K. has been the result of Government recognition of the significant shortfall in the number of doctors that are required to address the modernisation of the N.H.S.. In line with this, the Welsh Assembly Government has agreed an increase in the U.W.C.M. intake from 160 to 300 students over the next few years, with an additional 70 places in the proposed graduate entry scheme making a total of 370 students graduating each year.

The Royal Gwent Hospital will continue to increase its contribution to teaching in line with the increased intake to the College of Medicine.

The title of Gwent Clinical School is not the only form of recognition. Funding based on teaching activity has increased dramatically annually with a projected annual budget of over £2m by the year 2007/8. The money has enabled the organisation to improve facilities for teaching as well as to expand consultant numbers in response to teaching activity. The number of student attachments to the hospital and indeed to the Trust demands a teaching structure that enables clinical staff to dedicate time to this important development. This is a welcome development that has been requested by consultants in Newport from successive managements in the past and recognises that teaching takes time for which allowance has to be made from contracted service commitments. Since the creation of The Gwent Healthcare N.H.S. Trust, Dr. Stephen Hunter (Medical Director) and the Trust Board have been very supportive of these developments which have been given impetus from the Welsh Assembly Government.

The annual commissioning visit of the Dean of Medicine of the U.W.C.M., Professor Ken Woodhouse, and the Postgraduate Dean of Medicine of U.W.C.M., Professor Simon Smail continues to recognise the quality and quantity of teaching activity undertaken in Newport. One of the issues raised during these visits is the need to improve and expand the training facilities on the Royal Gwent Hospital site. As part of the birth of the Gwent Clinical School a Business case has been submitted to the Welsh Assembly Government proposing the building of a Health Science Institute on the Royal Gwent Hospital Campus.

Health Science Institute

It has been agreed to build The Health Science Institute on the site of 64 Cardiff Road (ref. Pull-out Plan 2 - Site 3).

This building has been in use for many years by The Royal Gwent Hospital and during some years before 1948 it belonged to The Workmen's Fund as its headquarters. *(information from Miss Blake, now aged 84, who worked in 64 Cardiff Road from 1935. -*

64 Cardiff Road boarded up in 2003 and awaiting demolition for the new Health Science Institute.

(photograph courtesy of Rex Moreton, Newport)

communication from Mr. Stan Jordan) From 1948 until 1974, it was the headquarters of The Newport & East Monmouthshire H.M.C. and then housed various administrative units under The Gwent Health Authority until it was closed.

The architect-designed building of the proposed Health Science Institute has recently received planning permission from the local authority and the business case has obtained approval from the Gwent N.H.S. Trust Board and the Gwent Health Authority.

Pending the approval of a detailed business case, Mrs. Jane Hutt AM, Minister for Health to the Welsh Assembly Government, has announced £6m to fund this important development. The building, which is due to be completed in 2006 will provide a state of the art library and other educational facilities both for postgraduate and undergraduate education. The building will have five levels with a total floor space of 2500 M² of which 600 M² will be occupied by a library and data centre. Other facilities will include a number of lecture theatres, seminar rooms, clinical skills training and examination rooms as well as being the administrative centre for the Clinical School.

Computerised projection of proposed Health Science Institute at the junction of Cardiff Road and Clytha Square.

(photograph courtesy of Estate & Works Department, Terry Gale)

The building will also provide common room and locker facilities for all undergraduate students on attachment to the hospital.

The Research and Development Unit will also be located within the building. The development of closer links between clinical research and medical education within the Gwent Clinical School is considered to be an essential component to the success of the project.

Undergraduate Education Structure of The Gwent Clinical School

The support structure and teaching activity are integral parts of the Gwent Clinical School.

The management structure includes a Development Manager for education, Ms. Linda Coe, who has been in post since October 2001. She heads an undergraduate department of three members of staff on the Royal Gwent site and they provide a focal point for the students as well as organising and co-ordinating the teaching activity within the Hospital. The undergraduate administrator, Ms. Maria West, is responsible for the important role of ensuring that all activity is organised and implemented smoothly within the Hospital as well as being a 'mother figure' for the students.

The Gwent Clinical School together with the College of Medicine has appointed a Senior Lecturer, Mr. Keith Vellacott, with responsibility for managing the teaching and assessment activity for the Royal Gwent Hospital site. To support him Lecturers have been appointed in the Departments of Medicine, General Surgery, Paediatrics, Reproductive Medicine, Orthopaedics, E.N.T., Ophthalmology, Anaesthetics, Dermatology and Pathology. Also, all consultants involved in teaching students are appointed as Clinical Tutors of the University of Wales College of Medicine.

Conclusion

As in the past, students and trainees from all disciplines continue to favour rotations to the Royal Gwent Hospital. This has always been due to the effort and enthusiasm over many years of clinical teachers within the organisation. There is every expectation that The Gwent Clinical School will flourish in the future and increase the reputation that the hospital has gained since the mid-1960s as a centre of excellence for clinical, research and educational achievement. The ethos of The Gwent Clinical School encompasses not only medical education, but includes education of nurses and professions allied to medicine.

Postgraduate Vocational Training for General Practice in South Gwent
Dr. Chris John, Postgraduate Organiser for G.P. Training

Prior to the advent of the N.H.S. the boundaries between General Practice and hospital medicine were not clearly defined. Many practitioners were involved in both areas. From 1948 on the roles diverged and general practice was a career route that required no additional training after the pre-registration year. The advent of vocational training in the 1970s brought a fresh impetus to postgraduate activities.

In 1972 a local G.P., Hywel Williams, developed the first training scheme for general practitioners. This was linked to hospital posts at the Royal Gwent and local practices and brought many future local GPs to the south Gwent area and enabled them to have experience of a close working relationship with local consultants and hospital career staff. *(It also enhanced considerably the quality of practice in the South of the County - Editor).* The Friars postgraduate centre was and still is the local focus for lectures and seminars for doctors in training for practice although the training scheme now encompasses the whole of Gwent.

The immense popularity of General Practice throughout the 1970s and 80s faded rapidly after the introduction of a new G.P. contract in 1990 and the South Gwent scheme collapsed leading to amalgamation with North Gwent in 1997. The revival of the scheme owes much to the dedication and hard work of two Pontypool G.P.s, Drs. Doug Dare and Hasmukh Joshi, who saw the Vocational Training Scheme through a very trying period.

More change is around the corner and we look to our local Postgraduate Centre and the proposed Heath Science Institute to keep the spirit of enthusiasm for learning alive in difficult times. The motto of the The Royal College of General Practitioners lives on - 'Cum Scientia Caritas' (Caring Supported by Good Science).

Chapter 11: Supportive Services

Hotel Services - Catering
Jeanette Dawes

for Patients

Before 1948, meals for patients were very basic, so much so that visitors would bring in food to support the meagre diet provided by the hospital. There was insufficient domestic staff to provide morning and daily hot drinks and this was left to patients to organise and implement. The Ward Sister would choose two 'up patients' who would collect money from the other patients who wished to participate in the scheme. They would then be called by the night staff before the ward woke in the morning, they would make the tea and take it around the ward. In the evening before the patients retired, another tea round would take place. The two patients also had the job of collecting the cups and washing up. When these two patients were discharged another pair would be chosen by the Ward Sister. There was no choice of drink as there is today - tea was the only beverage. *(Cliff Knight)*

The main kitchen was situated at the top of the building together with a Doctors' Dining Room. Food for patients was sent in specially heated containers to all ward kitchens where it was plated by the Ward Sister and served to patients. Ward orderlies made tea in the ward kitchen.

In 1937, the kitchen was reconstructed, enlarged and equipped at a cost of £4,700. Cooking was by gas, electricity and anthracite coal ovens and was carried out by one chef, two assistant cooks and kitchen hands working in shifts. They had to feed five hundred people each mealtime.

In 1968, Scheme 1 of the re-development programme included construction of a new kitchen and Dining Room in the 'New Hospital' (now Block 'B') and a new method of feeding patients was introduced. The hospital kitchen was fitted with a long conveyor belt, which had heated/cold, compartments along its side. Food for that particular meal was placed into the respective compartments by the chefs after preparation. Catering assistants served the food from these compartments onto a hot plate, which was placed on a tray on the moving conveyor belt. The tray contained a menu, which had been filled in by the patient up to three days before with their choice. A supervisor checked the tray at the end of the conveyor for visual acceptability, portion size, dietary correctness and appropriate cutlery. A lid was then placed on the hot food and the tray was put into an enclosed trolley for transportation to the wards by porters. The trolleys were insulated but had no means of temperature control.

In 1993 the Patients Association published guidelines for minimum standards of quality for food served to patients in hospitals. These standards included;

- an attractive presentation is very important in making food appetising to the patients who may not feel like eating, but need nourishment.
- patients should be able to order as near as possible to the time the meal is served.
- patients should be able to select a meal from a choice of dishes and decide whether they want a large or small portion at the time of ordering.
- hot dishes should in fact be hot and smell appetising, whilst cold dishes should be cold.

In 1994 the National Audit Office surveyed hospital catering with the following conclusions;

- ordering meals in advance - ordering two meals in advance was considered a reasonable maximum.
- attractive and appetising meals - the survey showed that standards of food presentation varied but were mostly poor.
- meal sizes - most meals served were found to be too large or too small, mainly dependent on the patient's age.
- the temperature of meals - hot food being served too cold due to insufficient cooking, faulty equipment or slow delivery and service.

The Citizens Charter noted that these should be well publicised and easy to use complaint procedures. However, patients surveyed were not aware of local catering service complaint procedures.

In 1992 the Royal Gwent Hospital, under the direction of Mrs. Siân Martin (Head of Operational Services) decided to change the way in which patients were being fed to fully comply with the above mentioned guidelines, and food safety and nutritional standards. A team of Operational Services Managers was tasked to design a new service that would encompass the three main jobs now being carried out for the patients by separate departments. These were;

- Movement of patients and goods by the Portering Department managed by the Portering Manager.
- Cleaning of wards and departments by the domestic staff managed by the Domestic Services Manager.
- Feeding of patients and staff by the Catering Department managed by the Catering Manager.

The team, which included the above managers, combined these three departments to form 'Hotel Services' and the staff were invited to volunteer to work on a pilot scheme to introduce the new service to the wards. Several changes of working pattern were introduced before this new service went 'live' in July 1993.

These were:
- introduction and training of a generic workforce (renamed hosts/hostesses) currently employed by the three separate departments, including Hotel Services Supervisors and Duty managers covering twenty-four hours, seven days a week.
- a new pay deal for the above and the introduction of new working rosters in conjunction with the Trades Union Council.
- to refurbish ward kitchens with new equipment capable of producing a continental breakfast with only limited involvement from the main kitchen to provide special dietary needs. Re-design of the main kitchens included a new cooking island with separate food preparation areas and dishwasher, together with a separate loading and washing area for the new food trolleys.
- purchase of bulk food trolleys capable of keeping hot and cold food at the correct temperature required by the law.

New staff uniforms highlighted the tasks involved in the new service such as food handling or cleaning. (A different coloured tabard was used to indicate which task the hostess was completing).

A same-day ordering service for lunch and supper was introduced with breakfast being chosen by the patient directly from the trolley.

A patient information booklet described the new service, the ordering system and the procedure for complaints.

The system was monitored through patient questionnaires and daily visits to the wards by the Head Chef ensured so that the service could be seen to deliver the high standard of quality that was expected.

New menus reflected current trends which included a roast meat lunch with a healthy and vegetarian alternative as well as a hot and cold choice for supper instead of sandwiches as had been provided previously.

Belle Vue Park Restaurant

The dining room for staff and visitors built in 1968 at the time of the Scheme 1 redevelopment of the hospital was upgraded in 1993 at the same time as the main kitchen. The new restaurant design was completed by a team of catering and works department managers and was officially opened on 13 December 1993 by Franco Taruschio, Chef/Patron of the Walnut Tree Restaurant in Abergavenny. Staff of the Hospital were invited to suggest a name for the new restaurant and the name Belle Vue Park was chosen.

The staff dining room built in the Scheme 1 development programme 1966.
(photograph courtesy of Cliff Knight)

The Artists in Residence, Carol Hiles and Wendy Lewis, designed and made a unique ceramic tile mural which was fixed on the wall at the rear of the food counters in the restaurant by Mr. Mattie Maloney from the hospital's Works and Estates department. The mural, measuring 9ft. by 40ft. was unveiled by the B.B.C. Radio gardening expert Mr. Clay Jones on 17 June 1994. The mural took 5 months to complete and a month to fix to the wall and comprised of over 1,000 hand-painted tiles based on scenes and plant forms from Belle Vue Park. The project was financially assisted by British Steel and the Post Office and the tiles were donated by H. & R. Johnson Limited of Stoke-on-Trent. Gwent College of Higher Education, Ceramics Department, fired the tiles.

The Belle Vue Restaurant.

The Mural in the Belle Vue Restaurant.

The newly refurbished Belle Vue Restaurant became so popular with staff and visitors that it became necessary to plan another catering outlet which would be situated at the Eastern end of the Hospital. A new Italian style café opened on 1 April 1998 together with a retail shop. Visitors to the hospital, staff and patients are now able to purchase gifts, toiletries, flowers, stamps, newspapers and magazines as well as enjoying hot and cold snacks and speciality coffee. The popularity of the café was such that the original opening hours were extended to include a night service from 9.00pm to 2.00am.

The Beechwood Café 1998.

(photograph courtesy of Cliff Knight)

The Hospital Chaplaincy Service
The Reverend Alan Tyler, Senior Chaplain

When the N.H.S. was established in 1948, hospital authorities were advised that special attention should be given to the spiritual needs of both patients and staff and to ensure that public worship was available regularly.

Advice was also given that when the size of a hospital justified it, a room should be set aside for use as a Chapel. Chaplains should be appointed from the various Christian denominations to provide for the spiritual needs of the patient and staff and also to officiate at public services each Sunday. Most chaplains would be part-time, working within a parish or church local to the hospital and dedicating time each week for work within the hospital community. In some instances where a hospital cared for more than 750 patients, the Board of Governors or Management Committee was encouraged to give serious attention to the appointment of a whole-time chaplain.

This guidance given by the government to hospital authorities recognised that the physical welfare of a patient could not be kept separate from their spiritual and mental well-being. It was also a serious recognition of the part played by the Christian church over many centuries in the provision of medical care to the sick and needy.

This situation remained the same until 1977 when the Department of Health produced a document PM 84 which acknowledged that a chaplain's duties depended not only upon the number of patients that he could be expected to see, but also should be related to condition of patients as acute, critical, or long-stay cases, for example. Consequently, the number of whole-time chaplains in hospitals throughout the country increased from 108 in 1976, to over 400 by the year 2000.

The Royal Gwent Hospital had for many years appointed sessional or part-time chaplains from those churches local to the hospital. St. Paul's Church at the lower end of Commercial Street provided an Anglican chaplain, (Church of Wales/England) and St. Mary's Church on Stow Hill, arranged for a resident Roman Catholic priest to visit the hospital regularly. The Free Church chaplain could be from any non-conformist tradition and was nominated to the hospital by the local Free Church Council.

By 1996 the increasing activity of the Royal Gwent Hospital led to a consultation process being initiated between the hospital and local churches to consider the appointment of a new whole-time chaplain. In August 1997 the first whole-time chaplain began to work on-site in the Royal Gwent.

The modern approach to chaplaincy seeks to provide for the wider spiritual needs of patients and staff, offering an ear to listen and counselling, as well as prayer and the sacraments. Pastoral care and patient support underpins all of the chaplain's work, recognising the vital importance of a holistic approach to healthcare.

The chapel is currently on Level 3, D-Block. The windows were salvaged from the original chapel of the old hospital when it was demolished in 1991 and were re-installed in their present position with a carefully designed internal lighting system. The original chapel had been donated in 1912 by Mrs. C.H. Bailey of Stelvio House as a memorial to her husband and the preservation and re-positioning of the stained glass was carried out by Mr. Terry Gale of the Building and Works Department.

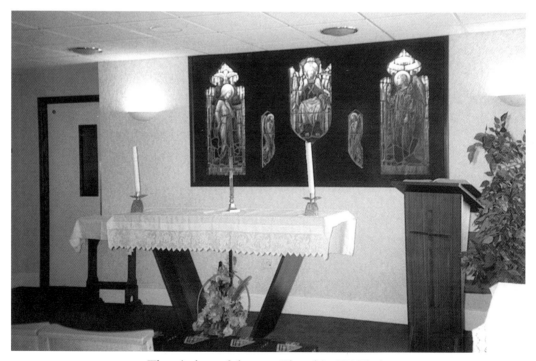

The windows of the new Chapel in 'D' Block.

(photograph courtesy of Cliff Knight)

The four current chaplains work every weekday and a Sunday morning in the hospital and provide an around-the-clock on-call facility for emergencies.

There also several volunteers who work alongside the chaplains to provide support for patients.

In 2003, arrangements were made for the Muslim population of the area to have access for Islamic spiritual support and assistance while in hospital. This is, of course, a timely recognition not only of the needs of the Muslim community in Newport but also of their increasing place and contribution in everyday life.

The Artists in Residence
Gwilym Griffith OBE FRCS

The Royal Gwent Hospital was one of the first hospitals in Wales to create posts of Artists in Residence. In a joint venture with The Welsh Arts Council, Carol Hiles and Wendy Davies were appointed to share the post.

Their work is to be seen throughout the hospital - in the main corridors, the children's wards, the Out-Patients and radiology departments. Mosaics in the Belle Vue Restaurant at The Royal Gwent and in the dining room at St. Woolos Hospital are much admired.

They gave much valuable advice about rescue from E.N.T. Wards in the old building of tiles depicting scenes from nursery rhymes before demolition. These have been referred to on page 126 where they are illustrated in their new site in the Children's Unit in 'D' Block.

They also provided valuable advice with planning the multi-faith chapel.

During the time that they have been in post, their work has succeeded in making the hospital less impersonal and forbidding, so achieving the primary aim of the new idea of Artists in Residence.

Hospital Porters and Domestic Staff
Cliff Knight

Portering is obviously a key element of hospital life otherwise goods, food and patients could not be moved around for their various needs. It is difficult to know exactly when porters as such began to function at the Newport hospitals. In an Annual Report of 1943, it was mentioned that 'special thanks be given to the voluntary stretcher bearers'. However, it is known that in 1944, Mr. W.F. Chadwick came from Llandough Hospital, Penarth to work at the Royal Gwent Hospital and was appointed Senior House Porter in 1946. This post was later renamed Head Porter and he supervised and organised the portering staff of the hospital.

In those days, the Head Porter was a person of considerable importance and was held in high esteem. For example, he would accompany the Mayor at his Christmas visit and he organised official functions of the hospital and helped to run and contribute to the hospital's Amateur Theatrical Society which was a major event during the Christmas period (see Chapter 13). In fact, his outstanding services to the hospital were recognised in 1963 with the award of the B.E.M..

Today, the role of the Head Porter has been replaced with a team of Hotel Service Supervisors working in shifts with the porters. They also look after the Domestic Service staff who keep the hospital clean night and day as well as Ward Hosts/Hostesses who serve patients with meals and beverages.

Chapter 12: Fundraising after 1948

It soon became apparent after 1948 that the State was not able, and could not be expected, to give total global financial cover for everything needed by The National Health Service. Therefore, in Newport, supplementary fundraising was accepted as a necessary and essential source for purchase of some amenities and smaller items that might lie outside the normal budget of the hospitals. Two organisations in particular have become the backbone of supplementary fundraising in The Royal Gwent after 1948: these are The Gwent Hospitals Contributory Fund and The League of Hospital Friends. *(Editor)*

1) The Gwent Hospitals Contributory Fund
information from Anne Dyer & Tony Gray MB BCh - Editor

In 1948, the reality of a free Health Service created a crisis of identity for the Gwent Hospitals Contributory Fund whose work had played a fundamental role, as The Workingmen's Fund, towards the revenue and capital of The Royal Gwent Hospital when it had been a voluntary institution. There is little doubt that without the support of the Workmen's Fund, the Royal Gwent Hospital would never have developed as it did and this close working relationship is illustrated by the location of its headquarters which has been,for many years, across the Cardiff Road opposite the main gate of the hospital.

Therefore, the problem in 1948 for the Directors of The Contributory Fund was two-fold. Firstly, was the Fund no longer needed as the hospital should, in future, be funded by the State? Secondly, should the Fund be wound up?

These options did not appeal to its members: they decided that the Fund would continue in a different role from the days when it gave financial support to The Royal Gwent as a voluntary hospital. It was resolved that the most reasonable course of action would be to substitute cash benefits for treatment costs and since then, in return for a subscription, members have been able to receive help when in need of medical care and amenities not available through the N.H.S.. Grants have been available for hospital patients, for maternity, for dental treatment, for optical treatment and even a funeral grant.

The Gwent Hospitals Contributory Fund 2003. Top row, left to right: W.C. Stanton, W. Young, R. Williams, A. McCarthy, H. Thomas, T. McNamara, J. Slade, W. Yates, D. Hire, D.B. Price. Front row: E.R. Owen, D.E. Sturdy (President), D. Clark (Chairman), P.J. McKim and W. Heaven.

The first full year's income in 1949 was £3,500 of which £3,200 was paid in benefits to two thousand claimants. The success of the Fund, since then, is self-evident for its income in 1974 exceeded £100,000 and in 1998 total contributions were £1,142,286 of which £821,523 was returned to the members in the form of benefits. The current worth of the Fund is approximately £2 million. The Chief Executive until recently was Mrs. Anne Dyer supported by an Executive Committee of members of the Fund.

In addition to providing help for individual needs, the Fund has been able through its charitable status to help many hospital-related causes such as the provision of a swimming pool for Llanfrechfa Grange Hospital and a Postgraduate Centre at the Royal Gwent Hospital.

One of its outstanding achievements was to found the Trevor Gray Memorial Nurses Scholarship which has enabled at least four nurses each year to gain a certificate for a month's training in the care of the terminally ill and dying patients. This was to honour the work of Mr. Trevor Gray who had been Secretary of the Gwent Hospital Contributory Fund from 1948 to 1984 and had built up the membership from a couple of hundred to nearly 20,000 subscribers. He became a most influential, and always modest, leader in many aspects of health care in Wales and nationally. For instance, he served as Chairman of The League of Hospital Friends in Wales, as Chairman of the National Association of Leagues of Hospital Friends and as Chairman of Wales Voluntary Bodies in the Health Service. Mr Gray was a member of The Welsh Hospital Board and, indeed, was a very good friend of the Royal Gwent Hospital in particular. It is not known generally that in 1974 he was the first Lay Member to be appointed to The General Medical Council. His son (Dr. Tony Gray) observed that Trevor Gray was very shocked at the severity of The General Medical Council towards its professional peers. He was also a Justice of the Peace for many years. For all these services, Trevor Gray was created a Member of The Order of the British Empire (MBE.) in 1973, a well deserved honour for a lifetime of service to others.

Very sadly, Trevor Gray died of cancer in 1985, the year after his retirement, at the age of 65 from leiomyosarcoma, a rare malignancy.

Trevor Gray and his family at Buckingham Palace for his investiture of an MBE. in 1973.

(photograph courtesy of Dr. Tony Gray)

2) The League of Friends of The Royal Gwent Hospital
information provided by Miss Beryl Griffiths and Mrs. June Price - Editor

The hospital's League of Friends is a registered Charity. It has been one of the mainstays of voluntary work for the hospital by fundraising from boot sales, sporting events, bed pushing, slimming contests, garden parties, sales of work, gifts, coffee mornings, concerts, jumble sales, fêtes, etc. However, a major source of monies arose from a mobile telephone service for In-Patients that League members took around the hospital.

The first recorded League of Friends was formed in Worcester in 1746 with the simple aim of caring for the health, comfort and dignity of patients. This was in the days when there was little medical help from local dispensaries or hospitals except perhaps for the more fortunate who were able to pay for treatment.

The modern movement of Leagues of Friends began in 1949 and a National Association of Friends was formed that year. This was welcomed by the Minister of Health, Aneurin Bevan, for the support that they gave to the new National Health Service through personal, voluntary efforts to raise money for patients in hospitals.

It was on the 29th November 1956 that a meeting was held in Newport, chaired by Mrs. Nancy Morgan, the wife of one of the hospital's consultants. This led to formation of the League of Friends at the Royal Gwent Hospital whose objective was to improve the quality of life of In-Patients by funding items which were not normally provided by the budget of the hospital from within The National Health Service. Initially, the members of the League were wives of consultants and it is of interest that this group of ladies got together in response to a statement of need from the hospital for their help. In fact, the League of Friends was a continuation of The Needlework Guild that had done so much work and fundraising for the hospital during its time as a Voluntary Hospital. The work of the Needlework Guild had ceased in 1948 following the view of hospital officials of the newly formed National Health Service that the Guild's services were no longer needed because the hospital had become self-sufficient. With time this view was reversed so that after a while the previous contribution of The Needlework Guild was resurrected as The League of Friends *(private information to Editor)*.

The League consisted entirely of volunteers (as it does today). In the early days of The League, gifts of toys to children in the hospital helped to make a child's stay in hospital less frightening and more comfortable. Even plates decorated with nursery characters were given to cheer the children up.

Toys for the Children's ward, and television sets for adults wards might be termed 'luxury items' as could pictures and flower arrangements in waiting rooms but the overall intention of The League's activities has been to reduce the impartiality and unfriendliness of hospital surroundings which can intimidate and frighten so many, especially children.

The League has no past records available before 1981 but since that date many funds have been made to purchase medical, surgical and technical equipment to support the work of doctors, nurses and other staff. These have included:

to 1996	£61,935 including £20,000 for the Lithotripter Appeal
• in 1997:	£63,175 including £10,000 to The Endoscopy Unit and £14,300 to Vascular Surgery
• in 1998:	£27,090 including £13,000 for Endoscopy research
• in 1999:	£26,693 including £20,000 for Endoscopy (instruments)
• in 2000:	£20,639 including £4,000 for pressure monitors (Radiology)
• in 2001:	£42,429 including £18,711 for a portable D.V.T. scanner

- in 2002:   £61,195 including £20,000 towards Dye Laser (Dermatology) and £22,500 for wireless capsule endoscopy
- in 2003:   £10,000 to fund a Treadmill and Hoist for the Physiotherapy Department and £10,000 for Prostate Tissue Morcellator for the Department of Urology in partnership with the Royal Gwent Hospital Golf Day.

This makes an incredible total of £323,156 donated to the hospital.

Other contributions have been toward:

- the rose garden in the hospital grounds,
- fittings and furnishings for the Maternity Department and the Nurses' Home,
- an E.C.G. machine costing £600,
- £2,100 towards the hospital radio service,
- £2,000 for the Postgraduate Centre at the Friars,
- £500 worth of toys for children attending the Oral/Maxillofacial Surgery Unit to occupy their time while they were waiting for their appointments,
- each Christmas the League gives a present to every patient both in the Royal Gwent Hospital and St. Woolos Hospital.

Unfortunately, in September 1998, a major source of income for The League stopped. For many years members of the League of Friends had provided a mobile telephone service to In-Patients so that they could make outside calls to relatives and friends. The charges for the calls were within the normal B.T. rates and this service was much appreciated generally. Income from this quiet and unassuming but widely used activity was frequently in the region of £25,000 or even £30,000 per year hence the ability of the League to contemplate major donations to various aspects of the hospital's work, as has been catalogued in the previous section of this article. The mobile telephone service was replaced by a commercial system offering a combined telephone, television and radio unit

Photograph showing the bedside communication system for In-Patients which offers an integral television, telephone and radio that can be operated by patients.

(photograph Nigel Pearce, Medical Illustration R.G.H.)

at each bedside in the hospital for which patients paid a hire charge to a central agency within the hospital. It was a management decision to install this system after due representation by the League of Friends had been made. It is not within the remit of this book to comment upon the popularity of this system with patients and their relatives or its success in terms of value for money but although its arrival has made funding of non-exchequer projects for clinical and house-keeping projects more difficult for The League, it has provided better opportunities for patients to keep in touch with their families and friends.

The League of Friends has no central office, but it took over the Buffet in the Main Out-Patients which is regarded as its base in the hospital. This became available when The Red Cross closed in 1998. There is also a Buffet in the Antenatal clinic run by members of the League. These are the current main source of income. There are up to 50 members who work on a rota basis. All members of the League consider it to be a great privilege to be able to serve those less fortunate than themselves, and generally appreciate the support that they receive from the local community so that they can help the work of the doctors, nurses and other staff at the hospital.

The League of Friends of The Royal Gwent Hospital. Front row, left to right: Miss Ruth Cook, Mrs. June Price, Mrs. M. Richards, Mrs. Mary Rees, Mrs. N. Jones, Miss B. Griffiths, Mrs. S. Price (Barclays Bank), Mrs. S. Williams, Mrs. Liz Gull and Mrs. M. Bennett. Second row: Mrs. G. Berry, Mrs. R. Morgan, Mrs. A. Hewes, Mrs. M. Walters, Mrs. J. Barnes, Mrs. M. Hamilton, Mrs. L. Jones and Mrs. Rita Cook. Third row: Mrs. G. Lee, Mrs. W. Banfield and Mrs. G. McNamara.

(photograph courtesy of The South Wales Argus, December 2000)

The work of Leagues of Friends was commended in 1995 by Stephen Dorrell, the Secretary of State for Health at the time, with the following statement: *'I have been extremely impressed by their achievements and the vital role played by Hospital Friends in cementing the links between local hospitals and the people they serve'*.

Chairmen of the committees of The League of Friends of The Royal Gwent Hospital have been:

Mrs. Glyn Morgan	(1956 to 1958)
Mrs. Betty Vernon Jones	(1958 to 1960)
Mrs. Olga Thomas	(1960 to 1962)
Mrs. Pearl Phillips	(1962 to 1972)
Mrs. Sally Hughes	(1972 to 1988)
Mrs. Ray Morgan	(1988 to 1994)
Miss Beryl Griffiths	(1994 to 1997)
Mrs. June Price	(1997 to 2001)
Mr. Mark Evans	(from 2001)

(The achievements of the League of Friends of the Royal Gwent have indeed played a vital role for the Royal Gwent in providing technology and other facilities that have enabled clinicians and others to give a service of the highest and most up-to-date quality for the local people. It is a remarkable story of achievement and service by volunteers - Editorial comment).

3) Other Fundraising

1) The Annual Cycle Ride in aid of the Cardiology Department, which has been led by Dr. John Davies since 1984, has raised over £500,000 since that date.

2) In 1991, a fund was set by Mr. Bill Sage, a local Estate Agent, to raise money to purchase a Lithotripter for non-surgical treatment of kidney stones. The target was £300,000 and Mr. Sage personally raised £220,000. This massive achievement was supported by funds raised by Mrs. Eleanor Gower (£30,000), a donation of £20,000 by The League of Friends, £20,000 from Research Funds of the Department of Urology which had accrued from clinical research studies and the remainder came from smaller individual donations.

Chapter 13: Some Aspects of Hospital Life

Years from 1948 to mid-1970s
Brian Peeling CBE FRCS

The previous chapters have been written about the social and political influences that changed the fabric and organisation of the Newport and district hospitals allied to increasingly rapid advances in science and technology that have created a revolution in healthcare during a relatively short period of time.

However, within the hospitals there has been a community of doctors, nurses, secretarial and support staff, engineers, porters, maintenance workers and others who together provide the structure that enables care of patients to happen. In Chapter 2, it was deduced from the specification in the design of the new hospital of 1901 of bedrooms for house surgeons, Matron and nurses, ward maids, engineers and porters, that these people lived and worked in a hospital-based community which was their home. For nurses, residential accommodation provided by the hospitals, but tightly controlled and disciplined, was the norm until the 1970s when nurses moved into Blocks 9 and 10 in Friars Field or were moved out of 'Springfield House' at St. Woolos Hospital. Similarly, junior hospital doctors were provided with Residential Quarters including their own Dining Room until the mid-1970s.

Therefore, it was natural for hospital staff in those days to create activities within the community of the institution. For instance, the Royal Gwent Hospital cricket team in the 1960s was made up of junior doctors, office and maintenance staff with a few consultants, and their favourite venue for matches was the cricket field at St. Cadoc's Hospital. The standard of play was unpredictable, and Derek Richards, who was a consultant surgeon at that time, would officiate from time to time as umpire with calculated fairness rather than informed objectivity. For instance, on one occasion, Dr. Johnny Thomas (a consultant anaesthetist) was run out about five yards from his stumps but as he had only been batting for a few minutes, Derek Richards after a minute or two of careful thought decided that Johnny hadn't had a fair run so pronounced him 'not out'. This resulted in a demonstration from the opposition which surely was a precursor of modern-day cricket. The umpire was not for turning.

There was also a tennis court at the present site of the car park for Management and Administration staff of Block 9. This was used frequently by all staff especially resident doctors and nurses.

As could be expected, the Residents' Mess was a focus for all medical staff. There were rooms in which junior doctors lived, a Sitting Room used by all medical staff in which tea with sandwiches and cakes were available at 4pm, a Dining Room with its own kitchen for meals and domestic staff to look after the living and catering aspects of the Residents' Quarters. In this day and age, there will be many who resent this mode of life as undue privilege but it has to be understood that traditionally, junior doctors were often on-call on alternate days and nights without resident back-up, that their rates of pay were very poor (in the 1950s a house officer's take-home pay was under £5 per week), and that almost all were unmarried so that the Residents' Quarters was their home.

Therefore, life in a Residents' Mess tended to be based within itself and, especially at Christmas time in the Royal Gwent and St. Woolos Hospitals there was much social activity, the highlight being a Staff Party in the Mess. This was hosted by the juniors for senior medical staff and registrars, ward nursing staff, administrators, porters and others. While such occasions inevitably developed a high decibel level, they were an opportunity for all levels of individuals to get together and were an undoubted asset to the morale and loyalty of the hospital staff as a whole. Furthermore, until the early 1970s, a formal Christmas Dinner was given by the Management Committee for the junior medical staff at The Royal Gwent which was much appreciated by the doctors as a gesture of goodwill.

The tradition of the Christmas visit to the hospitals by the Mayor and Mayoress of Newport still carries on. However, the tradition of a Nurses' Choir singing carols through the wards of the hospitals has fallen by the wayside.

Nurses in their uniforms carol singing at Christmas in one of the wards of The Royal Gwent Hospital. Note the caps and cloaks worn at that time (circa 1980).

(photograph courtesy of Mrs. Caryl Jones)

However, Christmas in the Children's Wards can still be a time of fun and happiness for youngsters and Father Christmas has also been seen in the Endoscopy Unit.

Father Christmas meeting youngsters in the Endoscopy Unit.

(photograph courtesy of Endoscopy Staff)

Another Christmas tradition that has disappeared is carving the turkey for lunch on Christmas Day. Each ward was provided with a roast turkey and its trimmings and the ward sister would invite one of the consultants who visited the ward to carve the bird for the patients. It was the custom to dress the consultant in a chef's hat and overalls and the consultant's children often obliged by serving each patient with a plateful of Christmas fare. Sometimes poor, indigent and lonely individuals would be admitted as 'emergencies' to stay in a ward over the Christmas period but in general, most patients who found themselves as In-Patients were too ill or recuperating from recent surgery to enjoy roast turkey and Christmas pudding although they invariably did their best. The downside for a chef-consultant was often over-generosity by the ward sister with the contents of a whisky bottle that reduced his capacity for lunch to follow at home. (That was before the hazards of drink-drive).

Mr. Derek Richards, consultant surgeon, operating at Christmas (circa 1966) in Ward 6 with Sister Marge Sully on the right.

(photograph courtesy of Cliff Knight)

In the mid-1970s, whole roast turkey was changed to turkey slices for Christmas lunch in the wards for financial reasons. Thus, consultants became freed of their carving obligations.

Those of us who remember The Royal Gwent and St. Woolos before the 1970s recall with great pleasure and amusement the Christmas Shows put on by the staff, partly for their own fun and partly for entertainment of patients. The Shows at St. Woolos were staged in the Main Dining Hall on a permanent stage and the lyrics and music were written in-house mostly by Brian Smart, husband of Sister Myris Smart, and the Shows at The Royal Gwent Hospital became an annual event on a large scale in the Out-Patient Hall. This was performed each year by The Royal Gwent Hospital Dramatics Group.

The Royal Gwent Hospital Dramatics Group
Mrs. Caryl Jones and Cliff Knight

In the late 1950s and early 1960s there was an active Amateur Dramatics Group at The Royal Gwent Hospital. This was run by Mr. R. Vernon Jones in addition to his responsibilities as Head of the Casualty Department. Vernon Jones had always been an accomplished pianist and had always had an interest in the stage and in music. During the war, he had his own band on the ship in which he served and for many years he directed and ran the popular and successful operettas produced by the Newport branch of Standard Telephone and Cable.

For the Hospital Dramatics Group, he got together a team of talented people from many departments - Charlie Borchaert (Chief Clerk), Alun Giles (Head Nursing Tutor), Walter Chadwick (Head Porter), Bryn Williams (Hospital Secretary), Dr. Vera Gammon (surgical registrar) and many others who returned to take part in the shows each year.

Ye Olde Gwent Minstrels pictured left to right Charles Borchaert, Alan Giles and Eddie Bennett. Alan Giles received the MBE for services to nursing.
(photograph courtesy of Cliff Knight)

It was no easy task to persuade all the participants to get together for rehearsals at the same time for these were scheduled for 9pm until 11pm after nurses and other tired hospital staff had completed their daily duties. Rehearsals could be disrupted sometimes by emergency calls to medical staff or even to Vernon, and a disaster may occur when half of the nurses in the chorus of twenty-two very attractive girls were put on to night duty!

Somehow, he coaxed and cajoled many medical and non-medical staff to join in as performers, to become craftsmen to build stage and scenery, and persuaded his daughters and wife to make and design costumes usually at their home.

Despite the difficulties, in the 1960s, the annual follies went ahead, and the Out-Patients' Hall, where the concerts were staged, was filled to capacity to enjoy a two and half hour production of light hearted fun with plenty of bright songs, dance routines and comedy sketches. The chorus was about thirty-strong, and supported a number of excellent soloists from their ranks. There were also six dancers who could be relied upon to produce clever dance routines. The compere was John Kane and the comedy team included Gladys Cooper, Jack Collier, Peter Foster, Wendy Morris, Kitty O'Shea, Janet Waters and Walter Chadwick (the Head Porter).

Vernon Jones produced the shows and also played the piano: in the orchestra was his daughter, Caryl, on the percussion who been appointed to the job at short notice by her father after thirty minutes tuition by Tony Henderson who led a local dance band! The violin part was played by Bryn Williams. A thankless task with choreography by Audrey Aston came from the men who appeared to have not two feet but four left feet.

The concerts had a 'mini-musical' and a 'grand finale'. These varied from 'The Student Prince', 'Desert Song', 'The Red and White Minstrels' Show'.

Red and White Minstrels Concert Party 1962-63 (founded by Mr. John Elgood in 1952). Caryl Jones, daughter of Vernon Jones was the piano and drums player and Mrs. Betty Jones was responsible for the wardrobe. Vernon Jones' head is just visible conducting.

(photograph courtesy of Caryl Jones)

The shows were always sold out and the Mayor always attended as did the hospital hierarchy. There was invariably a feeling of impending disaster - which rarely occurred - but many performers felt that the best performances were the Dress Rehearsals when the audience was made entirely of patients who were not only delighted to escape from the wards for a while but came to enjoy a good evening's entertainment. That was really the intention of all the hard work, and tears, of the Dramatics Group.

Then, in the New Year, the Dramatics Group would present their review at various locations in the town in aid of charities including World Refugee Year and the Adult Deaf and Dumb Mission. It was a very popular event in the town.

Similar Shows at Christmastime were put on in the large hall at St. Woolos Hospital in which medical staff were thoroughly lampooned by nurses, secretaries and others who took the opportunity to 'have a go'. The music and dialogue (if it could be called that) was always written and produced in-house, mostly by Brian Smart (husband of Myrys Smart sister of McMahon Ward). It could be slightly bawdy but was always harmless fun. As in the Royal Gwent, special performances were put on for patients who inevitably made their contribution to the back-chat.

It is sad that these annual occasions of fun gradually petered out in the 1970s as they were an opportunity for all staff, patients and families to get together. The hospitals are poorer without them.

However, one venture in recent years to give entertainment to patients in the hospital has been outstandingly successful and much appreciated. This has been 'Radio Royal Gwent'.

Radio Royal Gwent - Channel One
Cliff Knight

Radio first came to the hospital through the generosity of the *South Wales Argus* in 1926 when it provided radios to various parts of the hospital and replaced them in 1932 when they became worn out.

But it was in 1972 that some volunteers got together and with the co-operation of the hospital authorities set up their own broadcasting studio in Block 8. When this block was demolished they moved to Floor Two in the main hospital. Inside the studio they proudly boast of 52,000 items of recorded music from rock to opera which is used to broadcast to the wards from 6pm to 10pm each evening. Volunteers visit the wards before-hand to ask patients for requests which are sent out over the air with a mention of the patient's name and ward.

The studio has at present about forty volunteers with ages from 16 to 70 and as well as giving a welcome service to the patients, gives experience to potential radio broadcasters.

Occasionally interviews with well-known people are broadcast and what is going on at the hospital relayed.

The present Chairman is Des Morgan and his deputy Mike Williams.

Des Morgan Radio Royal Gwent 2001.

(photograph courtesy of Cliff Knight)

Chapter 14: The Centenary Year 2001

Cliff Knight and Eric Sturdy MS FRCS

Although the new hospital that became The Royal Gwent Hospital was opened in August 1901, it was decided to celebrate the Centenary of that occasion on 15th June 2001. A Centenary Group had been set up by Mr. Denis Jessopp, Chairman of the Gwent Healthcare N.H.S. Trust, to arrange events to mark the occasion and a committee was formed to write a record of the events that followed 1901 in the life of The Royal Gwent which has developed into this book.

Children's Parade 15th June 2001

The first event on Centenary Day, was a Children's Parade masterminded by Mr. D.E. Sturdy, retired consultant surgeon at The Royal Gwent Hospital. The Centenary celebration set out to replicate events of August 1901 when the Mayor of Newport led a procession of civic dignitaries and representatives of trade, industry, business, the Fire Brigade, Police, judiciary and militia from Newport Athletic Club to the gates of the new hospital, called in those days The Newport & Monmouthshire Infirmary. The theme for the June 2001 Parade was Newport's youngsters and a hundred schoolchildren from ten local Primary Schools, some dressed in early 20th Century costumes, marched along the same route from Rodney Parade to The Royal Gwent Hospital led by drums and fifes of The Boys Brigade. The Mayor and Mayoress, Councillor and Mrs. Ron Morris, joined the pageant at The King's Hotel and proceeded to the dedication ceremony at The Royal Gwent Hospital. There was one major hitch: whereas the procession in 1901 took ninety minutes to complete the walk, our schoolchildren covered the same distance in seventeen minutes! At the gates of The Royal Gwent Hospital, a short service of re-dedication of the Foundation Stone took place, followed in the evening by a re-union of staff from the past and present at The Friars Postgraduate Centre.

The children's procession.

(photograph courtesy of Jeanette Dawes)

Re-Dedication of the Foundation Stone

At the hospital a large crowd joined in the service which was led by the hospital Chaplain, the Reverend Alan Tyler. Passages from the Bible were read in English and Welsh and two hymns were sung, one by the children.

The Order of the Service was:

Welcome and Bidding: 'We have come together today to celebrate the centenary of The Royal Gwent Hospital. Through this past century this building, although constantly changing and developing, has stood as a symbol of healing and caring to the community it serves. Today, we gather to this foundation stone as a symbol of all that this building represents.'

Hymn: *'Be thou my vision, O Lord of my heart'*

Readings: *'Psalm 118: 19- 29 and 1 Peter 2: 4-8*

Prayer of Dedication: 'Heavenly Father, we give thanks for the work of healing, comfort and care that has been provided by The Royal Gwent Hospital this past 100 years, and we give thanks for the dedication and commitment of the staff who have rendered that service for the well-being of those who live in the community this hospital serves.

Now at this centenary, we celebrate the achievements and ask your continued blessing upon this hospital and its work.'

The Re-Dedication: 'O God, full of compassion and mercy, we dedicate this newly re-laid Foundation Stone as a symbol of the Royal Gwent Hospital's commitment to care for all who are sick, in the name of the Father, and of the Son and of the Holy Spirit. Amen'.

Prayers/Gweddi

Hymn: *'He gave me eyes so I could see'*

The Blessing

The Mayor of Newport, Councillor Ron Morris unveiled the re-laid Plaques from the ceremonies held in 1897 of the Foundation Stone and the opening of the new hospital in 1901. Mr. Denis Jessopp OBE, Chairman of Gwent Healthcare N.H.S. Trust, reminded everyone of the efforts of those who, well before the National Health Service was created, had the vision and determination to provide first class health facilities for the people of the Newport area. The children released hundreds of coloured balloons following the re-dedication to mark the occasion.

Staff Reunion

In the evening a reunion of staff past and present of both the Royal Gwent Hospital and St. Woolos Hospital was held.

Service of Re-dedication: The Mayor of Newport, Councillor Ron Morris and Mrs. Morris and Mr. Denis Jessopp OBE, Chairman of the the Gwent Healthcare N.H.S. Trust.

(photograph courtesy of The South Wales Argus)

Staff Re-union Pharmacy: Eluned Price, Jill Williams, Linda Parry, Marcia Moss, Norah Davies and Pauline Bowen.

(photograph courtesy of Jeanette Dawes)

Staff Re-union Midwifery: Margaret Goring, Beryl Wilson, Ann Hewes, Joan Rees, Gwenda James and Yvonne Wooten.

(photograph courtesy of Jeanette Dawes)

Staff Re-union: June Price, Sylvia Williams, Gwyneth Beavan, Theresa Dunn, Eileen Bartlett and Joan Barnes.

(photograph courtesy of Jeanette Dawes)

Staff Re-union: Eunice O'Hara, Beryl Tyler, Rosina Guy, Marjorie Roberts, Morfydd Poyntz, Pam Watson and Dorothy Hann.

(photograph courtesy of Jeanette Dawes)

Staff Re-union: Eric Sturdy, John Hughes, Gwilym Griffith and Sally Hughes.

(photograph courtesy of Jeanette Dawes)

238

Editor's Acknowledgements

It is appropriate to acknowledge first the *South Wales Argus*. The role of this newspaper as a major player in support for The Royal Gwent Hospital and its predecessors has been noted in this book on several occasions beginning from the date of its establishment in 1892 right up to 1948. Since 1948, the *Argus* has always been willing to lend its columns to publicise fundraising projects and for this book, the newspaper requested their readers to send in old cuttings and photographs about the hospital.

The Editorial Group also appreciates the support received from the Gwent Healthcare N.H.S. Trust which has underwritten the costs of publication and Adrian Hearn and Alison Griffiths who have directed marketing and sales.

However, the book is unlikely to have come about without the foresight of Cliff Knight whose extensive research into past and more recent events concerned with the hospital has provided a solid basis for many of the chapters. He has also been the source of many of the illustrations that have been used.

Particular gratitude goes to the many members of staff of the hospitals for their contributions about the many aspects of the work of the hospitals associated with the Royal Gwent. The Editor is most grateful to them for their goodwill, patience and their skill in presenting the evolution of the new order as it is in 2004.

Special thanks must go to departmental administrative staff who have compiled much information for the Appendices; these are Helen Hopcroft, Christine Everett, Samantha Salisbury, Susan Darlow, Bronwen Truman, Lynne Morgan, Suzanne Burt, Sandra Workman and Chris Jones.

Also, the Editorial Group thanks Mr. Stan Jordan for permission to include his watercolour painting of the Royal Gwent for the dustcover frontispiece and Reverend G.S. Harrison and members of Emmanuel Evangelical Church, Newport for an aerial photograph of the Royal Gwent placed in the 'end papers' of the book.

Much material has come from external sources, in particular Newport Museum and Mr. Roger Cucksey, the Gwent Record Office and Dr. Luned Davies with her colleagues (David Rimmer and Colin Gibson), the archives of the Gwent Healthcare N.H.S. Trust and Mrs. Gill Winstanley, The League of Friends and The Gwent Hospitals Contributory Fund.

My colleague and friend, Mr. Lewis Thomas, has given me much wise advice from his many years of experience in Newport and Cardiff and I have admired his stamina for he has read through three draft proofs of the book.

For the production of the book, my special thanks go to the management and staff at Old Bakehouse Publications for their advice, patience and good humour at all times even for re-writes. Also to Andrew Ponsford whose skills with digital processing of so many illustrations, often made within a short time-scale, have made these a central feature of the volume.

It has been a pleasure to work with the Editorial Group and we are privileged and honoured that Mr. Paul Murphy agreed to write a Foreword.

Finally, my thanks to Denis Jessopp for his support to see this project through and especially to my wife Audrey who, two years ago stopped asking *'when will that book be finished?'*.

Brian Peeling
Newport August 2004

Appendix 1
Senior Staff Appointments to the Newport Hospitals (from 1948)

General Medicine
E. Grahame Jones	1948 - 1975
P. Edward Dipple	1948 - 1975
John Swithinbank	1962 - 1975

General Medicine & Chest Medicine
Maldwyn Jackson	1949 - 1969
Norman V. Williams	1951 - 1983
E. Gerald Anderson	1969 - 1996
Susan G. Cotton	1972 - 1999
Ian S. Petheram	1979 - 2001
Ian Williamson	1996 -
Melissa Hack	1999 -
Alison Whittaker	2002 -
Patrick Flood-Page	2003 -

General Medicine & Diabetes
(P. Edward Dipple	1948 - 1975)
Howell J. Lloyd	1975 -
Owain Gibby	1983 -
Philip Evans	1998 - 2002
Peter Evans	2003 -
Kofi Obuobie	2003 -

General Medicine & Gastroenterology
Brian Calcraft	1975 d.1993
Miles Allison	1991 -
Manny Srivastava	1994 -
Thomas Yapp	2000 - 2003
Nimal Balaratnam	2003 -
Chin-Lye Ch'ng	2004 -

Cardiology
John D. Davies	1983 -
Shahid Ikram	1996 -
Nigel Browne	2001 -
M.K. Javed (A)	2002 -

Geriatric Medicine & Care of the Elderly
Morag Insley	1961 - 1976
Howard E.F. Davies	1975 - 1991
D. Jayasekara	1975 - 1985
Norman V. Williams	1983 - 1984
E. Anne Freeman	1984 -
Sarah E.M. Browne	1985 - 2004
Joe Toner	1987 - 2003
David Sykes	1989 -
Sanjeev Vasishta	2004 -
Jan Beynon (A)	1993 - 2002

Dermatology
Bernard Thomas	1948 - 1976
M.D. Mishra	1974 - 1994
Cynthia Matthews	1978 - 2003
Alex Anstey	1994 -
Caroline Mills	1995 -
Natalie Stone	2000 -
Richard Goodwin	2003 -

Genito-urinary Medicine
Bernard Thomas	1948 - c.1954
Joe Ribiero	c.1954 - 1976

David Beckingham	1976 - 1992
Robert Das	1992 -

Paediatrics & the Care of Children
Terrence Brand	1950 - 1965
Robert Prosser	1964 - 1991
Ralph Evans	1965 - 1970
John Cawdery	1970 - 1996
David Ferguson	1983 -
Sabine Maguire	1991 - 2001
Paul Buss	1993 -
Ian Bowler	1996 -
John Barton	1996 -
Peter Dale	1999 -
Hilary Lewis	2002 -
Michelle Barber	2002 -
Marion Schmidt	2003 -
Siddhartha Sen	2003 -

Psychiatric Services (Retired Consultants)
John Hughes
Val Evans
Peter Parsons
Dr. Johnston
John Lowther
Richard Bird
W. Waheed
George King
T.S. Davies
Eleanor Kapp
V.A. Wills
M.G.E. Morgan
I. Gonsalves
P. Ramachandran

Psychiatric Services (Consultants Recently Retired)
P.L.J. Jenkins
R. Huws
N. Warner
C.B. Dwyer
K. Moses
S. Seton-Brown
M. Rowlands

Psychiatric Services (Consultants in post 2004)
Stephen Hunter
Jennifer Davies
N. Jamil
N. Mirando
Ita Lyons
Pauline Ruth
K. Williamson
M.T.P. Reynolds
D.I. Williams
Prof. R.J. Williams
W. Barber
Pia Menzies
M. Griffiths
U. Sundari
R. Jacques

Rheumatology
Peter Williams   1974 -

Neurology
Gareth Llewelyn   1996 -

Renal Medicine (Hon. Appointments UWCM)
Eric Sanders   1976 - 1978
David Webb   1978 - 1985
John Williams (Professor)   1985 -
Aled Phillips   1997 -
Keiron Donovan   2001 -

General Surgery
R.R.S. Bowker   1948 - 1955
J.T. Rice Edwards   1948 - 1962
J. Elgood   1948 - 1961
Hywel G. Roberts   1949 - 1979
R. Derek Richards   1955 d.1968
Lewis P. Thomas   1961 - 1986
D. Eric Sturdy   1962 - 1993
W. Brian Peeling   1968 - 1974
Gwilym H. Griffith   1972 - 1998
J. Martyn Price-Thomas   1976 - 1995
Michael J. Butler   1979 d.1982
Kenneth Shute   1982 -
Keith D. Vellacott   1986 -
Brian Stephenson   1995 -
Christopher Gateley   1995 -
Wyn Lewis   1995 -
Philip Holland   2000 -
Kashav Swarnkar   2003-
Vincent Chamary   2003-

Vascular Surgery
Ahmed Shandall   1992 -
Ian Williams   1998 -
David McLain   2003 -

Thoracic Surgery
T.H.L. Rosser   1953 - 1979

Urological Surgery
W. Brian Peeling   1974 - 1995
Richard Gower   1985 -
Winsor G. Bowsher   1991 d.2004
Kenneth B. Queen   1996 -
Christopher P. Bates   1998 -
Adam Carter   2003 -

Ophthalmic Surgery
F.W. Robertson   1948 - 1962
George W. Hoare   1948 - 1976
Kenneth Barber   1962 - 1978
Vaughan Jones   1960s - 1973
Nigel W. Walshaw   1973 - 2000
Alec G. Karseras   1976 - 2000
A.D. Holt Wilson   1978 - 1999
Yunis Khan   1978 -
David S. Hughes   1997 -
Christopher Blyth   1998 -
Susan Webber   2000 -
Desmond O'Duffy   2000 -
Andrew Feyi Waboso   2001 -

ENT Surgery
D.B. Sutton   1948 - 1950s
P. Thorpe   1948 - 1950s
J.L.D. Williams   1948 - 1974
Gilbert B. Leitch   1960 - 1985
C.S. Viswanathan   1963 - 1978
I.T.G. Evans   1974 - 1998
Marcus J.K.M. Brown   1978 -
Malcolm Clayton   1988 -
J.M. Preece   1996 -
Duncan J. Ingrams   2000 -
Syed Ali Raza   2000 -

Oral & Facial Maxillary Surgery
Desmond Dalton   1948 - 1975
John Nicholas   1975 - 1983
John R.V.B. Gibson   1948 - 1970s
Alan Quayle   1976 - 1978
Max Gregory   1978 -
Simon Wigglesworth   1980 -
John Llewelyn   1995 -
Madura Sirikumara (A)   1987 -

Obstetric & Gynaecological Surgery
R. Glyn Morgan   1948 - 1955
Stan W. Beswick   1948 - 1976
Mary Smith   1948 - 1987
Jack M. Bowen   1955 - 1980
Arthur Williams   1961 - 1966
Israel Rocker   1963 - 1991
Pat Gasson   1966 - 1971
D. Gwyn Daniel   1971 - 2000
Robert H. Golding   1976 - 2002
Martin Stone   1980 -
Mrs. Jo Wiener   1991 -
Asoka Weerakoddy   1991 -
Mrs. Rohini Gonsalves   2000 -
Miss A. Wright   2002 -
Mrs Leena Gokhale   2003 -
Mrs Makiya Ashraf   2002 -
Mrs Ros Goddard   2002 -
Gareth Edwards   2002 -

Orthopaedic Surgery
N. Rocyn-Jones   c.1936 - 1966
T.C. Howard Davies   1953 - 1982
Raj Dutta   1971 - 1995
Hilton Harrop-Griffiths   1966 - 1988
Keith Tayton   1983 -
Witek Mintowt-Czyz   1985 -
D. Greg Jones   1988 -
Robert Savage   1990 -
Andrew Grant   1995 -
Philip Alderman   1996 -
Paul Roberts   1997 -
Kartik Hariharan   1997 -
Simon Hannaford-Youngs   1998 -
Rohit Kulkarni   2001 -
Ashok Mukherjee (A)   2003 -

Radiological Services
T.I. Candy   1921 d.1931
W. Howitt Hastings   1931 - 1949
T. Jack Thomas   1949 - 1954
R. Aneurin Williams   1954 - 1987

241

Rex Owen	1960 - 1987	Gwyn D. Thomas	1970 - 1995
J. Meek	1955 - 1960	Audrey M. Peeling	1971 - 1992
Harold Ansari	1965 - 1987	David O. Jones	1972 - 1995
Rosemary Anderson	1972 - 1990	Martin Sage	1972 -
Jean Guy	1974 - 1979	H. O'Dwyer	1979 -
Glaslyn J. Griffiths	1976 d.2002	John Butler	1983 -
Barbara A.R. Williams	1981 - 1996	Geoffrey Clark	1983 -
Brian A. Sullivan	1981 -	John Gough	1984 -
Anthony Jones	1982 - 1990	David Thomas	1984 -
J. Richard Harding	1982 -	Hywel M. Jones	1986 -
Richard Clements	1987 -	Alison Carling	1987 -
Gerald V. Thomas	1989 -	Christopher Callander	1991 -
Fiona Brook	1990 -	Stephen Dumont	1992 -
Mark Bernard	1992 -	Paul Nicols	1992 -
Nuala Kennan	1993 - 1997	Derek Dye	1994 -
Andrew R. Jones	1995 -	Ian Greenway	1994 -
Anne M. Wake	1995 -	David Jones	1994 -
David M. Jackson	1996 -	Tan Mian	1994 -
Nest Evans	1998 -	Tracey Haynes	1996 -
Peter Stamper	1999 -	Katherine Woods	1997 -
Jennifer Haslam	2003 -	Jillian Curtis	1997 -

Pathology Services

J. Fine	1948 - 1965	Dermot Hughes	1998 -
L Stern	1949 - 1952	Iljaz Hodzovic	1998 -
G.S. Andrews	1953 - 1982	Sarah Watson	1999 -
W.H. Beasley	1956 - 1962	Tzvetanka Stoilova	1999 -
J. Howard Jones	1962 - 1987	Sonia Wartan	2001 -
Margaret Davies (A)	1963 - 1987	Rachel Walpole	2002 -
Robin D. Gray	1970 - 1978	Jonathon Griffiths	2002 -
W. Hunt	1974 - 1980	Joanne Janes	2002 -
J. Glencross	1978 - c.1990	Iwan Morris	2002 -
Emyr W. Owen	1980 -	David Howells	2003 -
Colin Hewlett	1981 -	S. Krishnan	2003 -
Michael D. Penney	1983 -	S. Lloyd-Jones	2003 -
Windsor Fortt	1983 - 2002	Vimla Victor	2003 -
Elizabeth Moffatt	1988 -	K. Prasad (A)	1979 -
M. Hickey	c.1990 - 1994	R. Michael (A)	1987 -
Elizabeth Kubiak	1994 -	K. Zak (A)	1984 -
Al Shafi	1995 - 2002		

Plastic Surgery (St. Lawrence Hospital)

Abdul-Majid Rashid	1997 -	Emlyn Lewis	1950 - 1969
Ian Thompson	1997 -	Leonard Schofield	1953 - 1975
H. Jackson	2000 -	Michael Tempest	1969 - 1987
Elsie Wessels	2003 -	John Bennett	1974 - 1976
D. Oleesky (A)	2000 -	Michael Green	1976 - 1992

Accident & Emergency Services

R. Vernon Jones	1952 - 1980	Philip Sykes	1976 - 1999
W.J. 'Bill' Morgan	1980 - 2002	Stewart Watson	1981 - 1983
Gerry McCarthy	1995 - 2001	Martin Milling *	1983 -
Francis J. Richardson	1996 -	Adrian Sugar	1984 - 1997
G. Quinn	1999 - 2001	Michael Early	1985 - 1989
Ashok Vaghela	2002 -	Alan McGregor *	1992 -
Sally Jones	2002 -	Mark Cooper	1993 -
Rajan Raghupati	2004 -	Hamish Laing *	1995 -
Audrey Palmer (A)	1996 -		

(* consultants from Morriston Hospital giving sessional cover at R.G.H. since 1995)

Note: Associate Specialists designated 'A'

Anaesthetics & Pain Relief

Ken Thom	1948 - 1972
Harvey Nicholl	1948 - 1966
D. Glyn Davies	1955 - 1971
J.W. Thomas	1956 - 1985
Alan H. Phillips	1959 - 1991

(Editor's Comment: this data illustrates the response required to cope with the expansion and specialties recorded in Chapters 7 to 9. Consultant numbers were relatively modest for many years after 1948 but in recent years have accelerated to provide services to keep Newport hospitals at the forefront of healthcare.)

Appendix 2
Honours, Awards & Appointments

Honorary Physician to HM The Queen

	Dr. John Hughes FRCP FRC(Psych)	1972 - 1974

Honours/Awards

CBE	Professor Brian Peeling FRCS	2002
OBE	Mr. Philip Sykes FRCS	1984
	Mr. Alec Karseras FRCS	1995
	Mrs. Anne Pegington RGN	1997
	Mrs. Hazel Taylor JP RGN	1998
	Mrs. Vernesta Cyril RGN	1999
	Mrs. Jill Evans RGN	1999
	Mr. Gwilym Griffith FRCS	2001
	Dr. Owain Gibby FRCP	2002
	Mr. Denis Jessopp MBE	2003
MBE	Mr. Alun Giles JP RGN	1987
	Miss Valerie Martin RGN	c.1992
	Mrs. Beryl Wilson RGN	1997
	Mrs. Pat White	2000
	Mrs. Glenys Matthews	2002
BEM	Mr. Walter Chadwick	1963

Military Honours/Appointments

MC	Mr. R. Glyn Morgan	
TD OStJ	Dr. John Hughes	
Hon. Col. (RAMC)	Dr. John Hughes	(203 Welsh General Hospital)
Lt. Col. (RAMC)	Dr. D.E. Sturdy	(203 Welsh General Hospital)

Appointments to Professional Bodies

Royal College of Physicians

Dr. E.G. Anderson	Board of Examiners	1985 - 1996
	Visiting examiner, Hong Kong	1985 - 1996
Dr. H.J. Lloyd	Regional Advisor for Wales	2002 - 2004
	Member of Council	2002 - 2004
Dr. Miles Allison	Committee for Gastroenterology	2001 -

Royal College of Surgeons of England

Mr. L.P. Thomas	Regional Advisor for S.Wales	1977 - 1985
Mr. D.E. Sturdy	Surgical Advisory Committee	1981 - 1991
	Regional Adviser for S. Wales	1985 - 1989
	Secretary, Welsh Board of R.C.S.	1982 - 1986
Mr. G.H. Griffith	Regional Advisor for S. Wales	1989 - 1994
Mr. A. Shandall	Board of Examiners	2002 -
	Regional Advisor for S. Wales	2004 -
Mr. J. Llewelyn	Examiner, Oral / Maxillofacial Surg. (I)	2001 -
P.J. Sykes	Examiner, Plastic Surgery (I)	1985 - 1991
	(Chairman)	1989 - 1991
	Specialist Adv. Comm. (Plastic Surgery)	1990 - 1992
	Regional Advisor (Plastic Surgery)	1992 - 1997
	Welsh Board of R.C.S.	1996 - 1998
	(I = Intercollegiate Board)	

M.A.P. Milling	Specialist Adv. Comm. (Plastic Surgery)	1984 - 2001
	(Chairman)	1999 - 2001
	Member of Council (Plastic Surgery)	2002 - 2003
	Regional Advisor (Plastic Surgery)	1999 - 2004
	Welsh Board of R.C.S.	1999 - 2004
	Examiner, Plastic Surgery (I)	1999 - 2004

Royal College of Surgeons of Edinburgh

Dr. M.J.K.M. Brown	Regional Advisor for S. Wales	1992 -
	Board of Examiners	1984 - 2000
	Specialist Advisory Board	1991 - 2002
	Examiner (I)	1999 -

Royal College of Pathologists

Dr. M.D. Penney	Member of Council	2001 - 2004
	Member of Executive	2001 - 2004
	Regional Advisor for Wales	1991 - 2001
	Board of Examiners	1993 -
	Chairman, Regional Council for Wales	1991 - 2001

Royal College of Obstetrics & Gynaecology

Mr. I. Rocker	Postgraduate Committee	1978 - 1981
Mrs. Jo Wiener	Standing Joint Committee with	
	Royal College of Radiologists	2003 -
	Member, R.C.Q. Committee	2002 - 2003

Royal College of Radiologists

| Dr. B. Sullivan | Welsh Regional Advisor | 1997 - |
| Dr. R. Clements | Faculty Board | 2004 - |

Royal College of Ophthalmologists

| Mr. C. Blyth | Training Programme Director (Wales) | 2003 - |

Royal College of Nursing

Mr. A. Giles	Chairman R.C.N. (UK)	1979 - 1983
	Chairman R.C.N. (Wales)	1977 - 1987
Mrs. A. Pegington	Chief Executive Officer,	
	R.C.N. (Wales)	1978 - 1998

British Medical Association

Mr. J. Llewelyn	Central Consultants & Specialists Committee	2003 -
	Chairman, Welsh L.N.C. Forum	2003 -
	Member, Welsh Council	2002 -

British Thoracic Society

| Dr. E.G. Anderson | Treasurer/Member of Council | 1986 - 1989 |

British Association of Urological Surgeons

Prof. W.B. Peeling	Member of Council	1981 - 1984
	Ex-officio Member of Council	1992 - 1993
	St. Peter's Medal	1996 -

British Journal of Plastic Surgery

| Mr. M.N. Tempest | Editor | 1979 - 1985 |

Academic Appointments and Invitations

Dr. E.G. Anderson	Visiting Examiner/Lecturer to Univs. of UK Hong Kong and Kuala Lumpur	1988 - 1996
Dr. John Davies	Honorary Senior Lecturer, Brompton Hospital, London	1988 -
Prof. W.B. Peeling	Honorary Professor of Surgery/Urology. The University of Wales College of Medicine	1991 -
	Visiting Professor/Lecturer to Yale, Johns Hopkins, Stanford, Toronto, Hong Kong, Auckland, Bangkok, Heidelberg	
Dr. Owain Gibby	Member: Advisory Board, Warwick (Diabetes) Health Care, University of Warwick	
Dr. Hywel Jones	Associate Medical Director for Teaching and Sub-Dean to the University of Wales College of Medicine	2000 -
Dr. I. Hodzovic	P/T Senior Lecturer, University of Wales College of Medicine	1998 -

Appendix 3
Medical Books Published by Staff of the Newport Hospitals

Mr. Lewis P. Thomas	Editor and Co-Author (with David MacFarlane) *'Textbook on Surgery'*, Livingstone 1st Edition 1964/5th Edition 1989. ISBN 0 44302768 4
Dr. E. Gerald Anderson	*'Para malignant Syndromes in Lung Cancer'*. William Heinemann. 1973. ISBN 0 43300610 2
Mr. D. Eric Sturdy	*'Essentials of Urology'* John Wright & Sons. 1974. ISBN 0 72360355 3
Mr. D. Eric Sturdy	*'An Outline of Urology'* John Wright & Sons. 1986. ISBN 0 72360885 7
Dr. Anne Freeman	Co-author: *'An aid to the MRCP short cases'* Blackwell Scientific Publications. 1st edition 1986. ISBN 0 63201451 2 and 2nd edition 1999. ISBN 0 63203067 4
Mr. Israel Rocker	Editor *'Pelvic pain in women - diagnosis and Management'* Springer-Verlag. 1990. ISBN 3 540199594 7
Dr. M.C. Allison	*'A Colour Atlas of the Digestive System'* Wolfe Medical. 1989. ISBN 0 73240886 6
Dr. M.C. Allison	*'Diagnostic Picture Tests in Gastroenterology'*. Wolfe. 1991. ISBN 0 81510117 1
Dr. John Davies	'Practical Clinical Medicine' Butterworth/Heinemann. 1992. ISBN 0 7506002 66
Dr. Anne Freeman	Co-author: *'An aid to the MRCP viva'* Churchill-Livingstone. 1992. ISBN 0 44304659 X
Dr. M.D. Penney	*'Sodium, Potassium and Water'*. Clinical Biochemistry. 1995. Churchill-Livingstone. ISBN 0 44304341 8
Professor W.B. Peeling	*'Questions and Uncertainties about Prostate Cancer'* Blackwell Science. 1996. ISBN 0 86542965 0
Dr. M.C. Allison	*'Self Assessment Picture Tests in Gastroenterology.'* Mosby-Wolfe. 1997. ISBN 0 73242589 2
Dr. M.C. Allison	(principal author) *'Inflammatory Bowel Disease'* Mosby-Wolfe. 1998. ISBN 0 73241888 8
Mr. Winsor G. Bowsher	*'Challenges in Prostate Cancer'* Blackwell Science. 2000. ISBN 0 63205422 0
Dr. Anne Freeman	Co-author: *'Medical short cases for medical students'* Blackwell Science. 2000. ISBN 0 63205729 7
Dr. Anne Freeman	Co-author: *'An Aid to the MRCP PACES. Vol.1: Stations 1, 3, & 5'*. Blackwell Publishing 2003. ISBN 1 40510768 5
Dr. Anne Freeman	Co-author: *'An Aid to the MRCP PACES. Vol.2: Stations 2 & 4'*. Blackwell Publishing 2003. ISBN 1 40510662 X
Dr. Anne Freeman	Co-author: *'The Complete PLAB. Objective structured clinical examinations'*. 2003. Elsevier Science. ISBN 0 44307050 4
Dr. Anne Freeman	Co-author: *'The Complete PLAB. Extended matching questions'* Elsevier Science. 2003. ISBN 0 44307092 X
Mr. Winsor G. Bowsher	*'Challenges in Prostate Cancer II'*. Blackwell Science (in preparation at the time of Mr. Bowsher's death 2004): Editorship to be continued by Mr. Adam Carter and Mr. Christopher Bates.